"Reading *To Right Every Wrong* is like finding some lost compilation tapes by Bob Dylan and discovering a treasure trove of new versions of his greatest hits, lost gems, and some fresh material. Dave Andrews, the original Christi-anarchist, reflects on a lifetime of living among and serving the poor, and calling others to join him, and the result is operatic! A must for those who haven't been introduced to Dave's work before, and a joy to those of us who have drawn inspiration from him for decades."

—MICHAEL FROST
Missiologist, Morling College, and author of *Keep Christianity Weird*

"It's not every day one has the pleasure of encountering someone who has lived passionately, consistently, and courageously in the way of Jesus, but Dave Andrews is one of those people. *To Right Every Wrong* offers a rollicking series of stories, insights, and observations about following Jesus in the world sure to inspire any sincere seeker into deeper discipleship. Dave's story, like his life, is wonderfully all over the place, literally and figuratively, as he and his wife, Angie, seek solidarity with the poor . . . while engaging in an endless, energetic campaign of writing, speaking, breaking bread, and confronting injustice, in the world and in themselves. Rarely has the risky, dangerous life of authentic discipleship . . . [been done] 'with such grand gusto'!"

—WES HOWARD-BROOK
Author of *"Come Out, My People": God's Call Out of Empire in the Bible and Beyond*

"*To Right Every Wrong* is an encyclopedia of Dave's praxis: the sources shaping his own distinctive thinking along with a litany of examples of his activities arising from these ideas. If you want to understand what's inspired, shaped, and sustained Dave over his life, read this book. We met Dave and Angie in 1978 in India as they began developing community in Delhi with Indian nationals. Lynden and I were in our early idealistic twenties, exploring our own life vocation. Their welcome, vision, ideas, and commitment to living Jesus's kingdom life were compelling, encouraging, challenging, and transformational for us. Some forty years later, this continues to be so."

—MICHAEL PRINCE
Leadership Coach and Facilitator, Oasis People & Culture

"This book is classic Dave Andrews. . . . In it, Dave Andrews shares his thoughtful plea to follow Jesus . . . with a touching, reflective, extra personal touch. It is a great way to get to know Dave further—his life, his priorities, his struggles, and his mission—to live by the Christian anarchism he has been preaching. The numerous stories from his inspirational life are shared with confessional frankness, giving a vivid illustration of his efforts to take on the role of a modern prophet."

—ALEXANDRE CHRISTOYANNOPOULOS
Author of Christian Anarchism: A Political Commentary on the Gospel

"I loved reading Dave's story. Christians have struggled with the question of what it really means to follow Jesus. Secular people observing what Christians do have scratched their heads and asked the same question. Readers will find in Dave Andrews's life story an answer. And it is inspiring."

—TIM COSTELLO
Senior Fellow, Centre for Public Christianity, and author of A Lot With A Little

"I thought I knew Dave well . . . a man deeply devoted to living his life as a follower of Jesus, dedicated to service to others. . . . However, reading *To Right Every Wrong* provided me a deeper insight into his calling to be a prophet . . . who showed me, a devout Muslim woman, what it means to deeply love God by relating to others, and to live that love passionately and compassionately in today's quite often troubled world."

—NORA AMATH
Chair of Islamic Relief, Australia, and AMARAH

"*To Right Every Wrong* gives you the best chance you'll get to see . . . what's it like to have a pudgy Gandhi or aging Jesus . . . who saved the lives of so many—as he did mine—lounging on your sofa. I dare you to read it."

—ADRIAN REITH
Author of Act 3: The Art of Growing Older

"If there is such a thing as a 'page turner' that 'reads itself' this book is it! The many autobiographical anecdotes make this book so accessible. I couldn't put it down and finished it in a couple of days. By looking back in the autumn of his life, Andrews offers nuggets of wisdom mined from practical lived experience to other would-be 'improbable prophets.' *To Right Every Wrong* is engaging, challenging, and inspiring."

—JOHANNES M. LUETZ

Senior Lecturer, Christian Heritage College, Brisbane, Australia

"It was Socrates who asserted that an unexamined life is not worth living. Dave Andrews's frank examination of his own life story is highly instructive to all those who wrestle with questions of finding meaning in life within a faith-based framework. His book is replete with penetrative insights accumulated over a lifetime rich with varied experiences across cultures, religions, and continents. He has sincerely embodied the prophetic call to live compassionately, thereby transforming communities for the better."

—ADIS DUDERIJA

Senior Lecturer Study of Islam and Society, Senior Fellow, Centre for Interfaith and Cultural Understanding, Griffith University, Australia

"The making of a prophet is always in risky obedience to the prompting of the Spirit of God. Prophetic calling is both prophetic announcement and prophetic manifestation. Dave Andrews's book *To Right Every Wrong* is an honest recollection of the journey of a prophet where the messenger is always the message. A must-read for anyone who feels the urge of a prophetic calling."

—C. B. SAMUEL

Theologian, pastor, mentor, and former Director of EFICOR, India

"Dave Andrews is one of the present-day prophets in the world today. In *To Right Every Wrong* he has captured his prophetic journey from a place of deep reflection. He is a wonderful storyteller and has taken great care to make sure that the reader feels included in his story. It is wonderful to see the acknowledgement of his wife Angie's influence on his life and their journey together over the years. Dave Andrews has been a 'prophetic inspirator' to a generation of people in India, many of whom have led community organizations which are based on Jesus hospitality, love, and justice."

—ANUVINDA VARKEY
Executive Director, Christian Coalition for Health, India

"Dave Andrews, in his new book *To Right Every Wrong*, describes a lifelong call to the role of the prophet. I was bothered by Dave's self-identification as a prophet. Calling oneself a prophet smacks of . . . arrogance. But by the end of the book I thought Dave had proved his case through his stories about prophetic action and self-reflection. Dave identifies as an Anabaptist that claims, '*Jesus* is the centre of our faith, *Community* is the centre of our life, and *Reconciliation* is the centre of our work.' Dave's life story demonstrates his commitment to these three faith statements. Being an Anabaptist puts Dave on the margins of the church and society where prophets often thrive."

—MARK S. HURST
Pastoral Worker, Anabaptist Association of Australia and New Zealand

"Growing up in a caring family, with an equally radical, compassionate wife, Angie, and a faith that holds on tightly to Jesus, Dave practises what he preaches, prophetically challenging many to rethink the teachings of Jesus of Nazareth to be disciples and speak and act compassionately."

—PAX TAN
Pastor, Senior Director of Communication and Prison, Drugs, and AIDS, Malaysian Care

"Any encounter with Dave Andrews leaves one both deeply inspired and yet profoundly unnerved. Inspired because Dave is a person willing to put his body on the line for the cause of Jesus. Unnerved because one can never quite put this man in a neat little box—he blows your categories. Not surprisingly, reading this book has a similar effect."

—ALAN HIRSCH
Founder of Movement Leaders Collective, Forge Missional Training Network, and 5Q Collective

"Told in the language of prophets, Dave's latest book explores the radical compassion our world needs right now to find peace."

—BENJAMIN GILMOUR
Author of *Warrior Poets* and director of *Jirga*

"It was a complete joy to read this book. I couldn't put it down. Sometimes funny, sometimes serious, always honest and sincere. Dave and Angie have literally spent a lifetime in service of others. Through his unique approach, Dave has changed the hearts and minds of many, in all parts of the world, people of all backgrounds. This book gives a beautiful snapshot of his colorful life and his open-hearted approach to it. Enjoy the ride!"

—JULIE SIDDIQI
Muslim community educator and activist, United Kingdom

"Dave has the vision of a prophet. The book offers us an insight into his own self-reflective wrestling to make sense of his call. One cannot help but be transformed by his gracious challenge to all of us to re-embrace gospel fidelity. My favorite part of the book caught me by surprise. I was about ready to close the book, but then found the epilogue and thought I'd better read it. It was so beautiful and finishes with reminding us that it is all about the love of God as revealed in Jesus."

—JUSTIN DUCKWORTH
Anglican Bishop of Wellington, New Zealand

TO RIGHT EVERY WRONG

TO RIGHT EVERY WRONG

*The Making and Unmaking
of One Improbable Minor Prophet*

Dave Andrews

WIPF & STOCK · Eugene, Oregon

Wipf & Stock
An Imprint of Wipf and Stock Publishers
199 W. 8th Ave., Suite 3
Eugene, OR 97401

www.wipfandstock.com

PAPERBACK ISBN: 978-1-7252-8853-9
HARDCOVER ISBN: 978-1-7252-8854-6
EBOOK ISBN: 978-1-7252-8855-3

01/11/21

When we were young
I once believed we'd do what should be done
I once believed that all of us would right every wrong.
Long ago. When you and I were young.

Those days are gone.
But I still long for love to fill my soul.
I still long for love that floods my soul to overflow.
Like it did—so very long ago.[1]

–Dave Andrews, "I Still Long for Love"

1. Dave Andrews, "I Still Long for Love," (mp3). https://bit.ly/3aVz8eG

CONTENTS

Introduction to Dave Andrews
for the Dave Andrews Legacy Series (2012)

I KEPT SEEING THIS guy on the shuttle bus - long hair, graying beard, a gentle 60's-70's feel to him. He seemed thoughtful, intense, friendly, and quiet, like he had a lot on his mind, as did I. Even though I saw him nearly every time I boarded the shuttle bus, we didn't speak beyond him smiling and saying, "G'day" and me nodding and saying, "Hey" as we boarded or disembarked.

It was my first time at Greenbelt, a huge festival about faith, art, and justice held every August in the UK. I had always heard great things about the event and so was thrilled when I was invited to speak. I was just as thrilled to get a chance to hear in person some musicians and speakers I had only heard about from a distance, so I went through the program and marked people I wanted to be sure not to miss.

It was near the end of the conference when a friend told me to be sure to catch an Australian fellow named Dave Andrews. "I've never heard of him," I said. "Oh, he's a force of nature," my friend said. "Kind of like Jim Wallis, Tony Campolo, and Mother Teresa rolled up into one." How could I not put a combination like that in one of the last free slots on my schedule?

I arrived at the venue a few minutes late and there he was, the bearded guy from the bus. Thoughtful, intense, and friendly, yes - but *quiet* he was not. He was nearly exploding with passion - passion and compassion, in a voice that ranged from fortissimo to fortississimo to furioso. How could a guy churning with so much hope, love, anger, energy, faith, fury, and curiosity have been so quiet and unassuming on the bus?

He was a force of nature indeed, evoking from his audience laughter, shouts, amens, reverent silence, and even tears before he was done. He spoke of justice, of poverty, of oppression, of solidarity across religious differences, of service, of hope, of celebration, of the way of Jesus.

As I listened, I wanted to kick myself. This is the most inspiring talk I've heard at this whole festival. Why did I miss all those opportunities to get to know this fellow on the bus? Now the festival is almost over and I've missed my chance!

Later than evening, I boarded the shuttle bus for the last ride back to my hotel, and there sat Dave and his wife, Ange. I didn't miss my chance this time. I introduced myself and they reciprocated warmly.

I was a largely unknown American author at the time and hardly known at Greenbelt, much less in Australia, so I'm quite certain Dave and Ange had never heard of me. But they couldn't have been kinder, and as we disembarked, he pulled two books from his backpack and told me they were a gift.

The next day when I flew home from Heathrow, I devoured them both on the plane. First, I opened *Not Religion, But Love* and read it through from cover to cover. Then I opened *Christi-anarchy* and couldn't put it down either. When my plane landed, I felt I had been on a spiritual retreat . . . or maybe better said, in a kind of spiritual boot camp!

Things I was thinking but had been afraid to say out loud Dave was saying boldly and confidently. Ideas I was very tentatively considering he had already been living with for years. Complaints and concerns I only shared in highly guarded situations he was publishing from the housetops. Hopes and ideals I didn't dare to express he celebrated without embarrassment.

I think I gave him a copy of one or two of my books as well, and I guess he was favorably impressed enough that we stayed in touch and a friendship developed. I discovered that we were both songwriters as well as writers, that we both had a deep interest in interfaith friendships, that we both had some critics and we both had known the pain of labeling and rejection.

Since then, whatever he has written, I've been sure to read . . . knowing that he speaks to my soul in a way that nobody else does.

We've managed to get together several times since our initial meeting in England, in spite of the fact that we live on opposite sides of the planet. We've spoken together at a few conferences on both hemispheres, and I had the privilege of visiting him in Brisbane. I've seen the beautiful things he has been doing in a particularly interesting and challenging neighborhood there, walking the streets with him, meeting his friends, sensing his love for that place and those people. He's been in my home in the US as well, and we've been conspiring for some other chances to be and work together in the future.

In my speaking across North America, I frequently refer to Dave's work, but until now, his books have been hard to come by. That's why I'm thrilled to introduce 'Christi-Anarchy', 'Not Religion, But Love', 'A Divine

Society', 'Learnings', 'Bearings', and '*People Of Compassion*', being published by Wipf and Stock, to everyone I can in North America.

Yes, you'll find he's one part Tony Campolo, one part Jim Wallis, and one part Mother Teresa, a force of nature, as I was told.

You'll also find he is a serious student of the Bible and a serious theological sage - the kind of reflective activist or thinker-practitioner that we need more of.

In a book like *Christi-anarchy*, he can boldly and provocatively unsettle you and challenge you. Then in a book like *Plan Be*, he can gently and pastorally encourage and inspire you. Like the central inspiration of his life, he is the kind of person to confidently turn over tables in the Temple one minute and then humbly defend a shamed and abused woman from her accusers the next.

You'll see in Dave's writings that he is highly knowledgeable about poverty, ecology, psychology, sociology, politics, and economics . . . not only from an academic standpoint, but also from a grass-roots, experiential level. His writing on these subjects grows from what he has done on the ground . . . for example, nurturing a community network that is training young adults to live and serve among the poor, supervising homes for adults who are learning to live with physical and psychiatric disabilities, encouraging small businesses to hire people who others would consider unemployable and developing a non-profit solar energy co-op for local people.

Dave's writings and friendship have meant so much to me. I consider him a friend and mentor. Now I am so happy that people across North America can discover him too.

You'll feel as I did - so grateful that you didn't miss the chance to learn from this one-of-a-kind, un-categorizable, un-containable, wild wonder from Down Under named Dave Andrews.

Brian D. McLaren
author/speaker/activist (brianmclaren.net)

Introduction to Dave and Angie Andrews
for *To Right Every Wrong*

I HAVE KNOWN DAVE and Angie for almost 50 years. . . Together they have provided me with a framework within which to house the meaning of my life. They have stimulated me to be engaged with the people who are suffering around me.

In them I have experienced the deepest friendship and have been affirmed in all of my attempts to accomplish beauty, be it in my painting or in my writing or in the work I do with people in mental anguish.

I sometimes feel I fall short of the standards that Dave sets: my conscience pricks me for not being involved enough or empathic enough, for being frightened of public social action. And Ange's unending compassion for the plight of marginalised people is a tough standard to measure oneself against.

But then I remind myself that I am more introverted than they are and that is OK. And through it all, I have been loved and appreciated and cared for by these two, who together seem to me to be the voice of God in a world that is often cruel and unjust.

This book is an amazing retrospective of two lives lived with the earnestness and love, the courage and the zeal to translate the message of Jesus into contemporary culture.

Dr Nimmi Hutnik
Reader in Mental Health, Artist
Chartered Counselling Psychologist
Accredited Cognitive Behaviour Therapist

PROLOGUE

To Right Every Wrong started out as a series of personal reflections I was writing about the strange, crazy kind of "call" I felt to be a prophet.

For me this was never a "call" to be a special person. The prophet Moses himself once prayed, "Would that all the Lord's people were prophets."[1] The philosopher Jean-Paul Sartre argued that prophets aren't special, because in one sense, "all men (sic) are prophets,"[2] and the preacher, Charles Spurgeon, agreed, saying, "we are all at times unconscious prophets."[3]

For me a "call" to be a prophet was not a "call" to prominence, still less a "call" to popularity. The journalist, Tom Junod, says, "The first thing you learn when you busk in the New York subways: you immediately join the ranks of the marginalised, unhinged prophets,"[4] and the singer Paul Simon points to the fact that, "The words of the prophets are written on the subway walls and tenement halls and whispered in the sounds of silence."[5]

Let me be clear the kind of prophet I felt called to be was not an exalted *rasul* in the Islamic tradition, but a humble *nabi* in the Jewish tradition. This is what my boss at Baptist Community Services, Neville Eckersley—knowing nothing of my "call"— always called me.

The best description of the prophet I felt "called" to be in the Christian tradition is outlined by my friend, the radical, peace activist and priest, John Dear:

> First, a prophet is someone who listens attentively to the word of God . . . and then goes into the world to tell the world God's message. Second . . . in the process, the prophet tells us who God is and what God wants, and thus who we are and how we can

1. Numbers 11:29
2. https://www.brainyquote.com/topics/prophets-quotes
3. https://www.brainyquote.com/topics/prophets-quotes
4. https://www.brainyquote.com/topics/prophets-quotes 4
5. Paul Simon, "The Sound of Silence"

become fully human. Third, a prophet . . . sees the big picture—war, starvation, poverty, corporate greed, systemic violence, nuclear weapons, and environmental destruction [and] interprets these current realities through God's eyes, not through the eyes of pundits. . . . Fourth, a prophet takes sides . . . in solidarity with the poor, the powerless, and the marginalized. A prophet becomes a voice for the voiceless. . . . . Fifth, prophets . . . call people to . . . create a new world of social and economic justice, which will be the basis for a new world of peace. . . . Sixth, prophets simultaneously denounce and announce. They lay low the obsolete ways of violence and weapons and hold high the alternatives of nonviolence and disarmament.[6]

I hadn't planned for this project to become a book. I was too embarrassed by the subject to make it a book. But as I wrote, it seemed to grow into a book. It certainly wasn't intended to be an autobiography or a history of the groups I've been involved with, as it's far too selective, partial and incomplete. I beg forgiveness of the many people who have played an important part in my life who never get the mention they would deserve in a proper autobiography or history of those groups.

The structure that seems to have emerged is series of reflections in three parts—the personal, the prophetical and the paradoxical. The personal part explores my own experience of spirituality and my shared experience of spirituality with my wife, Angie. The prophetical part explores my embrace of the prophetic call I felt and the four roles through which I have expressed that prophetic call: as an interrogator, a protester, a practitioner and an inspirator. The paradoxical part explores my making and my unmaking as a prophet, first accepting and then rejecting some of the more confrontational prophetic roles that I've played in order to assume a more caring pastoral role in my community and the wider society.

The style is idiosyncratic. Some may say it is an eccentric mixture of the styles—prose, poetry and song—that I have used for my reflections. My friend Malcolm Doney says it is "part manifesto, part memoir, and part compilation album." Thankfully the quality of my poor text has been enriched through the alchemy of Karen Hollenbeck-Wuest's editorial art.

I would like to thank Brian McLaren for writing the introduction for the *Dave Andrews Legacy Series* series and Nimmi Hutnik for writing the introduction for *To Right Every Wrong*, which I expect will serve as the final text in the *Dave Andrews Legacy Series*.

---

6. Dear, *The Beatitudes of Peace*, 116–117 (edited).

I would also like to thank James Hurst for doing the detailed work of formatting for the text, and providing the bibliography and the general, author and scripture indexes.

I would like to dedicate this book to my long-suffering wife, Angie, who has said that on the Day of Judgment, God won't ask my fans, who haven't lived with me, for their judgment of me, but rather will ask her, my wife, for her judgment. Lord have mercy.

—Dave Andrews
(at home in Brisbane in my seventieth year towards heaven)

PART 1

THE PERSONAL

DAVE

My name is *Dave*, which is short for *David* in English, *Dawid* in Hebrew or *Dauod in* Urdu, as I have been called in Afghanistan, Pakistan, India and Sri Lanka.

The meaning of the name is uncertain, but my parents told me that *David* meant *Beloved*. In this sense I have grown up as a *David*, for I have grown up feeling *loved* by my father and mother and by the God whom my parents represented. Because I have been loved, I feel as if my identity is rooted in *being loved*, and my destiny is in learning to be able *to love others as I have been loved myself.*

I feel like I am a bit like Obelix, the cartoon character in the famous French comic book series *Asterix*, who is the protagonist's best friend. Like me, Obelix has long hair and a large girth; he is not particularly smart, but has superhuman strength. His power is derived from the vat of magic potion, brewed by a "druid," that he was fortunate enough to fall into as a child. I have no doubt that any power I may have is derived from the vat of the magic potion of *love*, brewed by my family, the "An-druids," which I was fortunate enough to fall into as a child.

The *sine qua non* of my life, the thing without which nothing makes sense to me at all, the beating heart of my songs, my books and my work, is that I am Dave Andrews—the *David*, the *Beloved of God*. That is the secret of my life. That is my experience, purpose, passion, hope and salvation. My name is *Dave, David, Dawid, Dauod, the Beloved*.

I was born David Frank Andrews in London on 20 May 1951, the second of four siblings in a small English family. My father, Frank, and my mother, Margaret, were Baptist Christians, and my father was a Baptist minister influenced by the Anabaptist tradition. After my family migrated to Australia in 1960, I was brought up in the Queensland Baptist Churches where my father served as pastor—Southport, Inala, Cairns and Sandgate.

In *Not Religion But Love*, I wrote about how my mother and father incarnated the love of God in their relationship to each other, their children, their neighbors and random strangers. They not only took people into their hearts, but also into their home. Home was always open for those in distress, and people going through difficult times stayed for a day, a year, or however long they needed.

As a young and impressionable boy, I can remember the excitement that some of those people brought to our house. A cat burglar who had just got out of jail showed us how easy it was to break into our house, and my parents never bothered locking the house after that. Not all encounters were exciting. Some were pretty scary for a kid like me with a vivid imagination.

Having a man who had stabbed someone to death sleep in the room next to mine made for some very restless nights and some very graphic nightmares. But my parents taught me to relate to and respect everyone as people—not just "robbers" and "murderers."

As I grew up I identified myself as a Baptist and identified myself with Anabaptists by becoming part of the Anabaptist Association of Australian and New Zealand. I have always understood the church to be a voluntary community of disciples who are committed to spirituality, simplicity, service, peace and justice, not episcopal in structure, nor aligned to the state. My nonconformist orientation became excruciatingly clear to me as a boy when I was encouraged to join Christian Endeavour and Boys Brigade. Looking back now I realize that they were both pretty daggy organizations, but I loved Christian Endeavour and hated Boys Brigade.

As I remember it, Christian Endeavour was a Young People's Society run by young people for young people "to promote an earnest Christian life among its members, to increase their mutual acquaintanceship, and to make them more useful in the service of God." I have been an "earnest Christian" all of my life. My Mum says I made a sincere commitment to follow Christ when I was four years old. So I was very interested in a young people's society that promoted an "earnest Christian life" that could make young people like me "more useful in the service of God." As it turned out I became particularly interested in the "service of God" that both preached "mutual acquaintanceship" and practiced "mutuality" by having everyone "be present at and take some part in every Christian Endeavour meeting."[1]

By contrast the Boys' Brigade was a Christian youth organization dedicated to "the advancement of Christ's kingdom among Boys and the promotion of habits of Obedience, Reverence, Discipline, Self-respect and all that tends towards a true Christian manliness." To develop this "Christian manliness" the Boys Brigade used military order, discipline and drills to run camps, gymnastics and scouting activities. (Scouts grew out of the Boys Brigade.)[2] Through attending Boys Brigade I discovered that I particularly detested uniformed hierarchies that instilled mindless obedience through "manly" marching drills.

Thus my affinity for anarchy— at least for mutuality over against hierarchy—was formed by my love of Christian Endeavour and my hatred of Boys Brigade. Nothing I have experienced in any Christian organization since has given me cause to change my mind—to the contrary, everything

---

1. https://en.wikipedia.org/wiki/Young_People%27s_Society_of_Christian_Endeavour

2. https://en.wikipedia.org/wiki/Boys%27_Brigade

has confirmed my convictions. Like Tolkien, the author of *The Lord Of The Rings*, I would say: "My political opinions lean more and more to Anarchy. . .. The most improper job of any man (sic), even saints, . . . is bossing other men (sic). Not one in a million is fit for it, and least of all those who seek the opportunity."[3]

This probably explains why I liked Inter-School Christian Fellowship during high school and Inter-Varsity Fellowship during college. Because, in my time, both were self-managed groups, with the gentle guidance of staff - nobody was bossing anybody about.

I attended state primary schools in Yeronga, Southport and Serviceton and state secondary schools in Inala and Cairns. I ran in long cross-country races and enjoyed playing football (often called "soccer"), which linked my Australian present with my English past. I enjoyed school, excelled in my studies, engaged in debates, won a Commonwealth Scholarship to attend university and was awarded the title "Far North Queensland Youth of the Year." But in spite of all these accomplishments, I was constantly confronted with Jesus' question: "What's the point of gaining the whole world, and losing your soul?" (adapted from Matthew 16:26).

In 1969 I moved down from Cairns to Brisbane to study at the University of Queensland, where I boarded at the Baptist Theological College in Hill End. When I moved out of the college to stay with friends in a flat in Highgate Hill, I attended a local early morning prayer meeting, where I met Ange.

ANGE

Ange was born Antonia Bellas in Brisbane on 16 February 1951, the first daughter of eight siblings in a Greek-Australian family. Her father, Jim, and mother, Athena, were devout evangelical Greek Christians, and Ange was brought up in the evangelical Greek Church in West End. She grew up singing the great hymns of faith in Greek, the language of her home and her heart.

Ange attended West End State School, where she made many friends, whom she still has today. Then she attended Brisbane State High, which she represented in regional sports as a sprinter. While going to "English" school, Angie and her siblings also went to Greek school and learned to read and write in Greek. After graduating Ange studied at college and worked as a manager for a broker.

3.. J.R.R. Tolkien, Letter to his son 1943, from *The Letters Of J.R.R. Tolkien.*

When she was eighteen years old, her beloved Aunt Olga died. Ange's life had been greatly impacted by her aunt, who had been struck down with multiple sclerosis and abandoned by her husband, but had endured her fate with great grace because of her faith. Determined to emulate her aunt's example, Ange decided to follow a "call" to walk in the footsteps of Jesus and chose to be baptized as an adult.

Ange's parents, James and Athena Bellas, operated the Star Milk Bar in downtown Brisbane, which was famous for its food and drinks. People would come from all over town for a fresh salad sandwich and a mango milkshake.

Every morning, very early, Ange's dad would open up the café, and it seemed like all the hobos round town would emerge from the hiding places where they had huddled during the night and make their way to the cafe. Ange's dad would welcome them, sit them down, serve them tea and toast and chat with them about the night they'd had and the day ahead.

If anyone needed a job Ange's dad would leave his brothers in charge of the café and go job hunting with them. If they got in trouble with the police, he would visit them in prison. He regularly visited those who got sick and wound up in hospital. When anyone friendless died, Ange's dad would go to the funeral so that no one would be buried without a friend. Often he'd be the only one there.

Ange's dad would invite folks home to share a meal with the family even though Ange's mum had eight children of her own to feed. If anything, meals at the Bellas' house were even more famous than the milkshakes at the Star Milk Bar, so there was never a shortage of people who were willing to take up the invite—or just invite themselves.

Ange's parents taught her the importance of being family to those who had no family, and how she could always enlarge even a large family to make room for one more. Not surprisingly Ange became the exceptionally kind-hearted, extraordinarily hard-working, enormously hospitable, wonderful human being that she is.

DAVE & ANGE

Ange and I were both brought up in homes that lived out God's love. Frank and Margaret Andrews and James and Athena Bellas were shining examples of those who are not preoccupied with themselves. As they made time and space for God, they made time and space for the people about whom God passionately cares. So Ange and I have unashamedly, but not slavishly, tried to copy our parents and also tried to set a similar example of divinely inspired, human compassion for our children.

Ange and I met at an early morning prayer meeting called the Quiet Time Association (QTA), which some friends and I had organized as a self-managed peer support group for people who wanted to sustain their spirituality.

The QTA played a significant part in shaping the development of my relationship with Ange. I was introduced to her by Jim Gibson, with whom I started QTA, and the vital, sincere, innocent spirituality of the group brought us together beautifully as friends.

One day I got a call from a pop star named Mike Furber, who was playing a gig at the famous Cloudland Dance Hall, asking if I could come with a friend to spend some time with him and his girlfriend after the show. At the time, Mike was one of the most popular male vocalists in Australia as the lead singer of Mike Furber and the Bowery Boys, who had hits such as "Just a Poor Boy," "You Stole My Love" and "That's When Happiness Began."

I had gotten to know Mike before he was famous, when he was an unwanted teenage migrant kid, who fled family violence to stay at our place for safety. Like many of the young men who stayed at our place, he slept in the spare bed in my room. We got to know one another quite well through the many chats we had in bed before we went to sleep at night. When he called, his solo career was on the skids, so he was feeling pretty depressed and wanted to talk.

I immediately thought that the best person to accompany me to Cloudland was the naturally easy-going, amazingly engaging Ange, and so I walked up to her house, which was around the corner, though I hadn't been there before. I skipped up the front steps, knocked on the door and was met by one of her six brothers, who asked me what I wanted. I told him the story, and he said I should come in and talk to his father. I told him the story and then asked if Ange might be permitted to go with me. Before I knew what was happening, I was being escorted out the door and down the stairs by Ange's brothers, leaving me in no doubt about how her father felt about my request.

So I went to talk with Mike on my own and did my best to support him over the next few months. Sadly, I eventually lost touch with him, but his visit brought Ange and me together in a way that we never expected.

One day shortly after the Cloudland gig, Ange came to my flat in tears, saying that she was Greek and, unlike the English, girls in her community were not allowed to go out with boys. She explained that they didn't go out on dates before they decided to marry; rather, they decided to get married, and then they were they allowed to go out on dates. But even then, according to their customs, all dates needed to be chaperoned, so there was no chance her father would let her go out with me on our own.

As I've said, I was an earnest, young Christian, and my earnestness was enhanced through Christian Endeavour, Inter-School Christian Fellowship, Inter-Varsity Fellowship and the Quiet Time Association. As a result of my extremely-naïve but exceptionally-sincere spirituality, I despised the dating game and deemed it to be manipulative and exploitative. So I told Ange that, given the cultural prohibition on going out before deciding to marry, I was open to discussing getting married before going out.

Ange was surprised, but not shocked, because we liked each other, got on well with each other, had a good connection, and she had been brought up in a culture that was disposed to discuss getting married before going out. So over the next few weeks we discussed what we should do and eventually decided we would talk to our parents about it. We'd start with my parents and then try hers.

My parents were very encouraging and said that having a shared faith, similar values and a solid friendship was a great basis for a long-lasting relationship. Having got the nod from my mum and dad, it was time to run the idea by Ange's mum and dad. However, because I had recently been thrown out of their house, we thought it would be better if Ange approached her parents on her own. Ange's mum was happy about the proposal, but her dad was very unhappy. For one, he and her mum had had an arranged marriage, and so he wanted to be the one to arrange a marriage for his elder daughter who was the pride of his life. Second, I was not Greek, but a "long-hairy-hippy-*Englesi*."

Being earnest young Christians, we turned to the Bible for guidance about how to resolve this conflict and read the words of Jesus in Matthew 18:15–16: "If a fellow believer hurts you, go and tell him—work it out between the two of you. If he listens, you've made a friend. If he won't listen, take one or two others along so that the presence of witnesses will keep things honest, and try again." We decided that the best "one" to take as a "witness" was Charles Ringma, who was not only a friend and mentor of ours, but, more importantly, a friend of Ange's father, who had known Charles and his wife, Rita, for many years and held them in very high esteem.

Charles and Rita Ringma lived in an old abandoned monastery in South Brisbane and ran the Good News Centre on Manhattan Walk opposite the South Brisbane Railway Station. In the early 1970s Charles and Rita had got involved with young people on the streets of the city, especially those who were lonely, vulnerable, destitute, desperate or doing drugs. Over time Charles and Rita's work with drug addicts morphed into Teen Challenge, a residential rehabilitation program for men and women.[4]

Ange and I wanted to live our lives incarnationally like Charles and Rita, and so it was natural for us to turn to them for help. They were what Ange and I wanted to be like in twenty years, and so we wanted to learn to live our lives as well as they did. We have always thought it was smart to learn from our own mistakes and wise to learn from older mentors so as to avoid as many unnecessary mistakes as we could.

Thus before Charles traveled to the USA for a nine-month training on running residential rehab programs, Charles spent his last night talking to Ange's dad and interceding on our behalf. But to no avail.

As a Greek, Ange saw marriage as something between families as much as individuals, and so she could not contemplate marrying me without the approval of both her mother and father. Therefore if we could not get their approval, we could not proceed with our relationship. We went to talk with my mum and dad to ask their advice, and they told us that they would go and talk with Ange's mum and dad.

A date was set for my mum and dad to visit Ange's mum and dad, but Ange's dad continued to insist that he wouldn't talk with them, so Ange and I got everyone in QTA to pray for a change of heart.

When the time came, my mum, dad and I presented ourselves at Ange's place, and her dad opened the door. Surprised and impressed with how polite, respectful and respectable my parents were, he invited us in. We all sat in the lounge room together, with Ange's parents and my parents in the inner circle, and Ange and I to the side. Over the next hour or so, our parents got acquainted, affirmed their common faith and their commitment to their families, especially regarding our welfare as their children. Then, somehow—I'm not sure how—Ange's dad was apparently satisfied, because he asked Ange and I to go to the kitchen to make tea for everybody while they arranged the marriage.

So it was that on 22 January 1972, Ange and I got married.

Discerning Our Call

As a boy I had been enchanted by the story of my namesake, David, the shepherd boy, who defeated the giant Goliath in mortal combat, armed with only his sling and a well-aimed stone, and then became a celebrated archetypal national hero. Apparently, at one time, the courageous, devoted, risk-taking David was also "a man after God's own heart" (Acts 13:22).

4. https://www.teenchallengeqld.org.au/history

The beautiful, heartfelt songs of David, the shepherd boy and singer-songwriter, have resounded through the centuries, touching the hearts of generations of people of faith even thousands of years after they were written. The Authorized English Version of Psalm 23 is, without a doubt, the most well-known, well-loved song in the whole Bible.

When I was young, Psalm 23 expressed my own deep, personal faith in a God of love, a good shepherd who leads, feeds and looks after his flock, each of whom, according to tradition, he knows by name. He protects them with his "staff" and provides for them "in green pastures" and by "still waters."

> The Lord is my shepherd; I shall not want.
> He maketh me to lie down in green pastures:
> he leadeth me beside the still waters.
> He restoreth my soul:
> he leadeth me in the paths of righteousness for his name's sake.
> Yea, though I walk through the valley of the shadow of death,
> I will fear no evil: for thou art with me;
> thy rod and thy staff they comfort me.
> Thou preparest a table before me in the presence of mine enemies:
> thou anointest my head with oil; my cup runneth over.
> Surely goodness and mercy shall follow me all the days of my life:
> and I will dwell in the house of the Lord for ever. (Ps. 23:1–6)

But as an adult, I became increasingly disenchanted with my namesake, David, who was God's beloved, but seemed to love no one but himself. I don't think David ever really loved the women in his life, and even though Jonathan "loved him as his own soul" (1 Sam. 18:1), and David said Jonathan's love for him "was wonderful, surpassing the love of women" (2 Sam. 1:26), David cynically manipulated and exploited the love of King Saul's son for his own purposes. When David became king, he used his much-loved status to unscrupulously consolidate his tyranny and cunningly take advantage of his devoted subjects.

By contrast I wanted to be a David who appreciated that I was "much loved" and who understood that "from those to whom much was given much will be required" (Luke 12:48). I wanted to be a faithful Dave who "loved others as much as I was loved."

In all religions the challenge is to love our neighbor as we love ourselves.

In Taoism the challenge is *descriptive*: "Regard your neighbor's loss or gain as your own loss or gain." In Jainism the call is *instructive*: "One who neglects existence disregards their own existence." In Hinduism, Buddhism, Zoroastrianism, Confucianism, Judaism and Baha'i the challenge is *imperative* and is framed *in negative terms:* "Never do to others what would pain you"; "hurt not others with that which hurts yourself"; "what is hateful to you do not do to your neighbor"; "do not impose on others what you do not yourself desire"; and "desire not for anyone the things you would not desire for yourself." In Islam, Sikhism and Christianity the challenge is *imperative* and is framed in *positive terms:* "Do unto all people as you would they should do to you"; "treat others as you would be treated yourself"; "do unto others as you would have them do unto you."

Jesus referred to this challenge as the old commandment. All people of all religions all over the world have always known that the basic rule for nurturing a healthy human family is to "do unto others as we would have them do unto us."

However, Jesus also gave us a *new* commandment: "A *new* commandment I give to you: that you love one another as I have loved you!"[5] In the old commandment we were challenged to "love our neighbor as we have loved ourselves." For most of us, trying to transcend our own egocentricity and ethnocentricity so that we can extend the same kind of quality of care to others as we extend to ourselves is a big enough challenge. But in the *new* commandment, we are challenged to love our neighbor *as Jesus has loved us.* This is the biggest challenge in my life—*to love others as I have been loved*—radically, deeply, personally, passionately.

Jesus loves tenderly, relentlessly, sacrificially throughout his life, but he illustrates this love most graphically and poignantly in his death. Jesus embraced both the pleasure and the pain of love in the real world. On the cross, when Jesus chose to love in the real world, he chose to be vulnerable to the savagery beneath the civilized surface of the real world. Jesus was resolute in his love. He absorbed the evil done to him, but refused to let that evil define him. Rather he overcame that evil with good. In him there was neither reaction, retaliation, nor retribution, but only *single-minded kindness.*

Throughout our life together, Ange and I have sought to flesh out this noble, bittersweet, beautiful, sorrowful, joyful, single-minded kindness that we see in the face of Jesus.

Embracing Our Call

After Ange and I got married in 1972, we wanted to discover how to live out this way of life as a family. Unfortunately many celebrated models of the faith were heroic individuals who either didn't have a family or who acted as if they didn't have a family and, more often than not, destroyed the family

5. John 13:34.

that they had. Fortunately, we had both been brought up in families that did not "sacrifice their families for the sake of the ministry," but whose ministry of incarnating the love of God started first and foremost in their families and then extended in ever-widening circles of radical compassion, including relatives, friends, neighbors and strangers. Ange and I wanted to do the same, just as we saw Charles and Rita doing, because for us, getting married not only involved responding to a "call" to be committed to a covenant to one another, but also to others.

The spiritually aware analytic psychologist Carl Jung says that while our call may come to us in our own words, our "vocation acts like a law of God. It makes demands upon us. It demands our best and, at times, even better than our best. To liberate, to redeem, to transform."[6]

Ange and I translated our sense of vocation into a set of vows. Taking a set of vows may seem a bit extreme, and I guess it probably is, but every time we talked about it, Ange smiled and replied, "We're simply trying to be moderate. But sometimes in this society, to be moderate, we've got to be extreme!"

Our first vow was *solidarity,* which involved committing ourselves to being open rather than closed to the suffering of those around us. It meant choosing to see the tears, to hear the cries and to open ourselves up to the agony of others.

Our second vow was *simplicity,* which involved committing ourselves to living, in spite of our relative wealth, as close as we could to the poverty line in our country. It meant not only that we experienced something of the struggle of the poor who live at the poverty line, but also that we committed to sharing any extra time and money that we had with the poor.

Our third vow was *service,* which involved committing ourselves to living a life of quiet help and loud protest with many marginalized groups, both rich and poor, who find themselves on the periphery of our community. This meant not setting any agendas, but being available to do anything we could to support those on the margins in their struggle for greater opportunity in our society.

When we got married, Ange and I were able to purchase a lovely little Queensland workers cottage on Rosary Crescent in Highgate Hill with money that Ange had saved from her salary and a gift that her dad gave so we could buy a house.

Then we read what Jesus said to a rich young person like us: "If you want to give it all you've got, go sell your possessions; give everything to the poor. All your wealth will then be in heaven. Then come follow me (Matt.

6. Jung, *Collected Works,* vol.12, 167–187

19:21, *The Message*). We decided that if we were going to take following Jesus seriously and "give it all" we had, we needed to "sell all our possessions and give everything to the poor"—our time, talent, energy and money.

Looking back this seems like an extraordinary decision for us to make, but in the late 1960s and early 1970s, the Jesus Movement was spreading throughout America, Europe and Australia, and many people were opting out of the system and exploring alternative lifestyles (like Charles and Rita).

We sold everything—house, furniture, carpets, appliances, my Ford Zephyr, Ange's Kenwood Chef Kitchen Mixer, our beautiful handmade bedspreads—and, over time, we gave most everything that we had away to the poor as we also began to work with marginalized and disadvantaged people.

At the beginning of 1973, Ange and I joined Floyd and Sally McClung, who had set up *Dilaram* (The House of the Peaceful Heart) in Kabul, Afghanistan to provide short-term support for travelers who were in acute distress.

Thus the first group of marginalized and disadvantaged people we worked with were Western travelers who had gotten waylaid as they were heading east on the Asian hippie trail. Some were weak because they had sold their blood at various stops along the way to pay for the next stage of their journey. Some were unwell because they had contracted dysentery from eating watermelons sold by the weight, which were made heavier by enterprising traders who injected them with dirty water from the fetid drains that ran by their stalls. Some were sick, because they had no resistance to diseases that they had never encountered before, such as malaria, cholera, typhoid and tuberculosis. While some enjoyed the unbridled delights of the best hashish you could buy in Asia, others got addicted to "brown sugar" and developed bruises, abscesses and hepatitis from careless sharing and shooting up with unsterile needles. Others were caught by the police and incarcerated in the inhuman hell-holes of some of the most brutal prisons in the world alongside some of the most brutalized and brutalizing prisoners in the world.

Then in the middle of 1973, after a revolution in Afghanistan, it was decided that Ange and I should go with a small team to set up another *Dilaram* community in New Delhi, India to offer long-term friendship, hospitality and rehabilitation.

The second group of marginalized and disadvantaged people we worked with were Indian young people, who mixed with the foreign young people who passed through Delhi, and had similar problems. One had dangerous hallucinations after eating magic mushrooms and stripped stark naked, then ran around campus acting crazy, freaking out the students at the Delhi University. Another had cannabis-induced psychosis, became acutely paranoid and hid out among the dead in the Hauz Khas tombs. Another had a schizo-effective disorder and was subjected to primitive electro-convulsive therapy, where he was strapped to a cot and given repeated shocks to the brain, which, without any anesthetic, was torture.

In 1978 Ange and I joined Nimmi Parambi, an Indian psychologist, and Susie Mathai, an Indian social worker, to set up an intentional community with and for Indians called *Aashiana,* which literally means "nest" in Urdu and figuratively means "a place of protection, support, nurture and sustenance," where broken people could take refuge, lick their wounds, begin life again and grow stronger before taking wing. We visited people in hospitals and prisons and invited young people in need to live with us. There were many who were addicted to drugs of all kinds, such as booze, morphine and heroin. One was so depressed he wouldn't speak to us at all. One was so distressed he sat constantly banging his head against the concrete wall. One pulled the wiring out of our front room, scraped the paint off the partition with his fingernails, tore his clothes into pieces, heaped them into a pile of scraps and shat on them in the middle of our apartment. One was so suicidal that he was driven to stab himself in the heart one night in our kitchen.

Working with locals rather than travelers, we needed to engage them as individuals within their own complex spiritual, cultural, social, economic and political worlds. Doing rehabilitation with Indian addicts meant, on the one hand, that we could draw from the rich resources of their spiritual, cultural and social traditions, and, on the other hand, that we could encourage them to engage both their own personal poverty and also the economic and political poverty in their context.

In light of this, the third group of marginalized and disadvantaged people that we worked with, in collaboration with the recovering addicts in our community, were among the most vulnerable people we had ever met—the devastated survivors in Burari, North Delhi, whose village had been totally wiped out by the worst flood in a century, and the destitute *Kanjars,* who had come from their villages to the big city in the hope of getting some relief from the grinding poverty they had endured, only to be forced to eke out their meager existence in the Gautamnagar slum in South Delhi by foraging for waste materials from the municipal garbage dumps to sell to scrap dealers. Under the auspices of *Aashiana,* our friends set up *Sahara* as a therapeutic community to provide a place of rehabilitation for addicts and *Sharan* as a community organization that could help manage emerging grassroots development programs in villages and slums.

In 1984 the Indian government changed its visa policy with regard to Commonwealth citizens and instructed Ange and I to leave India. In 1985, after we returned to Australia, Ange and I (along with our friends Chris and Ruth Todd) set up an intentional community to work with three groups of marginalized and disadvantaged people in West End, a neighborhood in our hometown of Brisbane. We called this community network the West End Waiters Union, or simply the Waiters Union, to reflect our desire to be like waiters, waiting in the background, available to help people in West End who needed a hand.

As the Waiters Union, we worked with indigenous people who had a strong association with Musgrave Park at the heart of West End—and have had that connection for as long as anyone can remember. Yet their presence in that space has been continually contested, and a proposal to build an Aboriginal Cultural Centre in the park was passionately opposed for years by the Greek Community Centre across the road. Young Aboriginals, who gather in the park, have continually been moved on unceremoniously by police officers at the behest of local property owners adjacent to the park. Aboriginal Elders have been unfairly racially profiled and falsely detained by security officers. Aboriginals and Islanders are ten times more likely to be imprisoned than the general population and fifteen times more likely to die in prison. After over a hundred "black deaths in custody" in the previous twenty years, the tragic death in custody of a young talented Aboriginal dancer in 1993 caused an unprecedented eruption of outrage by the local Aboriginal people, which left more than thirty people injured. Since then, not much progress has been made in closing the gap between us.

We also worked with refugees who had come by sea to our country, fleeing persecution, torture and war, only to be incarcerated illegally by the government in a system of clandestine detention centers. Already traumatized refugees have been further traumatized by officers in body armor and balaclavas, who force families with young children into prison-like compounds by using paramilitary-type operations, where the families are then subjected to demeaning treatment by guards in the name of security. All the children who have been detained for more than one year show signs of Post-Traumatic Stress Disorder, serious depression and suicidal ideation. Those refugees who are fortunate enough to be released from detention still have to face multiple barriers to meaningful integration into Australia, because many don't have the right work, and so they can't earn the income necessary to access affordable accommodations, basic services, essential education or community activities. Since the terrifying attacks on the World Trade Center in 2001, many Muslim refugees have had to face barriers to meaningful integration because Australians suspect that they are frightening harbingers of terrorism rather than vulnerable people fleeing terrorism. Many have been spat on, sworn at and told to go back to where they came from.

We also worked with people who have physical, intellectual and psychiatric disabilities who have been ostensibly deinstitutionalized, only to be locked up again in nearby Boggo Road Jail, or forced to stay in supervised hostel accommodations round South Brisbane or to sleep in the parks by the Brisbane River. Many of these people live with chronic and acute trauma. One woman had been so badly beaten by her father that she was left with serious brain damage, which affected her sight and agility. Another woman was so terribly abused by her brother that she poured petrol over him and set him on fire, only to be sent to detention for her trouble. Two women with disabilities had two children each, whom they couldn't adequately care for—even with our support and help—and so both women had their children removed by the state and fostered out to other families and consequently wanted to kill themselves.

Suicide attempts among these dear, traumatized people have been all too common. One time a woman leapt out of a car as one of us was driving and lay down in the road so that she would be run over by the car behind us, which couldn't keep from running over the top of her, and so crushed her ribs and shattered her limbs. Another time, over a three-week period, we knew three people who tried to kill themselves by jumping off the Kangaroo Point Cliffs overlooking the Brisbane River. The first man jumped head first and hit the ground at the bottom of the cliffs, killing himself. The second man jumped feet first, and when he hit the ground, he broke his legs, but did not kill himself. The third man fortunately tumbled into the water, which still injured him, but not too badly. Years later, a woman we knew well threw herself from South Bank into the river not far from the Kangaroo Point Cliffs and drowned herself.

Ange and I have been living in West End and seeking to find what it means to love all these different groups of people ever since.

PART 2

THE PROPHETICAL

PROPHETIC SENSIBILITY

A Call to Love

I have come to believe that the love we are called to is a sacrificial concern for the welfare of others, one that is not self-righteous, but self-forgetful. Love is not masochistic, but willing to make significant sacrifices spontaneously to ensure the welfare of others.

Love always works toward mutuality, but love requires sacrifice in order to create the possibility of reciprocity. Without sacrifice, there is no possibility of reciprocity. Thus even though love always works toward mutuality, its potential can paradoxically only be realized in reciprocal relationships, where concern for mutual advantage is not an issue that anyone fights for, but one for which everyone equally and joyfully makes sacrifices in the interest of the other.

Love is seldom considered a political virtue, but as Professor Edgar Brookes points out, "the world languishes because love is being tried so little." I agree with him when he says that love should not be left out of the political process because "it is imperative that it should be admitted to the field of politics."[1] If love were not only put onto our political agenda, but also put at the top of our agenda as the starting point for dealing with all issues, it would profoundly affect the way we do politics.

First, as the ecumenical leader Michael Cassidy says, love would remind us that "politics is all about people—ordinary people and, for the most part, very ordinary people." Second, love would help us remember that the practice of due process in politics starts here and now with us. "If I don't let it start in my own heart, I cannot expect it to start at all." Third, love would help us remember that, while due process in politics may start with us, it can never be consummated without the full, free and frank participation of others, including those who may oppose us. Fourth, love would help us recognize the humanity of our opponents in the midst of disputes and forgive the enmity that often erupts from unresolved disputes. As Michael Cassidy puts it, "Unless we build [on the basis] of forgiveness, we will lose the day!"[2]

A Call to Justice

Justice has no separate meaning apart from the meaning that love imparts to it. Justice is the concrete manifestation of love as policy in our political

---

1. Edgar Brookes, in Cassidy, *The Politics of Love*, 124.
2. Cassidy, *The Politics of Love*, 125–135.

economy. Love is the ideal and justice is our attempt to realize that ideal in our community. At best, our realization approximates our ideal. At worst, it parodies our ideal.

The transcendent ideal of love constantly challenges our concrete attempts to realize that ideal as we try to bring justice to disadvantaged groups of people, affirming any progress and confronting any compromises we may make along the way. Justice involves putting the people at the bottom of the heap on the top of our priorities and treating them in a way that will make them feel more loved and more able to love.

Justice is not a mass-produced, consumer product, but a craft product produced by the masses. Justice is not something that we can acquire ready-made, like a nice car; it is something that we can only achieve if we build it ourselves, like a good friendship. We don't achieve justice by taking rights that we consider to be ours without considering our responsibility to others. We act justly when we give ourselves to doing what we know is right by one another.

Justice that preserves people's self-respect by doing what is right by one another will always be a struggle as we seek to empower those who, hitherto, have been overpowered, so that people from every stratum of our society can move toward being less autocratic, more democratic and more active in seeking and finding the elusive synergy and serendipity of consensus through participatory processes of corporate decision-making in communities, both large and small.

The American theologian Reinhold Niebuhr reminds us that democracy is not a panacea. He describes it, rather ironically, as "a method of finding proximate solutions for insoluble problems." But democracy is nevertheless a very important process in our struggle for justice because, as he says, our "capacity for justice makes democracy possible, but [our] capacity for injustice makes democracy imperative." According to Niebuhr, "the highest achievement of democratic societies is that they embody the principles of resistance to government with the principle of government itself."[3]

The French Christian anarchist Jacques Ellul warns us not to take any such achievements for granted because "experience has shown the state will only retreat when it meets an insurmountable obstacle. The obstacle can only be citizens organized independently of the state. But once organized, the citizens must possess a truly democratic attitude in order to depoliticize and repoliticize" our society in terms of community. Ellul reminds us that "democracy becomes possible only through every citizen's will; it remakes

---

3. Harland, *The Thought of Reinhold Niebuhr*, 164.

itself every day, through every citizen. It must be forever started again, reconstructed, begun again."[4]

A Prophetic Calling

In the Hebrew Scriptures, the prophets spoke of what it would be like to begin again, "to do justly, love mercy and walk humbly with God" (Mic. 6:8). We may be able to begin again, but even at our best, what we can accomplish is only partial and temporary. We know there is a long way to go before the work of transformation that we are hoping for is permanent and complete. Prophets like Isaiah help us grasp a vision of God's promise of a "new heavens and a new earth" and hold on to that promise when all hope is gone.

> Behold,
> I will create new heavens and a new earth.
> The former things will not be remembered,
> nor will they come to mind.
> But be glad and rejoice forever in what I will create,
> for I will create Jerusalem to be a delight and its people a joy.
> I will rejoice over Jerusalem and take delight in my people;
> the sound of weeping and of crying will be heard in it no more.
> Never again will there be in it an infant who lives but a few days,
> or an old man who does not live out his years;
> he who dies at a hundred will be thought a mere youth;
> he who fails to reach a hundred will be considered accursed.
> They will build houses and dwell in them;
> plant vineyards and eat their fruit.
> No longer will they build houses and others live in them,
> or plant and others eat.
> For as the days of a tree, so will be the days of my people;
> my chosen ones will long enjoy the works of their hands.
> They will not toil in vain or bear children doomed to misfortune;
> for they will be a people blessed by the LORD,
> and their descendants with them.
> Before they call I will answer; while they are still speaking I will hear.
> The wolf and the lamb will feed together,
> and the lion will eat straw like the ox,
> but dust will be the serpent's food.
> They will not harm on all my holy mountain,says the LORD.
> (Isa. 65:17–25)

---

4. Ellul, *The Political Illusion*, 224–236.

In the new world order that God will establish, the prophets tell us that there will no longer be any tears—or, indeed, anymore cause for tears. The normal causes of pain for the poor will be totally eliminated. Infant mortality will be eliminated. Children will no longer die. Adults will live to a ripe old age. Unemployment, underemployment and exploitative employment will be eliminated. People will be able to work, enjoy their work and get a just reward for their work. Homelessness will be eliminated. People will be able to build their own homes and live in their homes. And there will be at peace at last!

I was always fascinated by the prophets' capacity not only to critique the status quo, but also to articulate an alternative vision of the future. As I read and re-read the Scriptures, reflecting on these proclamations of the prophets, I had a growing conviction that I was being called to be a prophet—not a major prophet, but a not-too-sure-of-myself minor prophet.

The American author, Franciscan Friar, Richard Rohr says "If we're going to talk about biblical prophets . . . our starting point is an . . . experience of . . . God . . . as we see in Isaiah 6, that . . . is so absolutizing that it has the effect of relativizing everything else. . ."[5]

The story of Hosea absolutely gripped my imagination as a young man and inspired me to be committed to a long-haul godly fidelity in the midst of general infidelity. When I reflected on what the Lord required of me, I thought it was exactly what he had asked of Micah: "To do justly, love mercy and walk humbly with God" (Mic. 6:8) I also thought that I heard the same call that had come to Jeremiah so long ago: "seek the welfare of the city . . . for in its welfare you will find your welfare" (Jer. 29:7).

I will never forget how the word of God that came through Amos echoed in my soul: "I despise your religious festivals; I cannot stand your assemblies. But let justice roll on like a river, righteousness like a never-failing stream!" (Amos 5:21, 24). Like the prophetic figure in Isaiah, I felt that "the Spirit of the Sovereign Lord is on me, because the Lord has anointed me to proclaim good news to the poor. He has sent me to bind up the brokenhearted, to proclaim freedom for the captives and release from darkness for the prisoners" (Isa. 61:1).

But lest I be considered presumptuous, I didn't tell anyone—except my best friend, who wisely advised me that if my calling had any merit, then time would tell, and others would recognize my calling without any prompting from me.

5.. Richard Rohr, "Understanding the Prophet," adapted from Rohr, *Prophets Then, Prophets Now.*

Up till now I never referred to myself publicly as a prophet because even though I have always affirmed the functions of apostle, pastor and prophet, I have also always had a visceral reaction to turning those functions into offices and conferring the people in those offices with titles. Jesus explicitly warned against elevating the status of ordinary mortals and specifically condemned the use of titles as a way of putting people on pedestals (Matt. 23:8–10, *The Message*). For this reason, I vowed from a very young age never to get a doctorate or to get ordained. I never, ever wanted to have a title. Though I felt called to be a prophet, I never wanted to be called a "Prophet." So I cherished the call quietly in my heart.

Revolutionary Sympathy

My understanding of a prophet has been shaped by Abraham Heschel, a Polish-born American rabbi who became one of the leading Jewish theologians of the twentieth century. Heschel was not only a professor of Jewish mysticism at the Jewish Theological Seminary of America, he was also active in the American civil rights movement, marching alongside Martin Luther King Jr. from Selma to Montgomery.

Heschel authored a number of widely read books, his most influential being a two-volume masterpiece, *The Prophets,* which was first published in 1962.[6] In the first volume, Heschel surveys the various messages of the different prophets in the Bible. In the second volume, he explores the singular essential prophetic experience that all the prophets share.

For Heschel the essential prophetic experience is "sympathy" with God, noting that the God of the Bible is not "apathetic" and "nonresponsive," but "empathic" and "compassionate." Heschel cites Jeremiah, who says that God grieves with us when we are hurt: "For the wound of the daughter of my people, is my heart wounded—my grief is beyond healing!" (Jer. 8:21–22). He also cites Zephaniah, who says that God rejoices over us when we are happy: "God . . . will rejoice over you with joy . . . he will joy over you with singing" (Zeph. 3:17). Thus the prophet is one who "sympathizes" with God in both his agony and ecstasy.[7]

Heschel argues that such sympathy with God is possible, not because God is "anthropomorphic" (where we make God in our own image), but because God is "anthropopathic" (God has made humanity in God's own image). As men and women who are made in the image of an "empathic," "compassionate" God, we are created to feel angry, along with God, when

6. Heschel, *The Prophets.*

7. Heschel, *The Prophets,* vol. II, 87.

we hear about injustice, and we are created to feel delight, along with God, when see justice being done.[8]

In my first book I asked the question, *Can You Hear The Heartbeat?* (as in, *Can You Hear The Heartbeat of God?*). I asked this question out loud to anyone who might hear me, but first and foremost, I addressed the question to myself as a wannabe prophet who was trying to follow in the footsteps of Jesus.

In *Not Religion But Love*, I wrote a chapter entitled "Revolutionary Sympathy," where I said:

> Being a devotee of Jesus is not a matter of subscribing to a certain set of dogmas, obeying rules and regulations, and getting others to subordinate themselves to them. The essence of being a devotee of Jesus is to live in sympathy with God as Jesus did, feeling the throb of God's heartbeat, and teaching our hearts to learn to beat in sync with the love that sustains the universe. It means developing our capacity to intuitively sense what causes love pleasure, and what causes love pain, and doing everything we can to enhance the pleasure, and to diminish the pain.[9]

This "revolutionary sympathy" is at the very heart of my prophetic spirituality.

Radical Compassion

Jesus played the part of a truly radical compassionate prophet.

From the moment he was conceived, his mother Mary knew that Jesus would be a revolutionary figure: a king who would not only overthrow other kings, but the very idea of kingship itself. He would stand with radical empathy against relentless cruelty for the sake of genuine inclusivity, equity and equality. As far as Mary was concerned, her son Jesus was going to be the answer to her people's prayers (Luke 1:46–55).

Mary is said to have sung a song of praise that reflected her deep, profound, personal faith in God and revealed her joyous and jubilant appreciation of God's great faithfulness to her as a person: "My soul praises the Lord and my spirit rejoices in God, my Savior, for he has been mindful of the humble state of his servant. From now on all generations will call me blessed, for the Mighty One has done great things for me—holy is His

---

8. Heschel, *The Prophets*, vol. II, 49–58.

9. Andrews, *Not Religion but Love*, 28.

Name. His mercy extends to those who fear Him, from generation to generation" (Luke 1:46–50).

Mary's song has been described by Stanley Jones as "the most revolutionary document in the world."[10] Mary celebrated her experience of God as a God of love and justice, whom she prays will one day overthrow the rich and the powerful and uphold the poor and the powerless: "He has performed mighty deeds with His arm; He has scattered those who are proud in the plans of their hearts. He has brought down the mighty from their thrones, but has lifted up the humble. He has filled the hungry with good things, but has sent the rich away empty. He has helped His servant Israel, remembering to be merciful to Abraham and his descendants forever, even as He said to our fathers" (Luke 1:51–56).

Jesus grew up with a compassionate concern for the welfare of his people, particularly those for whom no one else was concerned. He was passionately concerned about the plight of the poor, who were victims of the imperial system, and the predicament of the prisoners, disabled and disadvantaged, who were excluded from all meaningful participation in society by bars of steel and stigma. He was also passionately concerned about the condition of the lepers, both because of the pain of their ulcers and also the pain of their untouchability. And he was passionately concerned about ordinary people whose hope had been destroyed by their circumstances and who felt consigned to long days and even longer nights of utter despair.

For Jesus, a compassionate concern for people meant a passionate commitment to people. He became forgetful of himself, living in constant remembrance of the forgotten ones who gathered around him. He desperately wanted people to feel fully alive again, to revel in the joy of being loved and being able to love once more. He worked tirelessly to set them free from all that might debilitate them, breaking the bonds of exclusivity, poverty, misery and guilt. He welcomed the outcasts, helped the weak, healed the sick and forgave the sinner, giving everyone another chance at a new beginning. He didn't write anyone off, and he encouraged everyone that he met not to dismiss one another. He challenged everyone to tear up their prejudices, trash their stereotypes and just get their act together—mixing up the "in" crowd with the outcasts, the strong with the weak, the rich with the poor, the saints with the sinners—and to support one another in their common quest for their own humanity.

Jesus criticized people of all religions for promoting domineering leadership (Mark 10:42–43), acting as closed groups that were not open to others (Matt. 5:47) and practicing empty rituals without embodying

---

10. Barclay, *The Gospel of Luke*, 9.

practical compassion (Matt. 6:7). Jesus never intended to start a religion—particularly a monopolistic religion that would bear his own name and see itself in competition with other religions for people's allegiance. Jesus simply said that he came "to bring life and life in all its fullness" (John 10:10). Thus I think Jesus would affirm all that is life-affirming and confront all that is life-negating in all of the world's religions.

Jesus did not play the part of a reformist priest—because he was against the establishment. He did not try to play the part of a traditional rabbi—because he was against legalism. He did not try to play the part of a classical monk—because he was against asceticism. And he did not take up arms and fight as a guerrilla—because he was against violence, from both the left and the right.[11]

Rather, Jesus loved the world and showed people a revolutionary way that they could love their world just as he did. For Jesus, liberation could never come from Sadducean rules and regulations, Pharisaic rituals and ceremonies, Qumranic disciplines and practices or Zealot strategies and tactics. For Jesus, liberation could only come through real love—substantive, sacrificial, giving and forgiving love—for God and neighbor, for friends and enemies.

Prophetic Grieving

My understanding of a prophet has also been shaped by Walter Brueggemann, one of the most influential American Protestant theologians and biblical scholars of the last several decades. He is an important figure in the progressive Christian movement in America, whose work often focuses on the Hebrew prophetic tradition and the socio-political imagination of the church. He argues that the church must provide a counter-narrative to the dominant forces of nationalism, militarism and consumerism.

Brueggemann believes that God can "raise up prophets" anywhere, anytime, in any country, tradition or religion. But he believes that prophets are more likely to emerge in communities that are oppressed and longing for liberation. For him, Moses is the prophetic prototype and Exodus is the prophetic paradigm. Moses spoke out, in sympathy with God, against the brutal reality of an imperial regime that had enslaved his people, hoping for and imagining an alternative future, which did not yet exist, of a divinely constituted society of freed slaves. Brueggemann says that Moses embodied the two psychodynamics that characterize the psyches of all prophets to this very day: grieving and imagining.

11. Küng, *Christianity*, 34.

Over the years I have become increasingly sensitive to the world around me, and I have come to realize that all prophetic engagement must begin with grieving. Though there is much to grieve, not everyone mourns the current state of the world. What we feel depends on what we see and hear, and what we see and hear depends on where we stand in the world. If we identify with the top 20 percent of the world's population, who are "well fed" and "laugh" (Luke 6:25), we will probably "rejoice with those who rejoice" (Rom. 12:15). But if we identify with the other 80 percent of the worlds' population, especially the bottom 20 percent, who "go hungry" and "weep" themselves to sleep (Luke 6:25), then we will "mourn with those who mourn" (Rom. 12:15).

The Scriptures suggests that God identifies with all people because they are made in his image—both rich and poor alike (Gen. 1:26–7). Yet God has a special place in his heart for the poor who are treated heartlessly (Prov. 14:31). When God comes into the world through Jesus, he makes it very clear where he stands. He says, "whatever you do to one of the least"— those whom most people consider the least, including the marginalized, distressed, disabled and disadvantaged—you "do it to me" (Matt. 25:40, 45). God says that whenever you crush my people contemptuously, God takes it personally—as if you are actually crushing God and God is grieving it deeply. God says, "My people are crushed, I am crushed; I mourn, and horror grips me" (Jer. 8:21–22).

As God's people, we are called to love the world as God does, and given the state of the world, all who love the world as God does will mourn over the state of the world as God does. As we sympathize with God and empathize with our neighbors who are in pain, we will inevitably be moved towards compassion, which is "a deep sense of shared pain" (Luke 10:27). Jesus is our supreme example of compassion: "When he saw the crowds, he had compassion on them, because they were harassed and helpless, like sheep without a shepherd" (Matt. 9:36).

As the great German liberation theologian Dorothee Soelle says, there are three phases of grieving associated with a compassionate response to a world in pain: wailing, lamenting and crying out loud.[12]

The first phase, *wailing*, is when we agonize with the pain, either as a victim or as one who loves the victim. Jesus wailed with Mary over the death of her brother Lazarus: "When Jesus saw her weeping, and the Jews who had come along with her also weeping, he was deeply moved in spirit and troubled. 'Where have you laid him?' he asked. 'Come and see, Lord,' they replied. And Jesus wept" (John 11:33–5).

---

12. Soelle, *Suffering*, 73.

The second phase, *lamenting,* is when we analyze the pain, both its tragic causes and its catastrophic consequences, which we see in the psalms of lament. Jesus also lamented over Jerusalem:

> As he approached Jerusalem and saw the city, he wept over it and said, "If you, even you, had only known on this day what would bring you peace—but now it is hidden from your eyes. The days will come upon you when your enemies will build an embankment against you and encircle you and hem you in on every side. They will dash you to the ground, you and the children within your walls. They will not leave one stone on another, because you did not recognize the time of God's coming to you." (Luke 19:41–44)

The third phase, *crying out loud,* is when we criticize the groups and organizations that are the perpetrators of pain in our society so that the public is forced to confront the issues. Jesus cried out loud against the merchants in the temple:

> When it was time for the Jewish Passover, Jesus went up to Jerusalem. In the temple courts he found men selling cattle, sheep and doves, and others sitting at tables exchanging money. So he made a whip out of cords, and drove all from the temple area, both sheep and cattle; he scattered the coins of the moneychangers and overturned their tables. To those who sold doves he said, "Get these out of here! How dare you turn my Father's house into a market!" (John 2:13–16)

For Jesus, criticizing the groups and organizations that were the perpetrators of pain in their society included *crying out loud* about his own people's complicity in their own oppression. Jesus was painfully aware of the captivity of the political economy in which he lived, and he recognized that this captivity was perpetuated by a preoccupation with power, position, and property, at the expense of people's lives. "'What the world esteems,'" Jesus said, "'is disgusting to God!'" (Luke 16:15). His critique was universal, but Jesus actually chose to confront this captivity at a national level, rather than an international level. Jesus was more concerned more with the mechanisms of control that were being perpetuated by his own people, than with the mechanisms of control that were being perpetuated by others, for Jesus knew that unless these domestic mechanisms of control were dealt with, the foreign yoke might be thrown off, but the captivity would continue. So Jesus confronted the people in his own country—the people of his own culture, tradition and religion—with their responsibility for their own captivity, and for their own liberation. "'Don't judge others,'" Jesus said. "'Judge yourself'" (see Matt. 7:1–3). "'How sad it is,'" he said to the religious leaders of his day, that "'you neglect to do justice!'" (see Luke 11:42). He taught his disciples, "'What will it profit [you] if [you] gain the whole world but forfeit [your] life?'" (Matt. 16:26).

Prophetic grieving is not about whining, (or as we say in Australia "whingeing"), but something more profound: *wailing* (agonizing with the pain), *lamenting* (analyzing the tragic causes and catastrophic consequences of pain), *crying out loud* (criticizing the groups and organizations that are the perpetrators of pain in our society), and *facing the awful truth* (that we can be complicit in our own oppression).

Weeping As A Prophet

I weep over the twentieth century.

I am a child of the twentieth century, the bloodiest century in history. More people were slaughtered in the twentieth century than in all the centuries that preceded it put together. I weep when I face the terrible violence that was visited upon millions of innocent men, women and children.

In 2002 I visited the Armenian Genocide Museum in Yerevan with my good friend, Armen Gakavian, whose family was forced to flee the slaughter at the beginning of the twentieth century. We were reminded that the total number of Greeks, Assyrians and Armenians killed has been estimated at between 1 and 1.5 million people, which included half of the entire Armenian population.

Towards the end of the twentieth century, the Khmer Rouge killed between 1.5 to 3 million people. In 2009 I visited the Cambodian Genocide Museum based at Tuol Sleng, the site of a former school, which was used as the Security Prison 21 (S-21), the most notorious of the 150 torture centers that were scattered around the country. Torture, forced labor and mass executions led to the deaths of an estimated quarter of the total Cambodian population.

The "Jewish" genocide took place at the heart of the twentieth century. In this Holocaust, "the worst single atrocity that our world has ever known," Jewish men, women and children were systematically tagged with yellow stars, then dragged out, beaten up and shot or rounded up like animals, thrown onto cattle trucks and herded into concentration camps, where the "productive" were put to work in slave battalions and the "unproductive" were put to death in gas chambers. Six million Jews, representing about two-thirds of the nine million Jews who had resided in Europe at that time, were killed. Over one million of the Jews who were killed were killed in Auschwitz.

In July 2016, the sky was crying as I silently walked in and around the buildings in Auschwitz. I saw pages filled with the personal names of each of the six million Jews who were massacred in the Holocaust. I saw partitions filled with photos of the faces of old and young, strong and weak, dignified and terrified brothers and sisters who were all killed in Auschwitz—not only Jews but also Poles, Russians, Romani and Sinti, religious leaders, political dissidents, prisoners of war, people with disabilities, marginalized gays. I saw the wall where these dear people were shot, the gallows where they were hanged, the chambers where they were gassed and the piles of shoes, clothes, glasses and prosthetics that these dear people left behind. And like Jeremiah, "I wish[ed] my head were a well of water and my eyes fountains of tears, so I could weep day and night for casualties among [these] dear, dear people" (Jer. 9:1, *The Message*).

I also weep over the twenty-first century.

I remember writing an article for *The Westender*, my local newspaper in February 2014, lamenting the fact that "We Are Entering A New Dark Age." I went onto describe how, "lately, more than ever, I have been having a recurring nightmare—that the world is moving slowly but surely towards what I call 'A New Dark Age'. And, when I wake up every morning, I see every reason to believe this nightmare is becoming a terrible reality."

Jacques Attali, a professor of economics at the Polytechnique in Paris and president of the European Bank for Reconstruction and Development, wrote in 2003:

> By 2050, 8 billion people will populate the earth. More than two-thirds will live in the poorest countries. Seeking to escape their desperate fate, millions will attempt to leave behind their misery to seek a decent life elsewhere. But neither the Pacific nor the European spheres will accept the majority of poor nomads. They will close their borders to immigrants. Quotas will be erected and restrictions imposed. [Renewed] social norms will ostracize foreigners. Like the fortified cities of the Middle Ages, the centers of privilege will construct barriers of all kinds, trying to protect their wealth.[13]

As I looked around, I could see clear signs that a "New Dark Age" had begun. Some of the features of the emerging neofeudalism that I observed include the following. For one, there is an emergence of powerful, unelected or unaccountable leaders who act as "lords" by offering protection in return

13. Attali, *Millennium*, 74–78.

for subservience and services. People are either "for" or "against" these lords. Those who are for these lords live as vassals, waiting on the lords and living off the crumbs that fall from the tables of the lords. In exchange, they find refuge in times of danger inside the castles of their lords.

Those who are against these lords are branded as infidels. The lords wipe out all the infidels, either by leaving them to starve outside their gates in times of hunger or by slaughtering them in crusades. There are no universal basic human rights. The only right is might. Civilization is the private preserve of the lords and their vassals, and they justify this iniquitous "civilization" in the name of religion.

The Australian sociologist Ghassan Hage shares my view, observing, "Not so long ago the state was committed to the welfare of everyone within its borders. (We even called it 'the welfare state.') That is no longer so."[14] Nowadays, he says, "We seem to be reverting to neo-feudal times, when the boundaries of civilisation no longer coincide with the boundaries of the nation, but the boundaries of upper class society. . . ."[15] In such a society, "there are no universal rights—only the privilege of the elite."[16]

He goes on to say how "we are increasingly witnessing the rise of a culture that combines a siege (castle) and warring (crusade) mentality; by necessity it emphasizes the exclusion (and/or) eradication of the potentially threatening other."[17] As a result, "in each country now, there are first-world elites and third-world threats to the elites. In this neofeudal age the challenge is not how to integrate the marginalised, but how to rid ourselves of these third-world threats (the refugees and refugee claimants that we have on our doorstep.)"[18]

We have begun to build more and more of what we euphemistically call gated communities, which are citadels guarded by walls, infrared cameras, heat-sensitive alarms and private security companies. Purpose-built, as Mike Gore, the developer of Sanctuary Cove, puts it, to keep "the cockroaches" out![19]

The Australian government under John Howard turned the whole continent into a gated community like Sanctuary Cove. Millions of dollars, which were supposed to be dedicated to foreign aid, were spent on the "Pacific Solution," a flotilla of heavily armed patrols dedicated to preventing

14. Hage, *Against Paranoid Nationalism*, 20.
15. Hage, *Against Paranoid Nationalism*, 18.
16. Hage, *Against Paranoid Nationalism*, 20.
17. Hage, *Against Paranoid Nationalism*, 140.
18. Hage, *Against Paranoid Nationalism*, 20.
19. Summo-O'Connell, *Imagined Australia*, 75.

asylum seekers from ever setting foot upon our shore. This policy is neither "pacific," nor a "solution," but is meant to keep the queue jumping "cockroaches" out!

The Australian government under Kevin Rudd took the "Pacific Solution" further with its "PNG Solution," according to which, "any asylum seeker who comes to Australia by boat without a visa will be refused settlement in Australia, instead being settled in Papua New Guinea if they are found to be legitimate refugees." The policy includes "a significant expansion of the Australian detention facility on Manus Island, where refugees will be sent to be processed prior to resettlement in Papua New Guinea, and if their refugee status is found to be non-genuine, they will be either repatriated, sent to a third country other than Australia or remain in detention indefinitely."

The Australian government under Tony Abbot funded "a nasty little comic book intended to deter those seeking asylum from making the journey to Australia; the narrative culminates with images of asylum seekers languishing miserably in mosquito-plagued camps." After a series of tragic incidents in the Manus Island detention facility, Jeff Sparrow says, "Perhaps an updated version can now depict them being shot or hacked at with machetes. Why not? That's the logic of deterrence, isn't it? Continue to make refugees miserable until the oppression they face from Australians becomes worse than that which they're fleeing."[20]

Seeing these signs of "A New Dark Age" in my country, I joined with forty concerned Christian leaders from around the country on 17 June 2015 to converge on Canberra, occupy the Parliament House, and publicly grieve over the injustice done in our name. As Brueggemann says, "prophets are not lonely voices against the establishment but are representative voices that give social expression to engaged social constituencies."[21]

Before being physically removed by security, we joined hands in a circle and sang an updated Australian version of a traditional African American lament:

> Were you there when the kids were locked away?
> Were you there when the kids were locked away?
> Oh, Oh, Oh Oh,
> Sometimes, it causes me to tremble, tremble, tremble.
> Were you there when the kids were locked away?

---

20. Sparrow, *The Guardian* (18 February 2014).
21. Brueggemann, *The Prophetic Imagination*, 58.

Like Jeremiah, "I wish[ed] my head were a well of water and my eyes fountains of tears, so I could weep day and night for casualties [we have caused] among [these] dear, dear people" (Jer. 9:1, *The Message*).

Prophetic Imagining

As I have already said, Brueggemann, who profoundly shaped my understanding of the prophetic, authored a number of widely read books, the most influential being his classic called *The Prophetic Imagination,* which was first published in 1978.

In it, Brueggemann asserts how Moses embodied the psychodynamics that characterize the psyche of all prophets to this day: grieving and imagining. When speaking out in sympathy with God, Moses not only grieved the brutal reality of the imperial regime that had enslaved his people, but he also imagined an alternative future of a divinely constituted society of freed slaves. Though this society did not yet exist, God would one day make it a reality.[22] Brueggemann argues that "the depth of the prophet's grief is actually what allows the penetration of hope all the way down into the despair of the people," but it's the prophet's imagination that is "most important" in leading the people out of their despair.[23] The prophet's role in helping people move from grieving the dominating present to imagining a liberating future is crucial because, as the psalmist reminds us, "without a vision" of a liberating future, "the people perish" in their despair (Prov. 29:18).

Brueggemann describes the essential task of prophetic ministry as follows:

> . . .to nurture, nourish, and evoke a consciousness . . . [that is] alternative to the consciousness . . . of the dominant culture. The alternative consciousness to be nurtured, on the one hand, serves to criticize in dismantling the dominant consciousness. To that extent, it attempts to do what the liberal tendency has done: engage in a rejection and delegitimizing of the present ordering of things. On the other hand, that alternative consciousness to be nurtured serves to energize persons . . . by its promise of another time and situation toward which the community of faith may move. To that extent, it attempts to do what the [evangelical] tendency has done, to live in fervent anticipation of the newness that God has promised.[24]Moreover, he says that

22. Brueggemann, *The Prophetic Imagination.*

23. Brueggemann, *The Prophetic Imagination,* Kindle loc. 124.

24. Brueggemann, *The Prophetic Imagination,* 67–78.

the prophet "cultivates the collective imagination, which paves the way for God to redefine the people of God in their specific situation."[25] The prophet tells us that the God who "gives a new song to those who grieve, birth to the barren, and nourishment to the hungry will actually bring the new community to the edge of their seat, not grasping but waiting in anticipation of what God will do to generate newness in God's people."[26]

For me, Jesus is the archetypal prophet; his own prophetic imagination was stimulated by the Hebrew prophets, especially Isaiah, who inspired his message and whom he explicitly cites at the beginning of his ministry. Luke describes this moment in his Gospel:

> And [Jesus] went to Nazareth, where he had been brought up, and on the Sabbath day he went into the synagogue, as was his custom. He stood up to read, and the scroll of the prophet Isaiah was handed to him. Unrolling it, he found the place where it is written:
>> "The Spirit of the Lord is on me,
>> because he has anointed me
>> to proclaim good news to the poor.
>> He has sent me to proclaim freedom for the prisoners
>> and recovery of sight for the blind,
>> to set the oppressed free,
>> to proclaim the year of the Lord's favor."
> Then he rolled up the scroll, gave it back to the attendant and sat down. The eyes of everyone in the synagogue were fastened on him. He began by saying to them, "Today this scripture is fulfilled in your hearing." (4:16–21)

From that day on, Jesus began to name the new movement of the "Lord's favor," announcing the alternative future he imagined as the "gospel of the kingdom of God" or the "gospel of the kingdom of heaven." While Matthew primarily uses the "kingdom of heaven" and other Gospel writers use the "kingdom of God," it is clear that these two expressions mean exactly the same thing (compare Matt. 5:3; Luke 6:20).

The main message of Jesus was not being "born again" (which he mentions only twice in one Gospel), but the kingdom of God/heaven (which he mentions more than seventy times in the four Gospels). The Gospel of Mark

---

25. Brueggemann, *The Prophetic Imagination*, 67–78.

26. Brueggemann, *The Prophetic Imagination*, 67–78.

tells us that he "came . . . saying, 'The time is fulfilled, and the Kingdom of God is at hand; repent and believe the gospel'" (1:14–15).[27]

Jesus wanted people to imagine that the kingdom of heaven could come on earth, and he wanted them to imagine that they could make it a reality in their own lives. He advocated heaven as a way of life that people could experience here and now, on earth, in this life as well as the next by teaching them to pray, "May your kingdom come, may your will be done on earth as it is heaven," every day (Matt. 6:10).

In the Beatitudes, Jesus introduced his disciples to the vision of the kingdom of God that he imagined—where it would be possible to experience heaven on earth:

> Blessed are the poor in spirit, for theirs is the kingdom of heaven.
> Blessed are those who mourn, for they will be comforted.
> Blessed are the meek, for they will inherit the earth.
> Blessed are those who hunger and thirst for righteousness, for they
>   will be filled.
> Blessed are the merciful, for they will be shown mercy.
> Blessed are the pure in heart, for they will see God.
> Blessed are the peacemakers, for they will be called children of God.
> Blessed are those who are persecuted because of righteousness, for
>   theirs is the kingdom of heaven. (Matt. 5:3–10)

The first part of each verse is a *Be-attitude*, or blessed attitude, that Jesus encouraged people to practice as a way of incarnating the kingdom of heaven on earth. The second part of each of these verses is an actual blessing of the kingdom of heaven on earth. The Beatitudes start with the phrase, "Blessed are the poor in spirit, *for theirs is the kingdom of heaven.*" The Beatitudes finish with the phrase, "Blessed are those who are persecuted because of righteousness, *for theirs is the kingdom of heaven.*" Both are present tense, so Jesus is saying that if people practice the Be-Attitudes, they will experience the blessings of the kingdom of heaven on earth here and now!

---

27. Following are several other examples. In Luke 4:43, "He said, 'I must proclaim the good news of the kingdom of God to the other towns also, because that is why I was sent.'" Luke 8:1 says, "After this, Jesus traveled about from one town and village to another, proclaiming the good news of the kingdom of God." In Mark 10:14, "He said to them, 'Let the little children come to me, and do not hinder them, for the kingdom of God belongs to such as these.'" In Mark 10:15, he says, "'Truly I tell you, anyone who will not receive the kingdom of God like a little child will never enter it.'" Mark 10:23 says, "Jesus looked around and said to his disciples, 'How hard it is for the rich to enter the kingdom of God!'" In Mark10:25, he says, "'It is easier for a camel to go through the eye of a needle than for someone who is rich to enter the kingdom of God.'" In Matt. 6:33, he says, "'But seek first his kingdom and his righteousness, and all these things will be given to you as well.'"

Jesus envisaged the blessings of the kingdom of heaven on earth as a world where those who mourned would be "comforted" (v. 4), the meek would "inherit the earth" (v. 5), those who hungered and thirsted for justice would be "fulfilled" (v. 6), those who gave mercy would "receive mercy" (v. 7), the peacemakers would walk proudly as "sons and daughters of God" (v. .9), the pure in heart, from all over the world "would see God" (v. 8), the physically hungry would be "filled" (Luke 6:21), and those who had wept bitterly would "laugh" happily once more (Luke 6:21). This is surely the kind of world that I imagine most people would hopefully envision for their children and grandchildren.

Campaigning As A Prophet

In 2000, I began meditating on the Beatitudes more intentionally for some reason, and so when 9/11 occurred in 2001, I reflected on the attack and counter-attack in the light of the Beatitudes. Both the attack and the counter-attack were based on a traditional, reactive approach that demands "an eye for eye," based on the words of Moses (Exod. 21:24). I called this "Plan A."

Plan A treats others like they treat us. On 9/11, Osama Bin Laden ordered an attack on the twin towers of the World Trade Center at the heart of the American Empire. As the world looked on in astonishment, Bin Laden cried, "Here is America struck by God Almighty in one of its vital organs, so that its greatest buildings are destroyed."[28] In retaliation, George Bush ordered an attack on Osama Bin Laden in Afghanistan and also on Saddam Hussein in Iraq (who did not have any weapons of mass destruction or anything to do with the 9/11attack, but had tried to kill Bush senior.) Bush claimed, "God told me to strike al-Qaeda and I struck them, and then he instructed me to strike at Saddam, which I did."[29] As a result, over a hundred thousand innocent civilians have been killed—and we are still counting.

The trouble with the "eye-for-an-eye" approach of Plan A is, as Gandhi said, that, in the end, it makes us "blind," so we are unable to see the sort of things that will bring about peace, love and justice.

Over against Plan A, Jesus gives us an alternative transformative response in his second commandment: "You shall love your neighbor as yourself" (Matt. 22:39). I called this approach "Plan Be," where we seek to treat others like we would like to be treated rather than treating others like

28. Lincoln, *Holy Terrors*.
29. Austin, Kranock and Oommen, *God and War*.

they treat us. This ethic is expressed in what I refer to as the "Be-Attitudes of the Beatitudes."

Very few Christians framed their responses to 9/11 in terms of the Beatitudes. In "Cold Turkey," Kurt Vonnegut, the satirical American author, wrote: "For some reason, the most vocal Christians among us never mention the Beatitudes. But—often with tears in their eyes—they demand that the Ten Commandments be posted in public buildings and of course that's Moses, not Jesus. I haven't heard one of them demand that the Sermon on the Mount, the Beatitudes, be posted anywhere."[30]

The Plan Be Revolution

I became convinced that it was time, now more than ever, to campaign for Plan Be, calling all people to practice the Be-Attitudes, becoming the "people that be" over against the "powers that be" in order to, as Gandhi put it, "be the change we want to see in the world."

To begin, I wrote a series of articles on each of the Beatitudes for a Brethren magazine. In response to these articles, I was asked to lead a retreat for Servants in the Swiss Mountains, walking through the Alps and sitting on a hillside to talk about each of the Beatitudes.[31] I was then invited to share these talks at Greenbelt, an alternative Christian Festival, where I spoke about "Plan Be" to the largest crowds I'd ever preached to before. I also recorded a podcast on what I began to call the "The Blessed Be-Attitude Revolution." A publisher at Greenbelt heard my talks, saw the reaction of the crowds and suggested that I publish them. The talks became my book *Plan Be*.[32]

Plan Be was adopted by the Uniting Church in South Australia, who used it as a framework for their churches, colleges and schools, and TEAR Australia dedicated a whole edition of *Target* to *Plan Be*, promoted the *Plan Be* resources through their organization throughout Australia.[33] Then MICAH, a global coalition of hundreds of mission and development agencies, invited me to share *Plan Be* at their international conference in Switzerland. Thus the call for a Blessed Be-Attitude Revolution spread around the

---

30. Vonnegut, "Cold Turkey,."

31. The Swiss home team for Servants for Asia's Urban Poor.

32. After *Plan Be* became a bestseller, I published a prequel, *Hey, Be and See*, and also a sequel, *See What I Mean*. After the popularity of *Plan Be*, the Bible Society helped to publish complementary *Plan Be* study guides, journals, tracts, CDs, DVDs, and a website on http://wecan.be

33. They also published my book *People Of Compassion*, which gives encouraging examples of people who have practiced the *Be-Attitudes* throughout history.

world, challenging people to implement four important, simple, sequential practices.

Recite the Be-Attitudes

The first practice is to restore the Beatitudes to the memory of the church by reciting them in church every Sunday. Reciting creeds is not enough because they do not have any ethical content. If we are going to recover the ethics of Jesus, we need to recite the Beatitudes as well. By reciting the Beatitudes, we will regularly focus on the following groups of people, just as Jesus did:

1. *the poor*—or those who identify with the poor "in spirit"
2. *those who mourn*—or those who grieve over the injustice in the world
3. *the meek*—or those who get angry, but never get aggressive
4. *those who hunger and thirst for righteousness*—or those who seek justice
5. *the merciful*—or those who are compassionate to everyone in need
6. *the pure in heart*—or those who whole-heartedly desire to do what is right
7. *the peacemakers*—or those who work for peace in a world at war
8. *those persecuted for righteousness*—or those who suffer for just causes.

Enact the Be-Attitudes

The second practice is to encourage Christians not only to learn but also live out the Be-Attitudes in the Beatitudes by sincerely committing ourselves to do the following:

1. *identify* with the poor "in spirit"
2. *grieve* over injustice in the world
3. *get angry,* but never get aggressive
4. *seek justice,* even for our enemies
5. *extend compassion* to all in need
6. *act with integrity,* not just for the publicity
7. *work for peace* in the midst of the violence

8. *suffer ourselves,* rather than inflict suffering.[34]

Nurture the Be-Attitudes

The third practice is to organize "Be" groups to help people overcome socially acceptable addictions to riches, status and violence, just as A.A. and similar groups help people overcome socially unacceptable addictions to porn, alcohol and drugs. These groups also encourage people to incarnate the radical, personal-political Be-Attitudes that are at the heart of the Blessed Be-Attitude Revolution:

1. *Solidarity*
2. *Empathy*
3. *Self-restraint*
4. *Righteousness*
5 *Mercy*
6. *Integrity*
7. *Non-violence*
8. *Perseverance.*[35]

Share the Be-Attitudes

The fourth practice is to urge Be-lievers to share the radical, personal-political *Be-Attitudes* that are at the heart of the Blessed Be-Attitude Revolution with people of all religions. For example, in *The Jihad Of Jesus,* I envisage how the *Sharia Of Isa* might guide Christian and Muslim collaboration amidst the chaos of the ongoing "conflict of civilizations" in which we find ourselves.[36]

As I write, St John's Anglican Cathedral, along with, a number of other Anglican parishes in my hometown of Brisbane, have decided to use *Plan Be* for their Lenten reflections. [37]

34. In *Hey, Be and See,* I talk about how the Spirit empowers us to practice the Be-Attitudes.

35. In *See What I Mean,* I talk about how I try to practice each of the Be-Attitudes myself.

36. See http://www.jihadofjesus.com.

37. St. John's Anglican Cathedral recorded a special podcast on "The Blessed

PROPHETIC ROLES

In reflecting on my own prophetic engagement, I have found the prophetic framework put forward by Tim Catchim quite helpful.[38] In the book he co-wrote with my friend Alan Hirsh *The Permanent Revolution: Apostolic Imagination and Practice for the 21st Century Church*, they say that prophets tend to communicate about the "space" that exists between God's will and ours either by "criticizing" us for "the gap," on one end of a continuum, or by "energizing" us to "close the gap," at the other end of a continuum. Though prophetic engagement includes both criticizing and energizing, most prophets tend to emphasize one more than the other.[39]

Jeremiah is a classic example of a prophet who emphasizes by criticizing more than energizing. Jeremiah's primary role is to "root out," "pull down," "throw down" and "destroy" the old order, whereas the role of "planting," "growing" and "building" a new order is secondary (Jer. 1:10). Isaiah, on the other hand, is a classic example of a prophet who emphasizes energizing over criticizing. Isaiah's initial call is to "cease to do evil" (Isa. 1:16). But Isaiah's principal role is to invoke the creation of a "good future," a "new heavens and a new earth" (Isa. 65:17), a "new tomorrow" that is no longer a "place of sorrow," but a place that is "for its people a joy" (Isa. 65:18–19). A healthy prophetic engagement will always include both criticizing and energizing.

Catchim, drawing on the ideas that he developed with Hirsh, tell us that prophets also tend to communicate about the "space" that exists between God's will and ours either by passionately, powerfully and unapologetically "verbalizing" their message in order to "[expose] the gap," at one end of the continuum, or by imaginatively, inventively and ingeniously "visualizing" their message by "standing in the gap," at the other end of the continuum.

A prophet may engage the world in a predominately "verbalized" form through speeches, stories and parables. Nathan is a classic example of a verbalizing prophet who used a parable to expose the gap between God's will and David's.

Nathan was in a fix. David, the potentate, needed to be judged for committing adultery with a married woman and arranging for her husband to be subsequently killed. But according to custom, only a king could judge, and so the prophet had to find some way to get the king to judge himself. So he told a brilliant parable that recounted the king's actions in an intriguing,

---

Be-Attitude Revolution" for their parishioners, "On The Way," https://bit.ly/2G9x9pF/.

38. Hirsh and Catchim, *The Permanent Revolution*.

39. Catchim, *The Prophetic Ministry*.

disguised, parallel narrative, which got the king's attention and Nathan's hoped-for reaction—a condemnation. Nathan then courageously turned this condemnation back onto the king himself.

> The Lord sent Nathan to David. He came to him, and said to him, "There were two men in a certain city, one rich and the other poor. The rich man had very many flocks and herds; but the poor man had nothing but one little ewe lamb, which he had bought. He brought it up, and it grew up with him and with his children; it used to eat of his meagre fare, and drink from his cup, and lie in his bosom, and it was like a daughter to him. Now there came a traveller to the rich man, and he was loath to take one of his own flock or herd to prepare for the wayfarer who had come to him, but he took the poor man's lamb, and prepared that for the guest who had come to him." Then David's anger was greatly kindled against the man. He said to Nathan, "As the Lord lives, the man who has done this deserves to die; he shall restore the lamb fourfold, because he did this thing, and because he had no pity." And Nathan said to David, "You are the man!" (2 Sam. 12:1–7)

At the other end of the continuum, a prophet may engage the world in a predominantly "visualized" form through symbols, dramas and demonstrations. Hosea is a classic example of a visualizing prophet who stood in the gap by using his own life as an illustration of God's love: he married a promiscuous woman, who became a prostitute, and then remained faithful to her in spite of her infidelities.

The story of Hosea is set during the time of Israel's decline and fall in the eighth century BCE, a period when the people of Israel turn away from Yahweh. Though Yahweh had delivered them from slavery into the freedom of the land of promise and made a compassionate covenant with them of undying love and loyalty, they begin to prostrate themselves before Baal, a disreputable God of fertility.

So God asks Hosea to marry a woman named Gomer and to remain committed to her in spite of her many public betrayals. God says to Hosea: "Go. Show your love to your wife, though she is an adulteress" (Hos. 3:1). Then God asks Hosea to speak out of the pain he experienced because of his scandalously steadfast love for Gomer, in spite of her many public betrayals, so that the Israelites will recognize God's scandalously steadfast love for Israel, in spite of the pain God experienced as a result of Israel's many public betrayals. God tells Hosea, "The Lord loves the Israelites, though they turn to other gods" (Hos. 3:1). The drama of Hosea's love for Gomer is one of the most amazing demonstrations of God's scandalously steadfast love ever enacted in history.

The criticizing to energizing" continuum can be expressed in terms of "tone," and the verbalizing to visualizing continuum can be expressed in terms of "tactics." The crossover between these two continuums gives rise to four primary types of prophetic roles: the *interrogator, protestor, practitioner* and *inspirator*.[40] For the remainder of this section, I will reflect on my attempts to engage the world in terms of these four prophetic roles.

The Prophetic Interrogator

Richard Rohr says, "Prophets are people who speak out when others remain silent. They criticize their own society, their own country, or their own religious institutions." He says that true prophets "must first be true disciples of their faith." In fact, he says "it is their deep love for their tradition that allows them to criticize it at the same time. Their deepest motivation is not negative but profoundly positive." He states" There is a major difference between negative criticism and positive critique. The first stems from the need for power; the second flows from love." He insists true prophets are "both faithful and critical."[41]

The role of prophetic interrogators is "to study a script for a play, audit the performance of the script [and] ensure the intended meaning of the script is accurately communicated. They step in to the middle of a theatrical production and say, 'This is not what the author of this script intended to be conveyed in this scene.'"[42] Prophetic interrogators like me feel "passionate about making sure the Scriptures are lived out in ways that represent the heart of God, and incorporate 'criticizing' people, when they feel they go 'off-script,' [by] clearly 'verbalizing' their criticism" through their singing, preaching, teaching and writing.[43] After all, as the famous fearless preacher, Aiden Wilson (A.W.) Tozer, once stated: "We are not diplomats, we are prophets and our message is not compromise but ultimatum." [44]

---

40. Catchim *Prophetic Ministry,* Part 2.

41.. Rohr, "Disciples Prophets and Mystics" adapted from Rohr, *The Way of the Prophet*

42. *Prophetic Ministry,* Part 2. Note that I have changed the name of this role: Catchim refers to an interrogator as an "auditor."

43. Catchim, *Prophetic Ministry,* Part 2.

44. https://www.brainyquote.com/topics/prophets-quotes 4

I can remember one Sunday morning when I found myself playing this role almost exactly as Catchim describes it. I was invited to speak at a large regional charismatic church service, which started with a typical contemporary "worship" time, where everyone sang songs of praise over and over again for almost an hour. When I was eventually asked to speak, I began by asking the crowd to reflect on the songs they had been singing.

I wanted to open positively, so I picked a phrase from one of the songs that I liked. "Isn't that a great line?" I asked. "'Let the weak say I am strong in the strength of the Lord!'" The crowd cried, "amen."

"Do you love your times of worship?" I asked. They called out affirmatively. Then I asked, "I'm interested to know, how many time did Jesus call us to worship him?" They looked at me hesitantly. "What do you think— twenty times? ten? five?"

Then one lone voice shouted, "Never! Not once!"

"That's right," I said. "He received worship from Thomas when the disciple offered it, but Jesus himself never ever asked anyone to worship him. Never! Not once!" Then I asked, "If Jesus didn't ask us to worship him, what did he ask us to do?"

A few brave souls hollered, "Follow him."

"That's right," I said. "He never called us to worship him because he didn't want us to bow down to him like an idol, saying, 'You're so awesome, I can never be like you.' He called us to follow him because he wanted us to treat him as a role model, saying, 'I so admire you. I really want to be like you.' He wanted us to follow in his footsteps."

I concluded by stepping into "the middle of [the] theatrical production," as Catchim describes an interrogator's tactics, and saying, "How heart-breaking it must be for Jesus, whom we say we serve, that every week we gather to do something he never asked us to, and throughout the week, we forget to do the one thing that he asked us to do!"

There was awkward silence. Then the band played a favorite "worship" song, the congregation joined in singing and they moved on from the embarrassing moment.

Sometime later one Sunday evening a new doctor, who had moved into our neighborhood, came to our church because he said he wanted to work with "the poor and needy" and we had a lot of people in our church with diagnosed disabilities.

He sat next me during the service, so it gave me the chance to explain the way we do church. I explained that for us church was not about the performance of the ostensibly most abled, but the participation of everyone, especially those with so-called serious disabilities. I told him that very night a young man who was labeled "schizophrenic" would be preaching for the first time and, as he was very nervous, it was really important for us support him. He nodded as if he understood. But straight after this young man finished preaching, the doctor, who obviously felt he didn't do a good enough job, leapt to his feet and preached the sermon on the same text all over again, publicly correcting his "mistakes." I was enraged.

I waited till the end of the service, took the doctor on one side and castigated him. I said, "How dare you do that? I just told you that we are not concerned about 'excellence' as much as 'empowerment'; that we needed to support this man, no matter how faltering his efforts might be; but instead of supporting him, you shamed him." As I was scolding him, he crumpled and sprawled backwards. His glasses dropped off as he collapsed onto the floor, unconscious. Everyone turned to check out what happened. Some of my friends who knew how angry I was with him thought I must have punched him in the face. I lifted my open hands in the air to protest my in-nocence, saying, "I didn't touch him." It was as if, as my Pentecostal friends insisted, he had been well and truly "slain in the spirit."

Eventually the doctor came round. He put on his glasses. I helped him to his feet. And asked him if he was okay. He assured me that he was. He gathered his belongings and made his escape as quickly as he could. Not surprisingly he never returned to our church. He's not the only one to give me a wide berth if they see me walking down the road towards them.

Interrogating Through Singing

I've criticized people when they go "off-script" through my *singing*.

I remember being invited to speak at one of the biggest, richest, most successful Baptist churches in the western suburbs of Brisbane. I wanted to make sure that the songs we sang in the service reflected and reinforced my message, so I met with the band to teach them a song I wanted us to sing called "Let Justice Roll." I adapted it from the original version written by my friend Garth Hewitt.

They liked the music and were happy enough to play it. Then I showed them the lyrics. They refused to sing it. I told them the lyrics were quite sound, scriptural and biblically based, but I couldn't change their minds. They refused to sing the song with me.

In the end, I had to sing the song in this vast church with my shaky voice all by myself.

> We've silenced our prophets,
> We've shot down our dreamers,

Our lifeblood is money, we're exploiting the poor.
Oh, the people of the West just love to invest
In the system that keeps the poor world poor.
We have no compassion; our lifestyle is evil;
Higher living standard is the God we adore.
Oh, the people of the West just love to invest
In the system that keeps the poor world poor.
Let justice roll on like a river
Truth like an never failing ever flowing stream,
Then tears of rage will turn to laughter
And people become what they should be.

We ignore the ways of justice
Though we talk a lot about it;
We victimise the stranger seeking refuge in our land.
Oh, the people of the West just love to invest
In the system that keeps the poor world poor.
Greed is our mother, silence is our father,
Our epitaph is written in frustrated tears of rage.
Oh, the people of the West just love to invest
In the system that keeps the poor world poor.
Let justice roll on like a river
Truth like an never failing ever flowing stream,
Then tears of rage will turn to laughter
And people become what they should be.[45]

After the service was over, I went to greet people at the door, where I was met by a very angry man, who was tearing my books to pieces and screaming that I was possessed by the devil. Since that "disgraceful," "diabolical" public audit of so-called Western civilization, I'm told that the people of the West have gone on to invest in "bigger" and "better" things.

Interrogating Through Preaching

I've criticized people when they go "off-script" through my *preaching*.

I remember a friend asking me to speak at his large Brethren church. It was sometime after the invasion of Iraq, and I had been praying for an opportunity to speak in a church about the invasion. When my friend gave me the specific text for that Sunday morning, I felt this was my moment.

He had asked me to preach on Micah 4:1–4:

---

45. "Let Justice Roll," http://www.daveandrews.com.au/media/songs/02_let_justice_roll.mp3

In days to come
the mountain of the Lord's house
shall be established as the highest of the mountains,
and shall be raised up above the hills.
Peoples shall stream to it,
and many nations shall come and say:
"Come, let us go up to the mountain of the Lord,
to the house of the God of Jacob;
that he may teach us his ways
and that we may walk in his paths."
For out of Zion shall go forth instruction,
and the word of the Lord from Jerusalem.
He shall judge between many peoples,
and shall arbitrate between strong nations far away,
they shall beat their swords into plowshares,
and their spears into pruning-hooks;
nation shall not lift up sword against nation,
neither shall they learn war any more;
but they shall all sit under their own vines and under their own fig trees,
and no one shall make them afraid;
for the mouth of the Lord of hosts has spoken.

When I began to preach, I critiqued American interventionist foreign policy and Australia's willing complicity with an illegal "shock and awe" invasion that had led to the deaths of over a hundred thousand innocent civilians. I contrasted this with God's foreign policy, which is committed to international mediation ("judge between many peoples"), restorative justice ("arbitrate between strong nations") and sustainable peace ("beat their swords into plowshares, and their spears into pruning-hooks"; prevent "nation from lifting up sword against nation"; ensure that the nations do not "learn war any more"; all peoples "shall sit under their own vines and under their own fig trees, and no one shall make them afraid"). Then I asked, "why don't more of us, who claim to be 'God's people,' oppose the Coalition's program for aggression and support God's plan for reconciliation?"

As I preached, I noticed people leaving—one or two at first, then groups of three and four, then whole rows of people. When I had lost a third of the congregation, I said that if the rest wanted to leave, that was okay by me, but if they decided to stay, I wouldn't take it as a sign of agreement, but a gesture of willingness to listen to someone with whom they disagreed. After I assured them that staying did not mean agreement, most of the congregation resumed their seats and stayed.

At the end of the service, I went to the door to greet people on their way out, but no one would talk with me. Actually, one person did talk to me, but she turned out to be a visitor like me. When the friend who had invited me came up from downstairs, where he had been conducting kids' church, he discovered that I had managed to alienate everybody in his church. "I love you Dave," he told me, "but I will never be able to invite you back after this debacle!"

Interrogating Through Teaching

I've criticized people when they go "off-script" through my *teaching*.

Sometime back I was asked to lead a one-day seminar for one of the most highly regarded Christian aid and development agencies in the world. I decided I would use the opportunity to help audit their so-called "Christian aid and development."

When the staff assembled, I asked them to imagine that they were a group of people considering their aid and development strategy in the light of their mission philosophy. I asked them to imagine that some of them were church leaders, some a missionary committee, some a missionary society and some prospective missionaries who wanted to work in a Christian aid and development agency.

Then I told them that I was going to tell them about a radical mission strategy that was demonstrated in a controversial case study, which I was going to present to them in their roles as church leaders, missionary committees, missionary societies and prospective missionaries interested in Christian aid and development.

I told them that some of them might be familiar with this famous study, and I had changed some names so that they wouldn't be able to identify it readily. I wanted them to face the issues raised for them by this controversial case study afresh.

I set the case study in a politically repressive country called "Khuda-i-stan," which was under the yoke of a ruthless colonial regime that had a central government that regularly cut provincial insurgents to pieces. Hence political opposition was systematically destroyed.

I told them Khuda-i-stan was economically impoverished and had an underdeveloped agrarian economy. Land was its main capital base, and most land was owned by a few wealthy families. The few poor people who managed to have their own land struggled to pay 40 percent of their income in taxes, so many sold their land to the few wealthy families to pay their taxes and so became landless and had to struggle simply to survive.

I told them Khuda-i-stan was socially oppressive and had a rigid caste system, with a few high caste, some low caste, but most totally outcaste. The elite maintained their status by collaborating with colonialists while the masses had no status at all. The colonialists and their collaborators couldn't care less about the masses or their welfare.

I told them Khuda-i-stan was religiously conservative, with the majority of the population having very dogmatic beliefs. People worshipped in *mandirs,* and priests offered *puja* to their deity. The religious traditions supported the status quo—the political repression, the economic impoverishment as well as the social oppression. By all accounts, the religion was very anti-Christian.

Then I told them about the mission strategy that a man named "Mac" adopted to engage the oppression, impoverishment and repression in Khuda-i-stan.

Mac began by seeking to develop some basic credibility with the people. He went to a village and worked in a local manufacturing industry. He spent years there, just being part of the village life and using his trade in his village. Over time, he learned the language, spoke to his neighbors, listened to their stories and came to appreciate the plight of the many marginalized people in the village. The people came to appreciate Mac because he was compassionate and responsible, willing to work hard and he had a wonderful sense of humor.

Mac wanted to demonstrate the practical relevance of the gospel by showing the people the relevance of his faith to their life. He demonstrated the good news first through aid by giving food to the hungry, second through education by encouraging the rich to share their wealth with the poor, third through direct action by staging a protest against exploitation at the stock-exchange, fourth through development by organizing a viable credit co-operative, and fifth through transformation by empowering people to adopt cooperation as the model for collaboration in ordinary everyday life.

After some time, Mac disclosed the glorious secret of the gospel. He did not tell the people at first that he was a "Christian"—not only because they were anti-Christian, but also because they misunderstood the meaning of Christianity. He wanted to redefine the meaning of Christianity in their experience of transformation before he told them about the Christ.

In response to the questions that people asked, Mac began gradually to disclose the secret of the faith that he had already shown them was relevant to their lives. The people's responses to the gospel were amazing. Thousands joined him, and he organized them into hundreds of home groups all over the country.

But the authorities felt threatened by this mass movement of self-managed community groups, and it wasn't long before they accused Mac of being a member of the K.L.F. (Khuda-i-stan Liberation Front) and had him shot.

After describing the controversial case study, I divided the staff into four groups: church leaders, a church missionary committee, an interchurch missionary society and prospective missionaries who were interested in aid and development.

Then I asked each group to discuss the case study and answer the following questions from the perspective of their group: What are the strengths and weaknesses of Mac's strategy? How relevant is Mac's strategy to missions today? Would you encourage people to adopt Mac's strategy, or not?

After the groups had spent considerable time discussing the case study and answering the questions, I invited them to give their feedback. They all thought Mac's humble, vulnerable, culturally sensitive, bottom-up approach was a real strength of his strategy. However, the church leaders, missionary committees and interchurch missionary societies thought that Mac's unwillingness to be upfront from the start about being a "Christian" was a weakness. All four groups, especially the prospective missionaries, thought that Mac's staging of a public protest against exploitation at the stock exchange was his most serious weakness. After all, that protest got him killed!

Then we discussed the relevance of Mac's strategy. Not surprisingly, all four groups thought his personal approach was admirable, but his political approach of openly opposing the system was dangerous.

Then we discussed whether or not the groups would encourage others to adopt Mac's strategy. All four groups said they would not.

I observed how tragic it is that, even though we claim to be "Christians," when given a choice, a gathering of church leaders, missionary committees, interchurch missionary societies and prospective missionaries would deliberately reject the mission strategy of Mac, who is Christ!

Then I asked what we would need to change, both individually and institutionally, to be open to the high-risk, high-return mission strategy of Christ, who is Mac.

As I was leaving I overheard someone in the hallway say, "Who the hell does that old superannuated hippy think he is, talking to us like that?" Good question.

Interrogating Through Writing

I've criticized people when they go "off-script" through my *writing*.

I've published twenty books, and one of the most (in)famous is *Christi-Anarchy,* where I interrogate the shadowy track record of Christianity. I confess I was brought up to believe that Christianity was the "light in the darkness," but I've come to realize that Christianity has a dark side.

That dark side of Christianity is evident throughout history in all the ways that so many Christians have been so demonstratively un-Christlike in our behavior. So many of us have been dogmatic, judgmental, intolerant of political dissent and uncharitable towards disreputable minorities. Once Christianity becomes established as a religion with the support of the state, Christians are typically totally "unwilling to advocate crucial anti-establishment causes, like liberty, equality, and democracy for all."[46]

In order to make sense of this contradiction, I have found it helpful to look at the impact of two contradictory paradigms that people have used to try to interpret their relationship with Christ: a centered-set perspective and a closed-set perspective.[47]

A centered-set perspective is defined by the center and one's relationship to the center. From this perspective, Christians become part of the set by choosing to move towards the compassionate spirit of Christ, whom they have made the center of their lives. Being part of this set is about "turning towards Christ, whether we know him by that name, or not, beginning to judge our own lives for ourselves, in the light of his love, and beginning to trust his love to sustain us on the journey of personal growth and social change he is calling us to make." The journey is all about becoming Christlike and encouraging others to become Christlike, whether they become Christians, or not.[48]

A closed-set perspective is defined by an enclosure and who is included in that enclosure. From this perspective, Christians become part of the set by ascertaining whether their beliefs and behaviors are included within an enclosed set of boundaries. People can become part of the "in" set by subscribing to a certain set of circumscribed beliefs and behaviors, such as confessing Jesus Christ is Lord, and repenting of their sins. Those who conform become insiders. People who don't conform to these beliefs and behaviors can never be part of the "in" set. They are outsiders. If an outsider wants to become an insider, the only way to do so is by subscribing to the terms of the set. This is known as evangelism. If someone is inside the set, but doesn't want to subscribe to the set terms, that person will be

---

46. Andrews, *Christi-Anarchy,* 56–58.

47. Hiebert, "Conversion, Culture and Cognitive Categories"; Hiebert, *Anthropological Reflections on Missiological Issues.*

48. Andrews, *Christi-Anarchy,* 57.

put out. This is known as excommunication. "It is through defending these boundaries of belief and behavior that Christians define their identity as 'Christ-ians' or 'Christ's-ones.'" Hence closed-set Christians tend to fight to the death to defend these boundaries of belief and behavior because they believe that their religious identity and eternal destiny with Christ depend on the boundaries.[49]

In my mind, a closed-set perspective affords Christianity certain obvious advantages: "It is simple, precise, and portable; clear, concise, and communicable. To become a Christian all you have to do is confess 'Jesus Christ is Lord' and repent of your sins. Once you're a Christian, you're in. And once you're in, you're in. Saved! Secure, safe and sound." However, the serious disadvantages of the closed-set perspective significantly outweigh the advantages. Though it is straightforward, it is also superficial. It is essentially static, unchanging and unchangeable. As I write in *Christi-Anarchy*, "it is a homogeneous ideology that admits no questions, unless of course it asks and answers the questions itself. It is a uniform theology that demands complete conformity. There is no room at all for diversity, dissent or disagreement. It is reductionist: it reduces a relationship to Christ to a formula. It is exclusive, excluding anyone who cannot affirm the formula."

The closed-set perspective is not necessarily violent, but normally it is. I identify three reasons for this in *Christi-Anarchy*:

> Firstly, Christians tend to defend their boundaries to the death. Secondly, the best form of defense has always been attack. Thirdly, there are plenty of competing groups fighting for the right to define and defend their boundaries of belief and behavior for themselves. Thus the Closed-Set . . . rips the heart out of [Centered-Set] Christianity, replacing the warm, kind-hearted compassion of Christ with cold, hard-headed propositions about Christ, and relating to people in terms of an ideology of Christianity, rather than the love of Christ."[50] And that is always dangerous!

Unfortunately, the closed-set perspective has been the most definitive perspective for Christianity. While Christianity has sometimes served as "the opiate of the people," at others, it has acted as "'a benzedrine for brutality,'" which has unleashed such a rush of unconscionable cruelty on such a massive scale that Christians have shamelessly slaughtered entire

---

49. Andrews, *Christi-Anarchy*, 57.

50. Andrews, *Christi-Anarchy*, 56–58.

civilizations in frenzies of righteous indignation." As I say in *Christi-Anarchy,* "to the victims, this Christianity is the Antichrist!"[51]

When *Christi-Anarchy* was first published, it caused quite a bit of controversy. Some even claimed it was a denial of two thousand years of Christian tradition. At one time, Koorong, the biggest Christian bookseller in Australia, refused to stock *Christi-Anarchy* openly on their shelves lest it "cause offense" to their customers. One major Christian mission agency even threatened to sue me. Patricia Harrison, Missions Lecturer at Tabor College in Sydney, warned readers that "those afraid of moving out of their comfort zone are advised not to read this book."[52]

In spite of the controversy, *Christi-Anarchy* has become a bit of a cult classic. I wasn't surprised the book was received well by people who were disillusioned with Christianity, who used the book as a conversation starter with Christian friends. But I was surprised when so many nice, straight, middle-class, middle-of-the-road, evangelical and charismatic Christians responded to the book so appreciatively.

I will never forget the phone call I got from my elder sister, Ruth, an Australian Baptist missionary who happened to be a member of the large Baptist church where the band had refused to play "Let Justice Roll." I'd sent her a copy of the book and waited rather anxiously for her reply, as I was uncertain how she would take it. When Ruth eventually called me, all she could do was cry and say over and over again, "Thanks for writing *Christi-Anarchy*, Dave. It says what I think but what I've never had the words—or the courage—to say publicly myself.

The Prophetic Protestor

Richard Rohr says "A true prophet must be educated inside the system, knowing and living the rules. . ." He says "Only with great respect for and understanding of the rules can a prophet know . . . what (are) non-essential or not so important . . . (and) how to properly break those very same rules—for the sake of a greater purpose."[53]

The role of prophetic protestors incorporates criticizing people when they go off-script by acting out their criticism through symbols, dramas and demonstrations. Prophetic protestors are "provocateurs who devise creative, subversive actions that confront current scenarios. By providing

---

51. Andrews, *Christi-Anarchy*, 43–44.

52. Andrews, *Christi-Anarchy*, iii.

53.. Rohr, "Edge of the Inside," adapted from Rohr, *Way of the Prophet*.

an alternative point of reference, a visible deviation from the norm, they challenge our imaginations and question the legitimacy of the status quo."[54]

Jeanette Mathews says in *Prophets as Performers,* "When speaking of prophets, we might better describe them as performance artists than actors in a pre-set drama. Performance art is often focused on 'developing the expressive qualities of the body."[55] Yvonne Sherwood speaks about prophetic performance art as: crazy actions and crazy language are prophetic special effects designed to create the special effect of . . . *das Heilege,* which so frequently finds its expression—as Other—through the unnatural, abnormal."[56]

My mother was a prophetic protestor. I think her propensity for protest was formed in her by her father, who was a Scottish trade union activist in England, and fashioned in her by her faith as an active follower of the revolutionary Jesus.

My mum was in London during the Blitz in World War II, when the Germans were bombing the hell out of the English, and my mum's own next-door neighbor's house was blown to smithereens. So it came as no surprise when an enemy aircrew that had been shot down were not lavished with provisions from the scarce resources rationed throughout the city while they were in captivity. But my mum protested their mistreatment by getting food from her own rations, taking it to the detention camp and sharing it personally with those prisoners of war. Some people who came to know what she was doing called her a traitor. She admitted she was a pacifist, but insisted she was a patriot—and to prove it, she ran messages above ground between below ground air-raid shelters during the air raids, when the skies were raining bombs.

After the war, when my more activist mum married my conservative dad, they embarked on a jointly agreed mission of pastoral ministry together. Throughout their marriage my mum happily channeled her energy into her role as a pastor's wife. However, when my dad died in a car crash, my mum prayed she wouldn't merely survive his death, but thrive after his death, and in answer to that prayer, she felt free to recover a passionate prophetic role that she had not been able to play for years. As an energetic septuagenarian, she joined TEAR Australia, became an active member of a TEAR support group committed to social justice, advocated for people seeking asylum in Australia and got involved in a series of political protests, which culminated in her personally presenting a national petition demanding human rights

54. Catchim, *Prophetic Ministry,* part 2.

55.. Carlson, *Performance,* 110.

56.. Sherwood, 'Prophetic Performance Art (editorial)', 1.2, author's italics.

for refugees on behalf of TEAR Australia to Philip Ruddock, the minister for immigration at the time.

My mum taught me that, as a follower of Jesus, I needed to practice justice, protest injustice and be committed to nonviolent direct action. I was brought up not to carry arms, not to use drugs or alcohol, not to hide my identity behind a hood or a mask, not to resort to physical violence or verbal abuse and not to misuse facilities or damage any property in an intervention. Instead, I was brought up to dress neatly and tidily, to act in an exemplary manner, to respect my opponents as well as my supporters, to be strong but gentle, calm and constructive, to use good manners and good humor at all times, to adopt a dignified, friendly approach towards all, to render assistance to those most vulnerable and to resist the powers that oppress people.

Protesting Through Intervening

I've protested the "status quo" by *intervening* nonviolently in violent situations.

One of the earliest interventions that I can recall, which I initiated myself, was at my school in Inala. In those days Inala was considered to be one of the most deprived and dysfunctional outer suburbs in Australia based on socio-economic indicators of disadvantage. When my father accepted a call to the Inala Baptist Church, our family moved into the neighborhood, and I was sent to study at Inala State High School, which was as rough and ready and aggressive as the neighborhood in which it was embedded and enmeshed.

As a follower of Jesus, I intentionally tried to make friends with all the kids in my class, especially those who seemed to have few friends. One quirky kid was quite isolated, which made him vulnerable to attack. The class bully was a big boy who was a boxer. He practiced his boxing skills by punching the concrete posts around the school building with his bare fists. As a result, his knuckles were covered in bloody raw callouses. He took every opportunity he could to assert his total dominance in the class by beating up on the more defenseless kids. And I felt constrained to intervene on behalf of the quirky kid who was at risk.

Every time the bully attacked the kid, I would step between them, protecting the kid and asking the bully to back off and give the kid a break. As the bully got increasingly annoyed with me, he used to take a step forward instead of a step back, and then he'd get in my face and punch me in the head instead of the kid. This had become a bit of an unhappy pattern. As a follower of Jesus, I thought the best way to break the cycle of action and reaction was to befriend my enemy, so I invited the bully to the games night at our church youth group. Unfortunately for me, the bully saw this as an opportunity to break the cycle of action and reaction by seizing the chance, outside of school, to smash my attempts at resistance completely by bashing me into submission.

He came up behind me while I was standing outside on the church steps and hit me in the back of the head. I fell down the steps and sprawled face down, flat out on the street. While I was defenseless, down on the ground, he "kicked the shit" out of me, as they say in Inala. Fortunately for me, some passersby intervened, stopped the stomping and called for an ambulance. While the paramedics were carrying me to the ambulance on a stretcher, I remember saying to the bully, who was standing nearby, "Listen mate, no matter what you do to me, you can't make me hate you. We'll sort it out when I get back."

I was rushed to hospital, where I underwent emergency surgery on a suspected ruptured spleen. After I recuperated, I returned to school and learned that the bully was now isolated and universally despised for hitting me from behind and "kicking the shit" out of me. The situation provided a perfect opportunity to befriend my now friendless enemy. We reconciled, and I was able to help him get reintegrated into the class.

Over years I have learned a lot about how to intervene nonviolently in a violent situation. I generally take the following steps:

1. Take a deep breath.

2. Assess degree of risk.

3. Don't react to provocation.

4. Act or ask for help.

5. Approach while keeping distance.

6. Attend to the antagonist/s by: listening empathically to complaints and speaking peacefully to their concerns.

7. Try to deflect and diffuse their aggression.

8. Try to work towards a "win-win" solution.

9. If necessary, take a deep breath and go through this process again.

10. If I can't de-escalate the aggression, Ange calls the police. (In my experience, if the police do come, it's often too late.)

To give a typical example of how I seek to intervene nonviolently in a violent situation, let me tell you about the time I once heard someone screaming and saw a huge white man beating a fragile black woman with a lump of wood in the middle of the road. I turned to my younger daughter who was with me at the time and asked her what she thought I should do. "You should help that lady, daddy!" she said. I took her to the far side of the road, sat her safely on the curb, and told her, "I will. Watch what I do."

I walked up to them (I always walk, never run), stopped two meters away (I never get in a perpetrator's face) and greeted the man (I always address the perpetrator rather than the victim, because he has the power) by saying, "G'day mate. Can I help you?" (I always present myself as polite, respectful and helpful).

He turned to me (I had already distracted him) and said, "The bitch stole my purse" (now he was talking to me rather than beating her). I said, "If you let me speak to her, maybe I can help you sort that out" (I wanted him to see my intervention as a possible way for him to solve his problem—as well as hers). He nodded, stepped back to give me space to approach the woman (who lay bleeding on the road) and said, "She can keep the purse. I just need my puffer." (Apparently, he'd gotten an asthma attack from beating the woman.)

I asked her for the puffer, and she opened her purse, gave the puffer to me and I gave it to the man (I was playing a mediating role). He grabbed the puffer, took a puff, and stomped off (the immediate threat was neutralized). I called my daughter Navi to come over, we helped the woman up, walked with her to the side of the road and started to tend to her wounds. I asked her what she wanted me to do (restoring her power). "Call a cab so I can go to my relatives," she said. So I called a cab and waited with her on the side of the road until the cab arrived (just in case the man came back). She jumped in a cab and drove to her relative's house (where she felt she would feel safe).[57] Navi and I walked home.

Because we intervene in violent situations on our streets our attempts are always on public display. Once a man bashing a woman in the front seat of the car he was driving, lost control of the vehicle while turning the corner and crashed into our neighbor's concrete wall. I called my elder daughter Evonne and we rushed out to see what we could do. As the man was still punching the woman, we knew we needed to separate them as quickly as possible. So my daughter went to the woman's side to get her out of the car and as far away from the man as possible, and I went to the man's side to get him out of the car and as far away from the woman as possible. It was easy

---

57. Andrews, "My Struggle For Good Against Evil," 3–4.

for Evonne to extract the woman from the vehicle and escort her safely to sit on the curb on the far side of the road. It was not so easy for me, as the man who emerged from the vehicle was a giant angry beast of a human being, who now directed his redirected rage towards me. And a crowd of inquisitive neighbors gathered round us to see how this drama would play out.

As you can imagine, as the man got closer I kept stepping back, staying near enough to divert his attention from the woman sitting on the curb with my daughter, but far enough to keep a distance so he couldn't readily punch me in the head. As he cursed I did my best to listen as empathically as I could to deflect and diffuse his aggression. "Sure, man." I said, "I'd be upset if I'd crashed my car, Especially a nice new expensive car like yours."

I thought I was doing pretty well, dancing back and forward to keep my distance and divert his attention, when someone came up behind me and suddenly gave me a shove. I turned round to see who pushed me, and a bright red haired woman screamed at me saying, "Don't back down you coward. That man beat that woman. You should bash him. If you don't, I will." As she made to push by me to take him on, I pushed her back. "Don't push me, you bastard." She said. "Look," I said, " He's two times my size and three times your size. If we take him on he'll beat us to a pulp. Let me deal with it." Providentially she let me get on with it. So I kept on dancing back and forward, keeping my distance and diverting his attention, until eventually he calmed down. And so it was that by the time the police finally arrived they found us calmly chatting in the middle of the street.

This street theatre became local folklore. As neighbors talked about the incident different individuals took away different lessons about nonviolent community intervention. (And the bright red haired woman became a good family friend.)

The lessons people were learning loomed large before our very eyes late one night in the street outside our house. A young local boy had broken the brand new display window of Marie's Pizza Shop across the road, someone had grabbed him before he had escaped, and had dragged him back to face the music in front of a bunch of vigilante neighbors who now surrounded him. "What shall we do?" they asked. "We should call the cops," one said. "No we should deal with it ourselves," another said. "After all we are a community." My activist heart beat faster. But my nonviolent activist heart soon broke when someone else said: "Yes. You hold him down. We'll break his legs."

I took a deep breath. Waiting, hoping and praying that someone, anyone, would say something to challenge the violence of this suggestion. All of a sudden, Jon, who had recently got out of prison for making illegal martial arts weapons, and so wasn't generally regarded as the neighborhood peace freak, said: "No. Let's hug him!" "Hug him? You've got to be joking." The crowd cried. "No, I'm not," said Jon. "Lets all tell him how pissed off with him we all are, get him to promise to pay for a new window, and then give him a hug." As I watched I saw the mood of the crowd transformed, somehow Jon's words softened their otherwise hard hearts with kindness.

One by one people confronted the kid with their complaints, mainly about his petty thieving, then gave him a hug. Until it was Marie's go. Now Marie was not a woman to be messed with. She was big, she was strong, drove a large four-wheel drive utility vehicle and played rugby league as a tough front-row forward. When she let rip at the kid, he quivered with fear. But the boy stood there and took it like a man. Then before he knew it Marie embraced him in her ample bosom. He almost suffocated in her abundant embrace. When he finally lifted his head from between her breasts, he took a desperate breath, and with tears streaming down his cheeks he apologized and promised to pay for the repair of the window he'd broken. Halim, the Sufi coffee shop owner, offered to give the kid a job during the week to earn the money to pay Marie back and my son-in-law Marty invited him to play goalie on the weekend in the local Blackstar soccer team. Later that year the kid even got the chance to play goalie for Australia in the street people's world cup. Thanks to Jon, instead of having a lynching, we had a love-in.

The most dramatic example of my attempt to intervene in a very dangerous life-threatening disturbance took place when I was in India in 1984. Two Sikh bodyguards had assassinated Indira Gandhi, the Prime Minister of India, and many in the majority Hindu community had turned against the minority Sikh community in Delhi. Within forty-eight hours, up to five thousand innocent Sikhs were slaughtered in the city.

For more than twelve years, my wife Ange and I, along with our two children, had lived happily in the cosmopolitan city of Delhi. Then on this one day, all hell broke loose. People went crazy and took to the streets. Wherever they could find Sikhs, they would grab them by their long, uncut hair, hold them down, pour petrol over them and set them alight. Mobs stopped buses and stormed trains, searching for Sikhs, pulling people off at random and cutting them to pieces as they struggled to escape from their captors.

The police were either completely unprepared or totally outnumbered. The mobs of weapon-wielding maniacs ruled the streets. Driven mad by grief and anger from years of suppressed frustration, they looted and burned everything that crossed their paths. Billowing columns of smoke rose from all the vehicles, petrol stations, department stores, factories and houses that had been set ablaze. People clambered to their roofs to watch buildings all over the city burn like thousands of funeral pyres as thousands of Sikhs were slaughtered senselessly and needlessly on the streets of Delhi.

We knew we had to do something. Ange remembered an elderly Sikh builder who was living at a building site across the road and sent me to get him. I crept across the road, snuck him into our house and hid him under the bed in our bedroom.

This was *good*, but I knew it wasn't really *good enough*. It was a *passive* rather than an *active* approach to intervention. If Mahatma Gandhi, who had taken Jesus more seriously than most Christians I knew, had been alive, I imagined that he would not settle for such a passive approach when an active nonviolent intervention was so desperately needed.

I knew this was my moment of truth, and yet, at that very moment, I was tempted to do anything but take the risk I knew I had to take to make a stand. To my shame, I must admit, I was terrified, and doing nothing seemed infinitely preferable to doing something so scary.

But I knew that if I didn't do something, right then and there, to stand by my Sikh neighbors against the Hindu backlash, it would be a complete contradiction of everything I had ever said about my dream of "neighborhoods, where people relate to one another genuinely as good neighbors."

I discussed this with my wife, Ange, and we decided we had to do something. We didn't know what to do—just that we had to do something.

To start, we organized some houses in our locality to be made available as sanctuaries for Sikhs who were seeking refuge. As the word spread, Sikhs fled to us. We closed the windows, drew the curtains, locked the doors and prayed the mobs would pass by us. Next I hopped on my motorbike with my mate Tony and went in search of Sikhs whom we could rescue. As we rode around a corner, we drove straight into a large mob of people who were wielding knives, swords, wooden clubs and iron bars. We stopped the motorbike, took a deep breath to calm our nerves and stepped over to talk to them.

"What are you guys doing here?" I asked.

"We're here to kill some Sikhs!" they yelled. "What are you doing here?"

"Well, believe it or not," I said, "we're here to stop you." They laughed, and so I laughed too, acknowledging that it was rather ridiculous to think that a couple of unarmed men could do anything to prevent an armed mob from going on a rampage.

"Let's see what happens," they said. "We are going to wait here for a bus, check out the passengers and when we get our hands on one of those Sikh bastards, we're going to cut him to pieces. It'll be fun to see what you're going to do about that!"

While waiting for the bus, I did my best to try to make friends with the mob, asking people about their families, talking to them about my own, discussing the schools their children attended. I discovered that some of their kids went to the same school as ours and hoped that when the confrontation came, they'd remember our common humanity.

When a bus came along, they jumped aboard and searched high and low, but there were no Sikhs. They got off, disgruntled. Another bus came along, and they jumped aboard and searched high and low, but there were still no Sikhs. When they got off, their anger turned to rage, and they marched off to a shopping center and started smashing the shops and setting them on fire. Then they abandoned the shopping center and rushed toward a housing estate up the road. They wanted blood, not loot.

So Tony and I jumped on the motorbike and raced ahead of the mob to see if we could organize some neighborhood resistance to the immanent attack.

"They are going to kill the Sikhs!" I cried.

"Serves them right!" the Hindus replied.

We were pacing up and down in panic, wondering what to do next, when a shout rang out. The mob had come across an address that indicated there were Sikhs in residence, and they had broken into the house. The family had fled to the roof and were calling for help. We raced to the spot, pushed our way through the crowd and took our stand at the bottom of the stairs between the mob and the family.

Facing the mob, with our hands held together in a gesture of peace, we pleaded for the lives of the family. The mob broke down the door, busted up the furniture and threatened to butcher us if we didn't let them through.

We waited, and for a moment, our fate hung in the balance. The mob hesitated, and then the moment of danger passed as quickly as it had come. One by one, the members of the mob broke ranks, spat curses at us, turned their backs on us and walked away.

Then armored carriers arrived and deployed squadrons of armed soldiers all over the area, so the mob turned on their heels and fled.

The family clambered down from the roof, and we greeted each other, hugged and wept on one another's shoulders.

In terrifying times such as these, I'm often tempted to think that there is nothing I can do or that whatever I try to do won't make much difference, but I need to remember that sometimes the little I can do may well make the difference between life and death.[58]

58. Andrews, *Building A Better World*, 31–33.

Protesting Through Demonstrating

I've protested the "status quo" by *demonstrating* for justice in unjust situations.

I remember how just after I got back to Australia from India, my friends and I were discussing how political parties pandered to people's greed by promising to put more money in their pockets rather than seeking to meet people's needs by proposing to provide more adequate services for the most disadvantaged among us. We decided that a crazy way to dramatize this greed was to advertise that we'd give away a thousand dollars in two dollar notes in the city mall and see how many people would turn up to grab the cash. Some suggested that the amount of money was so small we'd only get a small crowd, but when the time came, hundreds of people showed up, circling us like sharks in a feeding frenzy, snatching the cash from our outstretched hands. It almost turned into a riot. We got to talk about our dramatic exposé of the dynamic of greed in society in mainstream papers and on prime-time television.[59]

I also remember when our community in West End was preparing for the impact of Expo 1988, which was going to be held on a seventeen-hectare site in our local community. A $625 million World Fair, it was the largest event of the bicentennial and was expected to attract more than 15 million visitors to Australia. As a local publication reported, "Landlords and developers saw the opportunity to make some quick cash during the event and foresaw that, post Expo, real estate in West End would increase in value. In the lead up to this World Fair, many tenants were threatened with eviction."[60]

As we approached Christmas in 1987, we thought of a crazy way to dramatize the difficulty that low-income people were going to have to get accommodation in our area. So we borrowed a domesticated donkey, got a couple of people to dress up as Joseph and Mary, and arranged for them to walk round West End together, searching for affordable accommodation on Christmas Eve. We sent out press releases in the form of large gold stars, addressed to the "Wise Men and Women of the Media," telling them where they could find Joseph and Mary looking for a place to stay in West End. Needless to say they were turned away by all the real estate agents, and the story was featured on all the TV news bulletins that night.

---

59. "Generous Dave will pass the bucks," *The Daily Sun* (25 June 1987); Perkins, "Dollar Distribution Targets Our Greed."

60. http://www.streetwalkersguidetowestend.com/uploads/1/3/2/0/13201772/street_walkers_guide_to_west_end_no2_lr.pdf

However, it took a lot more than a clever public relations coup to confront the serious crisis in affordable accommodation we were facing as the landlords in our neighborhood went into a rent-hike frenzy. The vulnerable people in our locality, who were dependent on cheap rental accommodation for their survival, were freaking out.

So we organized a number of community meetings to come up with a plan to solve the problem. One person suggested guerrilla warfare, led by chainsaw-wielding storm troopers who would cut the power brokers off at the knees, an idea that brought about an avalanche of applause. But after it was over, everyone acknowledged that the prospect was repugnant.

I sat there trying to think of an approach that would be acceptable both to Christ and the community and eventually the idea of a fast came to me. I told everyone I felt I needed to go on a "hunger strike" to fight against the greed that was wrecking our community and to fight for the rights of everyone in our community, whether rich or poor, to have affordable access to secure tenancy. As people clapped, I continued, "I'm not going to break my fast until fifty landlords promise not to increase their rents by more than ten percent, fifty tenants promise to support responsible landlords and expose irresponsible landlords and fifty residents promise to help landlords and tenants negotiate a just settlement of this dispute by publicly commending those who do and publicly condemning those who don't!" People cheered, so the plan was carried.

I decided to sleep outside my house during the hunger strike to dramatize the tragedy of the local people we knew who were being evicted from their houses.[61] Each day Chris Hawke and Ann Rampa who had joined me on my hunger strike, joined me in Boundary Street, collecting signatures of landlords, tenants and residents who promised to help us to solve the rental problem in West End.

One landlord agreed not to raise his rents at all. Another landlord, responding to an appeal by his tenants over an increase in rent, imposed a real estate agent, then fired the real estate agent and fixed the rent back at the original rate. Yet another owner, upon discovering that his tenants were going through a tough time financially, actually reduced the rent for a period of time.

All these landlords were presented with flowers to commend their sense of responsibility to the community. The presentations took place on national television to encourage them and others like them to continue to act as responsible citizens in our community.

---

61. "Dave starves, shivers, in protest on poverty," *The Telegraph* (3 July 1987).

However, not everybody responded well to the challenge. One land-lord proved to be totally ruthless in his pursuit of a profit and beat up his tenant, a woman named Kimberly Williams, because she could not pay the inordinate rent he demanded. Then he literally threw her down the stairs in his haste to get her out of his flat as fast as he could.

As Ange and I listened to Kimberly's story, we became convinced of its veracity, assured her of our support and became firm friends. Then Ange and I went to talk with her landlord, but he was not interested in anything we had to say. He told us that he had the right to run his business any way he wanted. We tried to suggest that he had the right to run his business any way he wanted—as long as he did not infringe on the rights of others to safety and security. He told us we had no right to call him to account since he was only accountable to himself, his family and his bank balance. When we chal-lenged that, he told us to get out, then threatened to kill us if we came back. As far as he was concerned, we had become mortal enemies.

Because we were afraid, we felt like backing off, but we felt constrained to be faithful to the cause in spite of the death threat hanging over our heads. So we organized a group of residents to camp on the doorstep of the recalcitrant landlord and bring home to him the reality of the homelessness that his callousness was causing. While we were camped on his doorstep, we discussed the issues with the landlord, his family and his neighbors. Though some of his neighbors were very supportive and some of his family were very sympathetic, the landlord was totally unwilling to negotiate.

Eventually we took the landlord to court on a charge of the assault he had committed against Kimberly. When he was found guilty, we asked the judge to give him six months of community work with us as a sentence, hoping that we could sort things out by serving the community together. Unfortunately, the landlord never did figure us out and remained furious with us till the day he died. Though the landlord did not end up lower-ing Kimberly's rent, she moved in with Anne Rampa and her husband Jim Dowling for several years until Kimberly got a housing commission flat of her own.[62]

After nine days of our hunger strike, we had the backing of fifty land-lords who promised not to increase their rents by more than ten percent, fifty tenants who would support responsible landlords and expose irrespon-sible landlords, and fifty residents who would help landlords and tenants negotiate a just settlement of the dispute. These people not only did a lot themselves but also put a lot of pressure on various levels of government to do even more. By working together, we were able to organize a series

62. Andrews, *Christi-Anarchy*, 183–186.

of community consultations, which marked the most comprehensive town planning process in which the Brisbane City Council had ever engaged. As a result, affordable accommodation was put back on the agenda for our area. Then on the tenth day, Chris Hawke, Ann Rampa and I broke our fast with doner kebabs at a local Lebanese restaurant.

An occasion to raise awareness about our selfish disregard for the suffering of marginalized peoples in other parts of the world arose in September 1987, when there were catastrophic floods in Bangladesh. Bangladesh is highly vulnerable to floods due to its geographical location at the deltas of the Ganges, Brahmaputra and Meghna rivers. More than 80 percent of the annual precipitation of Bangladesh occurs in the monsoon period between June and September, and the monsoon rains often cause extremely large floods. In 1987 there was calamitous flood (followed by another in 1988 and another in 1998), which inundated 70 percent of the country and displaced over 24 million people.[63]

I bought copies of our local newspapers to read further reports about the floods in Bangladesh, only to find there was no mention, either in *The Courier Mail* or *The Telegraph*. I phoned the editor of *The Courier Mail* to ask why there was no report, and he said that he had no information. So I got the latest updates from AAP and Reuters and sent them to him. The next day I checked *The Courier Mail* to see the report they had printed, only to find that there was still no mention of the floods. I phoned the editor again to ask why there was still no coverage, and he said that his target audience had no interest in a story about floods in Bangladesh. I pushed back, saying that it was his responsibility to print the story and to keep the public informed, but the editor wasn't interested and hung up on me.

From that point on, I decided to combine the approach of the two most famous activists of the twentieth century: the American Saul Alinsky and the Indian Mahatma Gandhi. In many ways, Gandhi and Alinsky could hardly be more different in their approach to protest.[64] Everybody

---

63. https://link.springer.com/article/10.1023/A:1021169731325

64. Gandhi was an idealist who believed that "means" and "ends" were convertible terms. He saw the "means" as the "ends" in the making. He said, "The means may be likened to a seed, the end to a tree, and there is just the same inviolable connection between there means and the end as there is between the seed and the tree. . . . We have always control over the means but not over the end. Impure means result in an impure end. I feel that our progress towards the [end] will be in exact proportion to the purity of our means. One cannot reach truth by untruthfulness. Truthful conduct alone can reach Truth."

Alinsky was a realist who believed that "the means-and-end moralists always end up on their ends without any means." He said that "means and ends are so qualitatively

who knows me knows I am a fan of Gandhi, who followed the example of Jesus more closely than most Christians, but I realized I needed to combine both the creative tactics of Alinsky with the overall ethical praxis of Gandhi.

So as Alinsky would say, I picked the editor as my "target" of my "campaign"—that is, I wanted him to publish an article about the floods. Though I would seek to "freeze," "personalize" and "polarize" him as my target, unlike Alinsky, I would never treat him as my "enemy" nor seek to "kill" him, and I would never use "ridicule" as my "most potent weapon."

Instead, like Gandhi, I would seek to treat my editor "opponent" with the same respect that I hoped he would extend to the Bangladesh people, whose plight I was trying to promote. Thus I had to make sure that my "demands for change" would be "reasonable requests." While Alinsky would argue that any campaign should be accompanied by a "threat" in case the change is not forthcoming, I knew that "the threat is usually more terrifying than the thing itself." However, as Gandhi would say, I also needed to make sure that my "demands for change" were "proactive, not reactive," and "always constructive" so that the "education of the public, the participants, and the opponent in the art of constructive action" would be an "integral part of the process of engagement."

As Gandhi would say, I knew that if my editor "opponent" was "unwilling to change," I needed to "move slowly, but surely, into the successive stages of a campaign" by seeking "a peaceful settlement at every stage of the campaign" in order to "destroy the enmity" but "not the enemy" so that I could work "out a settlement with my opponent without compromising my principles." At the same time, as Alinsky would say, my campaign could not be "a drag," but needed to "keep pressure on the opposition," while being one in which my supporters would have the "experience" and "expertise" to pull off the creative demonstration we had planned if the editor did not respond.

After talking to my friends, we decided that I should write an open letter to the editor of *The Courier Mail,* saying that he should publish a report about the floods in Bangladesh for three reasons. First, it was a major human interest story about what was happening to people in a neighboring country in our region. Second, the story was a tragedy on a scale that his target audience would relate to, since the number of people who had been left homeless was roughly equivalent to the entire population of Australia. Third, there

---

interrelated that the true question has never been the proverbial one, 'Does the end justify the means?' but always has been, 'Does this particular end justify this particular means?'" In his book *Rules For Radicals,* Alinsky advocates a non-purist, anti-puritanical, pragmatic modus operandi based on this framework: if a "means" achieves the specific "end" that is sought, it is okay.

were very likely many people in Brisbane who would want to provide aid for such a disaster, but they wouldn't be able to do so if he didn't tell them about it and they didn't know anything about it. I said that I expected him to publish a substantial article about the floods in Bangladesh—a fifth of page three or a third of page five—within the week. If not, my friends and I would bring the news about the floods in Bangladesh to the notice of his readers ourselves by building a Bangladeshi refugee camp on the steps of *The Courier Mail*. To ensure that the refugee camp got coverage, I would keep *The Telegraph* informed, along with local radio and television stations.

Each day for the next week, I sent the editor the latest update and asked him to publish a report on the floods in Bangladesh, reminding him that if he didn't, we'd build a Bangladeshi refugee camp on the steps of *The Courier Mail*. Each day I would be interviewed on the popular Radio Station 4QR to check his response. Each day the editor refused to publish an article, and so the pressure increased and public intrigue around our campaign intensified. At the end of the week, a Friday morning, we informed the media that we were going to build the refugee camp on Friday afternoon in order to bring the story to the attention of the people of Brisbane.

That Friday, 25 September 1987, fourteen adults and kids from our families, dressed in beautiful *sarees* with *dupattas*, colorful *kurtas, pyjamas* and *chappals* (sandals), carrying *jhola* bags with mats,[65] a collection of musical flutes and even a bantam chicken, walked together to the offices of *The Courier Mail* at on Campbell Street in Bowen Hills to build a Bangladeshi refugee camp. I went ahead of the group to assure security that we weren't going to abuse anybody, damage any property or block entrances to the building. Security allocated a space to one side, where we built our camp, constructed shelters, laid out mats, squatted with our kids and the chicken and played music while we waited for our much-anticipated meeting with the editor. *The Telegraph*, the competing newspaper, sent a reporter and photographer to cover the meeting, along with several major radio stations and television networks.

Many visitors to *The Courier Mail* taunted us as they went to and fro, but many more smiled, waved and hailed our humble and peaceful little protest. To our surprise, when the editor finally appeared, the first thing he did was to apologize for not taking the story of the catastrophe more seriously. He thanked us for our persistent but consistently respectful campaign and, with the nation's media bearing witness, he promised that he would run the story. I apologized for having to "target" him personally, but explained I felt I had no alternative. He assured me that in the future he would not

65. My apologies for the Hindi terminology; I don't speak Bengali.

only cover floods in South Asia, but would also add the details of any aid agencies involved in providing relief so that readers could contact them to offer support. I thanked him.

Gandhi says that "in working out a settlement, participants need to cooperate with their opponents as much as they can, without compromising principles." Alinsky says that 'the price of a successful attack is a constructive alternative."[66]

That night the national news on Channel 7 opened with their coverage of the demonstration, which then led into a lengthy presentation of the impact of the flood in Bangladesh. The next day *The Telegraph* published an article on the protest at *The Courier Mail,* and *The Courier Mail* published a substantial article on the floods in Bangladesh and how Aussies could support the Australian aid agencies that were providing relief. *On Being* magazine also ran a feature, referring to the campaign as "Prophetic Kingdom Action."[67]

The next week, the owner of a Bangladeshi Restaurant on Clarence Corner, near Woolloongabba, hosted our families for a wonderful Bangladeshi meal as a token of appreciation for our campaign in support of his country. He was really pleased when we told him that three of our friends, Chris and Ruth Todd and Nigel Lewin, whose families had taken part in our campaign, were going to fly to Bangladesh with TEAR Australia to take part in the flood-relief effort.

A year later, in September 1988, there was another disastrous flood in Bangladesh. True to his word, the editor of *The Courier Mail* covered the flood and flood-relief efforts extensively. I called and thanked him.

When I returned to Australia from India, I wanted to demonstrate an ongoing commitment to the struggles of our brothers and sisters in the majority world. So in 1985 I joined TEAR Australia, a Christian aid and development agency dedicated to making "biblically-shaped" responses to global injustice by helping Christians in Australia develop a biblical framework for advocacy along with strategies, tactics and resources for specific advocacy campaigns.

Through TEAR we worked in coalition with the Micah Network, a growing global network of over three hundred Christian relief, development and advocacy agencies in seventy-five countries, who are committed to calling, influencing and leveraging the leading decision-makers in all our societies prophetically in order to "maintain the rights of the poor and

---

66. Alinsky, *Rules For Radicals*, Rule 12.

67. *On Being* (November 1987): 19.

oppressed [and] rescue the weak and needy" (Ps. 82:3–4), particularly in the two-thirds majority world.

The key challenge of the Micah Network leading up to the year 2000 was to champion the Jubilee 2000 campaign, which was an international campaign calling for the cancellation of third-world debt by 2000. The concept derived from the biblical idea of the year of Jubilee, the fiftieth year during which those who were enslaved because of debts would be freed, any lands lost because of debt would be returned, and any community torn by inequality would be restored. The campaign aimed to wipe out $90 billion of debt owed by the world's poorest nations and to channel those funds into basic health, welfare and education.

One of my roles in TEAR was to establish support groups, consisting of about six to twelve people, who met regularly, to foster a nurturing, encouraging and challenging culture in which people of all denominations could come together to help each other respond to God's call to practice compassion and rally people around the country to demonstrate their concern for Jubilee 2000. Through these groups we trained people to speak in their churches, write to newspapers, chat on talkback radio, run forums, circulate petitions, meet with their MPs and organize demonstrations around the country in order to promote the Jubilee 2000 campaign in collaboration with the Drop the Debt Coalition.

I can remember being part of a demonstration at Parliament House in Canberra with delegates from all over Australia, which presented the largest foreign policy petition ever tabled in Australia, with over 450,000 signatures. This was also a significant contribution in terms of the total global Jubilee 2000 petition, which (according to Guinness World Records) holds two world records: the largest petition ever signed (with 24,391,181 signatures) and the most international signatures (with people from 166 countries signing).[68]

Jubilee 2000 also staged demonstrations at the 1998 G8 in Birmingham, England. At the Birmingham meeting, focusing on achieving sustainable economic growth in the context of environmental protection and good governance, between 50,000 and 70,000 demonstrators participated in a peaceful protest to put debt relief on the agenda. The protestors made headlines around the world by forming a human chain around the entire Birmingham city center.

The demonstrators caught the attention of Prime Minister Tony Blair and Chancellor of the Exchequer Gordon Brown, who met with the directors of Jubilee 2000 to discuss the issue. Subsequently, the Prime Minister

68. https://en.wikipedia.org/wiki/Jubilee_2000

publicly expressed his personal support for debt forgiveness. While the UK's move to cancel significant third-world debt was also influenced by the millennium development goals, Gordon Brown's decision to support debt cancelation at a Jubilee 2000 rally at St. Paul's Cathedral underlies the role of the movement.

In the end Jubilee 2000 led to the global cancellation of $100 billion of debt. In 2001, as a result of pressure from Australian Jubilee 2000, the Australian government pledged one hundred percent debt forgiveness for countries that qualified for relief under the International Monetary Fund and World Bank Heavily Indebted Poor Country scheme. Moreover, in 2004, the government cancelled the bilateral debts of Nicaragua (worth $5.4 million) and Ethiopia (worth $7.9 million). In 2007, Jubilee secured $75 million of debt forgiveness for Indonesia so that they could invest in tuberculosis treatment and prevention programs.[69]

Protesting Through Identifying

I've protested the "status quo" by *identifying* with what Brueggemann calls oppressed "subcommunities that stand in tension with the dominant community."[70]

When Ange and I returned to Australia after our years in India, we intentionally sought to identify with First Nations people who were seeking restitution, those fleeing persecution and seeking refuge and those from other religions who were seeking protection and recognition.

We landed in the West End community, which is a distinct, vibrant, urban village that is bounded by a bend of the Brisbane River. Musgrave Park is at the very heart of West End and as long as anybody can remember, it has been a significant meeting place for Indigenous peoples. People from all over Moreton Bay used to come to *Kurilpa,* the place of the Water Rat, to feast communally on its wild fruits. In spite of dispossession, the community in *Kurilpa* has survived, and their tradition of hospitality has shaped West End.

Though there are always mobs of *murris* round West End, many locals don't notice them, let alone connect with them—and even fewer relate to them with respect. Fortunately for us, Aunty Jean Philips, an Aboriginal leader who attended our church, introduced us to local Aboriginal people. Twice a year, for more than twenty years, Aunty Jean helped participants in the community orientation courses we have conducted identify with the

69. https://www.jubileeaustralia.org/about-jubilee/our-mission/history-of-jubilee

70. Brueggemann, *The Prophetic Imagination,* Kindle location 154.

struggles of Indigenous people by recounting the story of her people and their painful dispossession. She also took them with her to meet her people—some in maximum security prisons, languishing in their cells; others working with human rights organizations, fighting for the release of these prisoners and their basic human rights.

Aunty Jean introduced us to Sam Watson, who has helped us identify with the struggles of Indigenous people. Sam was born and raised in Brisbane and descended from the *Munnenjarl* and *Biri Gubba* tribal nations with blood ties to the *Jagara, Kalkadoon* and *Noonuccal* peoples. Sam worked full-time with the Tribal Council and other organizations that served the Indigenous community through health, housing, education, employment and legal aid. In 1971 Sam and his comrade Dennis Walker launched the Brisbane chapter of the Black Panther Party, and throughout the 1970s, Sam protested against both the state and federal governments. In the early 1990s Sam became involved with the state and federal Indigenous legal services. He was also a cofounder of the first Aboriginal and Islander political party (The Australian Indigenous Peoples Party) and contested elections at both the state and federal level. In recent years Sam worked tirelessly for Reconciliation, the Stolen Generations and Aboriginal Deaths in Custody.[71]

Through Aunty Jean, we were invited to identify with the Indigenous community in West End by getting involved with their proposal for an Indigenous cultural center in Musgrave Park, which was across the road from the Greek Club. Being Greek, Ange thought the Greek community might support the proposal for the Aboriginal community to have a similar center of their own, but she discovered that the Greek Club was actually circulating a petition against the Aboriginal community's proposal. They had no inclination to support "the *mavri*" (the blacks).

Ange felt it was unjust for the Greeks, who had received government funding for their club, to oppose the Aboriginals's proposal to receive government funding for their club. So Ange began circulating a counter-petition in support of the *mavri,* which caused an uproar in the Greek community. Here was "one of their own" acting as a "race traitor" and "betraying" them. Ange's relative, who worked for the Greek Club, was particularly upset. With the support of her gutsy mother, Ange engaged in multiple spirited exchanges.

Each year the pride of the Greek community is on display at the *Paniyiri* Festival, which celebrates Greece's cultural offerings to the world. Though it has always been held in Musgrave Park, Aboriginals haven't always been

71. http://macquariepenanthology.com.au/SamWatson.html

included. In recent years, however, Indigenous people have been invited to open the festival with a smoking ceremony, and Aboriginal dancers have been invited to join Greek dancers in featured *Paniyiri* performances. Over time, the Greek community has gradually changed its attitude to the *mavri* and has supported the Aboriginal community's proposal for a cultural center in Musgrave Park.

We had a special opportunity to identify with the Indigenous community in Australia during the 1988 celebration of the bicentenary of the arrival of the First Fleet of convict ships to settle the British colony in 1788. On Australia Day, Sydney Harbor hosted a re-enactment of this event, which "triggered debate on historical interpretation, Australian identity and Aboriginal rights. The Uniting Church in Australia wanted people to boycott the event unless Aboriginal rights were recognized. More than 40,000 people, including Aboriginals from across the country, staged the largest march to Hyde Park in Sydney since the 1970s Vietnam Moratorium demonstrations."[72]

We participated in demonstrations in Brisbane and then talked to Aunty Jean about how to respond to the issues of colonialism that the bicentenary raised for the *murri* community. She suggested that we organize a mixed camp of non-Aboriginal and Aboriginal people and invite the non-Aboriginal people to listen to the Aboriginal people talk about what living in colonized Australia has meant to them. We organized a camp of forty non-Aboriginal people and twenty Aboriginal people to get together for a weekend camp of listening at Mount Tamborine, which proved to be a powerful colonial bicentenary counterpoint experience. The Aboriginal people reported that it was an extraordinary experience to be able to speak so freely and be taken so seriously for a change. The non-Aboriginal people reported that hearing the stories was an excruciating face-to-face encounter with some of the most destructive consequences of the neocolonial regime with which we have been complicit—and from which we have benefitted at the expense of the Indigenous people.

Searching for a heartfelt response to the pain we confronted, the non-Aboriginal people asked if we might wash the feet of the Aboriginal people, and the Aboriginal people, most of whom were Christian, understood the ritual of foot-washing as a unaffected act of apology, humility and homage. As we washed the feet of our Aboriginal brothers and sisters, the tears began to flow. But when our Aboriginal brothers and sisters reversed the roles and unexpectedly—and embarrassingly—began to wash our feet, the

72. https://en.wikipedia.org/wiki/Australian_Bicentenary

whole gathering was reduced to tears that could not be stopped. We wept with one another, embraced one another and prayed for one another. This counterpoint bicentenary experience was not another event in celebration of a triumphal empire, but in the spirit of decolonizing compassion.

In November 1993, I remember Daniel Yock, an eighteen-year-old Aboriginal dancer, died in the back of a police van shortly after he was arrested in Musgrave Park. There had been over a hundred "black deaths in custody" over the previous two decades, and the senseless death of this up-and-coming performer was too much for our local Aboriginal community to bear. In response, they staged "a violent protest outside Brisbane police headquarters." Aunty Jean called on volunteers from our community to help her keep the protesters and police apart, but scuffles broke out all over the place, "leaving more than 30 police and demonstrators injured."

On 17 November, Aboriginals gathered in Musgrave Park from all over South East Queensland to stage a tribute to Daniel Yock. Sam Watson expressed concern that outside extremist elements might try to provoke further confrontation. Fearing reprisals from a growing mob of hundreds of angry Aboriginals, the police station in West End shut up shop. However, contrary to expectations, the city of Brisbane witnessed Aboriginal leaders direct over four thousand people in a powerful and disciplined silent protest.

"Marching up to 15 abreast in some streets, the protesters obeyed pleas by Aboriginal elders for a 'silent tribute' to Daniel Yock. "The marchers laid a wreath near Musgrave Park to mark the spot where Mr Yock was arrested. 'This is exactly the sort of demonstration I hoped it would be,' said Inspector Don Gardner, who made sure [the] police [kept] a low profile."[73]

Ange and I had another opportunity to stand with the Aboriginal community in Brisbane when we joined over 50,000 people in the People's Walk for Reconciliation in Brisbane on 4 June 2000, which proceeded across the William Jolly Bridge and concluded with a wreath-laying ceremony in King George Square. Reporting on the events of that day, the *Koori Mail* said, "The march was larger than organisers expected, with only about half of the marchers able to fit into King George Square for the ceremonies. As the marchers made their way to the square, an aeroplane wrote 'Sorry' in the sky. Among the marchers were Queensland Premier Peter Beattie and Brisbane Lord Mayor Jim Soorley. Soorley told the *Courier-Mail*, 'We have seen

---

73. "A peaceful 4,000: Marchers pay a silent tribute to Daniel Yock," https://trove. nla.gov.au/newspaper/article/127525002

today thousands of people in Brisbane come out to say we are sorry for the past injustices inflicted on Aboriginal people and we want to be reconciled and able to create a future together."[74]

On 13 February 2008, I went down to Musgrave Park to join the local *murris* who were gathering to watch a telecast of Prime Minister Kevin Rudd make a formal public apology on behalf of the Australian Parliament to Australian Aboriginal and Torres Strait Islander peoples, particularly the Stolen Generations—the Indigenous Australians who had endured immense suffering due to past government policies of forced child removal. This national apology to the Stolen Generations had come about as a recommendation from the National Inquiry into the Separation of Aboriginal Children from their Families, which had highlighted the suffering of Indigenous families under the federal, state and territory Aboriginal protection and welfare policies.

Aunty Jean and many of the older Aboriginal women were standing together around the large screen as I stood with Noritta Morseu-Diop, the cofounder of the Gallang Place Aboriginal and Torres Strait Islander Counselling Services, which seeks to enhance culturally appropriate health, healing and well-being for Aboriginal people. The event was described by SBS News as "one of the defining moments in modern Australian history." Seventy-nine-year-old Aunty Lorraine Peeters, one of the many thousands who were part of the Stolen Generations, was four years old when she was taken from her family an placed in an institution. She told SBS News, "Oh, we were so excited. We were out of our skin. We couldn't wait. It was a day I will never, ever forget in my life because we were being acknowledged as a group of people."[75]

We all stood there together around the big screen, watching and listening intently as the Prime Minister said, "We apologise especially for the removal of Aboriginal and Torres Strait Islander children from their families, their communities and their country. For the pain, suffering and hurt of these Stolen Generations, their descendants and for their families left behind, we say sorry. To the mothers and the fathers, the brothers and the sisters, for the breaking up of families and communities, we say sorry. And for the indignity and degradation thus inflicted on a proud people and a proud culture, we say sorry."[76] As we heard these words, we all wept together.

74. http://blogs.slq.qld.gov.au/jol/2017/05/31/peoples-walk-for-reconciliation-4-june-2000/

75. https://www.sbs.com.au/news/we-say-sorry-today-marks-more-than-a-decade-since-kevin-rudd-s-national-apology

76. https://www.australia.gov.au/about-australia/our-country/our-people/

I have the opportunity to publicly identify with my Aboriginal neighbors every year on 26 January. Non-Aboriginal people celebrate 26 January as "Australia Day" and remember it as the beginning of the European settlement of Australia. Aboriginal people commemorate 26 January as "Invasion Day" and remember it as the beginning of the European colonization, dispossession and expropriation of their land. On 26 January, I often join the Invasion Day rally in Brisbane, which begins outside Parliament House, proceeds through the city, stops now and then for speeches and chants, crosses Victoria Bridge and ends in Musgrave Park.

But sometimes supporting a "blackfella" protest against "whitefella" oppression can be complicated. One year I turned up to try to do my bit by carrying the "Always Was, Always Will Be Aboriginal Land" banner, and much to my surprise, I was publicly singled out by Aunty Jean. In front of a very angry mob of "blackfellas," she asked me, a "whitefella," to pray for everybody before we started.

I was gobsmacked. I didn't know what to do. It seemed that no matter what I did I would be, as we say in Australia, on a hiding to nothing. If I didn't do what Aunty Jean asked, it would prove that I was a "conceited white bastard." But if I did do what Aunty Jean asked and actually prayed for the assembled mob of "blackfellas," it would prove that I was "a condescending white bastard."

On balance, I thought it would be better for me to do what Aunty Jean asked, and so I said a prayer for the protest, doing my "whitefella" best to voice the heartfelt cries of all the "blackfellas" who were gathered.

When I opened my eyes I was gratified to see fists raised in a black power salute.

As older people Ange and I were expected to stay in self-isolation because of the pandemic, so we were unable to attend the Black Lives Matter - Stop Black Deaths In Custody protest in Brisbane on 6 June 2020. We were so pleased our dear seventeen-year old granddaughter was able to go on our behalf. Lila spent days preparing her placard with the names of many of the 432 First Nations people who have died in custody, which she carried to the protest when she accompanied our friend, Grace Eather, who is one of the famous Stingray Sisters from Maningrida, in the fabled Arnhem Land of the Northern Territory, whose "mob," her large extended family, had all stayed with us in our house for two weeks the year before. The Black Lives Matter - Stop Black Deaths In Custody 30,000 plus protest was the biggest that most

apology-to-australias-indigenous-peoples

people had ever seen in Brisbane, and a photo of the large multi-colored mask-wearing socially-distancing multitude featured in the lead into a story of global protest in *The New York Times.*

Protesting Through Resisting

I've protested the "status quo" by *resisting* serious prejudices in our society.

For example, over the last thirty years, my wife and I have intentionally sought to embrace people who are seeking asylum in Australia from other countries as beloved members of our extended family. Yet most Australians have a primal, historical and often hysterical fear of "boat people" coming to our country and dispossessing us. Australian anthropologist Ghassan Hage suggests that this is because our forebears came to this country as boat people and dispossessed the Aboriginal people who lived here before us, and so we fear that the next wave of boat people may do the same to us. He says that Aussies have an underlying fear of retribution for the genocide that our ancestors committed, either through decolonization by Aboriginals or recolonization by migrants and refugees.[77]

As a way of resisting this hysterical culture of fear, we organized the West End Migrant and Refugee Support Group in 1989 to help settle refugees in our local area. We also initiated a refugee airfare loan scheme to provide loans for airfares to help reunite over a hundred families. (These loans were eventually repaid without default.) To advocate for vulnerable people seeking asylum and facing deportation orders that would send them back to life-threatening persecution, we formed a torture and trauma support group in our home. Over the last few years, we've been involved in a movement of Christians from around the country who are seeking to resist Australia's inhumane asylum seeker policies.

Yet the primal historical and hysterical fear of boat people in Australia has been deliberately manipulated and exploited by successive governments for their own political purposes. To protect us from this carefully constructed and manifestly exaggerated "danger," the government stops the boats of refugees who are fleeing war, oppression and persecution to seek asylum on our shores and deports them to Manus Island, where they will be kept in detention in dehumanizing conditions until they are deported, repatriated or settled elsewhere. The government has intentionally and systematically misrepresented asylum seekers as "illegals," "queue jumpers" and "security threats" so that Aussies would vote them into power to ensure "border security" by "stopping the boats," regardless of the evils of indefinite detention.

77. Hage, *Against Paranoid Nationalism*, 48–52.

As the psychologist David Benner says, fearful people "may appear deeply loving, but fear always interferes with the impulse to love. Fear blocks responsiveness to others. Energy invested in maintaining safety and comfort always depletes energy available for others."[78] Similarly, psychotherapist Wayne Muller says that "when fear arises, we harden our bodies and our hearts, closing inward to protect ourselves. We build walls, call up armies, and pay governments to protect us from danger."[79]

In response to the government's indefinite detention of asylum seekers, in 2014 the Australian Churches Refugee Task Force encouraged Aussies to resist the government's policy because it is basically "State-Sanctioned Child Abuse."[80] In spite of ongoing resistance from churches over many years, successive governments have refused to change the detention policy[81] and continue to isolate detainees and deny them access to their lawyers and support networks.

I gave the following keynote address at a Refugee Action Collective protest in 2014, which was held at King George Square outside City Hall in Brisbane.[82]

I began by saying, "To be human is for our hearts to beat with the desire to love and be loved. If there is a single universal rule of ethical human conduct recognized by the whole of humanity, it is that 'we ought to love our neighbors as ourselves.' The greatest threat to our love of our neighbor is our fear of our neighbor."

78. Benner, *Surrender to Love*, 40.

79. Muller, *Legacy of the Heart*, 18.

80. For example, in 2015, there were more than two thousand asylum seekers in Australian detention facilities, including 127 children. Over a previous two-year period, there were more than four thousand reported incidents of actual, threatened or attempted serious self-harm in immigration detention facilities and twelve deaths, six of which were suicides. See James Carlton, "Immigration detention is 'state sanctioned child abuse:' church leaders," interview with Very Rev. Peter Catt (31 July 2014), abc. net.au/radionational.

81. For example, in 2014, the Uniting Church offered to care for the thirty unaccompanied children on Christmas Island who were going to be sent to Nauru, but Minister Scott Morrison dismissed the offer in a press conference. Similarly, the Baptist Union of NSW and ACT offered to temporarily house seventy detainees at Villawood so they would not be moved to the extremely remote Curtin detention center in West Australia, but the detainees were moved anyway. See "Children in Detention: Advocacy Brief" (November 2014), unitingjustice.org.au; Sophie Timothy, "Uniting Church offers to accommodate asylum seeker children" (4 March 2014), biblesociety.org.au.

82. This speech was later published as "Letting Our Humanity Get The Better Of Us."

I went on to address Aussies' primal, historical and hysterical fear of asylum seekers, which prevents us from treating them the way we would want to be treated if we were seeking asylum ourselves.

"This should—and this does—make many of us angry," I continued. "However, while anger is understandable, agro protests are not helpful." I said that to bring about a change in policy, we needed to change public opinion, and to change public opinion, we needed to create a culture of love rather than a culture of fear. "Anger does not encourage love," I said. "Anger engenders fear." I said that the government would exploit any fear "to justify the need for greater security and to rationalize the expansion of the very policies we oppose." I talked about how we could only win this fight by winning people over, drawing them to our cause by expressing our concern with laughter, tears, reason and strong but gentle pleas.

I explained how many asylum seekers are Muslim and I had recently gone to the Sunshine Coast with a Muslim friend to engage in a public conversation about how Christians and Muslims could live in peace. "You would have thought we were setting up a Caliphate on the Coast," I said. "All hell broke loose. Heaps of people turned up, many to protest, carrying signs that said, 'The Muslims are coming' and 'Resist Islam.'" I described how the police turned up and said that an anti-racist, pro-refugee counter-protest would have been totally counterproductive.

I discussed how we needed to acknowledge people's fears of difference, conflict and change. I said we needed to accept people with their fears—and to help them explore their fears without making them afraid of us. I said that we need to arrange ways for Aussies to meet refugees face to face so that they could see the "boat people" as people rather than "illegals," "queue jumpers" or "security threats," and Aussies could begin to move from fear towards "fair dinkum"[83] love.

"There are no quick fixes. There are no short cuts," I said. To create a culture of love over our politics and policies of fear, "we all need to take on the exceedingly important, excruciatingly painstaking work of encouraging one another" so that "our humanity [can] get the better of us and [we can] learn to love our asylum-seeker neighbors as ourselves."

I concluded by saying, "The policies will change only when the people change."

Over the Easter weekend in 2014, I joined Tri Nguyen on the last leg of his thirty-five day walk from Melbourne to Canberra. Tri Nguyen had set

83. "Fair dinkum" is a traditional Aussie phrase for something that we say is "the real deal."

out, towing a wooden boat through Benalla, Wodonga and Wagga Wagga to meet ordinary Australians, introduce himself as a "boat person" and plea for better treatment for boat people.

When Tri was eight, he remembers his fear of the men with guns who captured his refugee boat as he fled from Vietnam in 1980. With sixty-eight other refugees, he was taken to a Malaysian island and housed in a fenced compound, where everyone was fed one cup of rice a day and strip-searched at night. His uncle later told him that the women refugees were raped. Now a Brunswick Baptist pastor, Tri has "blocked a lot out" from the experience, but he remembers hearing the "screaming."

Tri also remembers that after he arrived in Australia in 1982, he and his father (Nang) and sister (Trang) were shown kindness at the Midway hostel in Maribyrnong, where there was no barbed wire. Locals taught his family English, gave them clothes and meals and helped Nang find a job with Australia Post. Eight years later, a group from the Moonee Ponds Baptist Church helped bring his mother and two younger brothers to Australia from Vietnam. At 2 AM, sixty strangers came to welcome them at Melbourne Airport. Tri says, "We were traumatised and had a really rough journey but were just immersed in love and hospitality."

Tri said that he had embarked on his long walk because he "wanted to thank Australians for giving him the gift of refuge when he came with his family on a boat from Vietnam thirty-two years ago." He was also carrying a message to the heart of the nation: he wanted to ask Australians to give the same gift of refuge to others, such as Linda, Daniel and Majid, other asylum seekers who accompanied him on his walk. Tri aimed to arrive in Canberra on Good Friday, donate the little boat to Parliament, then attend an Easter Sunday ecumenical service on the shores of Lake Burley Griffin. The small boat was made by Nang and was partly inspired by a "profound" Leunig cartoon of a man and a duck towing a trolley.

I felt deeply honored to support such a sincere, strong and gentle campaigner in his walk of resistance. At the Easter Sunday ecumenical service, Tri quietly reminded us, "We are at our best when we show compassion. I hope in thirty years' time, we have more refugees wanting to say 'thank you' rather than us wanting to say 'sorry.'"[84]

His small boat found safe harbor in Lake Burley Griffin.

I was also involved in a specifically Christian NonViolent Direct Action movement called "Love Makes A Way," which started in 2014 to protest the government's treatment of asylum seekers. Love Makes A Way is committed

84. Webb, "Give the Gift Of Refuge."

to Jesus as "the center of our faith, life and (enemy-loving) activism, willing to suffer for the sake of others." The movement seeks to join in the struggle alongside brothers and sisters from all Christian traditions through radical prayer, "not merely us asking God to change things, but God changing us that we might better reflect Christ's love and compassion in the world." The movement also works through nonviolent action, a pacifist, but not passive, "way of struggling for peace, justice and compassion." As Daniel Berrigan puts it, it is "a way of living and being and expressing the truth of our soul in the world," which can "be symbolized by the two hands of nonviolence: one hand pushed outward, as if to say 'Stop! we will stand in the way of the evil that is being done,' and the other hand held out with an open palm, as if to say 'Come, we invite you to join us in seeking what is right,'" a gesture that includes the perpetrator as well as victim, "even our enemies. . .(we think Jesus meant that bit)."[85]

In 2014 Love Makes A Way organized twenty-two nonviolent civil disobedience actions to challenge Australia's inhumane asylum-seeker policies. These actions included a twin sit-pray-in, which was held in the offices of Prime Minister Tony Abbott and Opposition Leader Bill Shorten, and a National Day of Action in six cities.

While I coordinated the Brisbane chapter of Love Makes A Way we organized a prayer vigil with eleven Christian leaders from various denominations in the office of Federal Health Minister Peter Dutton in Strathpine to raise awareness about our concerns for the plight of children held in immigration detention. Our group included three Anglican priests, a Catholic priest, a nun, ministers from the Uniting and Wesleyan Methodist Churches and lay people from various denominations.[86]

We sent out a press release at 11 AM that stated our intention to remain in prayer in the minister's office until he acted quickly and decisively to remove all children under the age of eighteen, who were being held in onshore detention or offshore detention on Christmas Island or Nauru, and to place them into community care. At 5:25 PM, we were detained and then escorted out of the building, but released later without charge.

On 17 June 2015, the tenth anniversary of the day that John Howard, the prime minister at the time, promised to release children from immigration

---

85. http://lovemakesaway.org.au/who-we-are/

86. Those involved in the vigil were Prof. Charles Ringma (University of Queensland), Rev. Kenn Baker (Wesleyan Methodist), Rev. Nicholas Whereat (Anglican), Rev. Geoff Hoyte (Anglican), Rev. Mary Smith (Anglican), Rev. Jenny Busch (Uniting), Rev. Fr Terry Fitzpatrick (Catholic), Sister Deloris (Sister of Mercy), Dr Jason McLeod (Quaker), Linda Page (Baptist) and myself. See press release at https://bit.ly/2Zga2kc

detention centers in Australia, I gathered with forty other Christian leaders as part of the Love Makes a Way movement for a prayer vigil in the lobby of Parliament House to express our frustration that nothing has been done politically to respond to our constant community campaigns to call the current government to release all children being held in detention. As BuzzFeed reported, the Australian government "celebrated by booting" us out of the Parliament House. As we "were forcibly removed from Parliament by security guards," we sang updated lyrics to the tune of an old African American spiritual, "Were you there when the kids were locked away?"[87]

Over the last four years, over two hundred Christian pastors, priests, nuns and laity have been arrested or detained for taking a nonviolent stand for compassion. Sam McLean, former national Director of GetUp, observed that Love Makes A Way "is the only effort cutting through [the public consciousness] at the moment. They are brave, but more than that, they're smart, careful, and deliberate. They have consistently generated public attention, but the real art has been to do so in a way that is on their message and their terms. Nonviolent love-in-action cuts through fear, spin and self-interest with a message of hope, empathy and compassion."[88]

Love Makes A Way has resisted the Australian government's inhumane policies through nonviolent protest and persuasion, formal statements, public speeches, petitions and letters, banners, leaflets, and posters, social media, radio and television interviews, lobbying, picketing, sit-ins and pray-ins. Nevertheless, Home Affairs Minister Peter Dutton has repeatedly insisted that no amount of protest would persuade the government to change its policy.

So many of us in Love Makes A Way decided it was time to call for a national campaign of nonviolent noncooperation. We called for social noncooperation with government ceremonies and economic noncooperation through boycotts by workers, producers, consumers, investors, owners and managers of Transfield and strikes by administrators, professionals and personnel in all detention centers. We also called for political noncooperation through slow obedience, disguised disobedience and open civil disobedience, refusing to cooperate with government agencies, rules and regulations in relation to the implementation of the current asylum seeker policy. Many other Australians also believed the time had come to move beyond protest and persuasion to civil disobedience and social, economic and political noncooperation.

87. https://www.buzzfeed.com/alexlee/why-are-children-still-in-immigration-detention#.bhmGGY477

88. lovemakesaway.org.au/lmaw-story.

On 11 October 2015, "doctors at the Royal Children's Hospital refused to discharge asylum seeker children back into detention. Doctors at the hospital are concerned about the welfare of their dozens of patients and say it would be unethical to discharge them to unsafe conditions that could compromise their health."[89]

In early February 2016, one-year-old "Baby Asha" was treated at Brisbane's Lady Cilento Children's Hospital after she was injured in an immigration detention on Nauru. Asha's injuries healed, but doctors refused official demands to discharge her to be returned to detention on Nauru, saying it was not a safe home for the baby. The child's fate focused the attention of Australians who were concerned about the government's treatment of the children of families seeking asylum. The federal president of the Australian Medical Association (AMA), Brian Owler, used Twitter to garner support for the doctors and nurses at Lady Cilento. On 13 February, a broad coalition of protesters led by the Refugee Action Collective, including Love Makes A Way, rallied outside the hospital to support the doctors and nurses who were refusing to obey the demands of the immigration department officials.[90]

On 17 February, a coalition of Christians hosted a candlelight vigil at Lady Cilento Hospital called "Light the Dark" to demonstrate our support for the #LetThemStay campaign for Baby Asha, her parents and the nearly three hundred mums, dads and children who were being threatened with removal to the unsafe conditions on Nauru and also to show our support for the brave doctors, nurses and other staff of the hospital who were risking their careers to defy federal directives in order to protect Baby Asha.[91] The Very Rev. Dr. Peter Catt, Chair of the Australian Churches Refugee Taskforce and Dean of St. John's Anglican Cathedral in Brisbane, declared that a group of churches and faith communities across Australia, including St. John's, were committed to offer sanctuary to the families who were seeking asylum and being threatened with a return to Nauru. "This is a hugely significant action for any Australian church to take," Peter said. "Historically, churches have afforded sanctuary to those seeking refuge from brutal and

89. http://www.theage.com.au/victoria/royal-childrens-hospital-doctors-refuse-to-return-children-to-detention-20151010-gk63xm.html#ixzz3plDVkznW

90. https://www.abc.net.au/news/2016–02-21/protesters-vow-to-block-cars-if-baby-asha-is-deported/7187278

91. Led by Love Makes A Way, the coalition included the Australian Churches Refugee Taskforce, the Brisbane Refugee and Asylum Seeker Support network (BRASS), the Ecumenical Social Justice Group (Western Suburbs), the Edmund Rice Centre and St. John's Anglican Cathedral, Brisbane.

oppressive forces. We offer this refuge because there is irrefutable evidence from health and legal experts that the circumstances asylum seekers, especially children, would face if sent back to Nauru are tantamount to state-sanctioned abuse. This fundamentally goes against our faith, so our church community is compelled to act, despite the possibility of individual penalty against us." Peter was prepared to go to prison himself.

On 20 February, "hundreds of protesters surrounded exit points at the hospital amid reports there were plans to move Asha and her family to immigration detention." Protestors said "they would put their bodies on the line to prevent Asha's offshore removal." A representative of the Refugee Action Collective told reporters that protesters "were stationed at hospital exits and using mobile phones to communicate" and said they were "stopping police cars coming out of the hospital on Saturday night to check the child was not inside." He insisted that the group was "good natured" and "had shown no aggression."[92]

Our group was willing to accept moving Baby Asha to community detention in Brisbane, where she could be housed safely with her mother. Finally, on 22 February, Baby Asha was released from Lady Cilento hospital into community detention in Brisbane, a solution that both sides could claim as a victory: the government claimed its policies were unaltered, and those supporting Baby Asha were assured that she was not being moved to Nauru.[93]

After the candlelight vigil for Baby Asha, Peter asked Love Makes A Way to run public meetings for those interested in supporting St. John's offer of sanctuary. In my presentation, I said, "We are called to protect the vulnerable against violence. St. Paul says, 'love always protects and always preserves' (1 Cor. 13:4). Direct nonviolent intervention is the most loving way to do that, as it is least likely to incite further cycles of violence and counter-violence. However, nonviolence should not be used as an excuse for nonintervention. [Because] nonviolent direct action is the most loving proactive response, Love Makes A Way is committed to this practice alone."

I said that the archetype of NonViolent Direct Action (NVDA) is Jesus Christ and how my friend Rabbi Zalman Kastel says that what he finds most confronting in the teaching of Jesus is his commitment to unflinching nonviolence in the face of violence, based on his commitment to love friend and foe alike. I also talked about how Gandhi said that Christ was the archetype

92. https://www.abc.net.au/news/2016–02–21/protesters-vow-to-block-cars-if-baby-asha-is-deported/7187278

93. https://www.abc.net.au/news/2016–02–21/protesters-vow-to-block-cars-if-baby-asha-is-deported/7187278

of NonViolent Direct Action for all people, not just for Christians. I quoted from Gandhi, who said, "The gentle figure of Christ—so patient, so kind, so loving, so full of forgiveness that he taught his followers not to retaliate when struck, but to turn the other cheek—was a beautiful example of the perfect person." Gandhi also said that Christ, the "martyr, was an embodiment of sacrifice, "and the cross is "a great example of suffering." Though "Jesus lost his life on the cross," he didn't lose the battle, but won—"as the world's history has abundantly shown." Consequently, Gandhi said that "the example of Christ" is a crucial "factor in the composition of my underlying faith in nonviolence."

I said that Jesus was a prophetic activist who embodied nonviolent revolution: he criticized the authorities for their corruption and oppression (Luke 13:32) and wanted to transform the status quo creating a new society in the midst of the old (Luke 6:19–22). He sought to establish an upside-down system, which would put the first last and the last first (Mark 9:35). He drove the rip-off merchants out of the temple, using a whip on their animals, but not on the people (John 2:15). He said that he came not to bring acquiescence but change, which would cut through other obligations like a sword (Matt. 10:34). Yet he specifically begged his disciples to put aside their weapons, "for all who live by the sword will die by the sword" (Luke 22:36–38). He urged his friends not to take life, but to give their life for others: "For there is no greater love than this—than to lay down your life for your friends" (John 15:13).

I also said that many famous exponents of nonviolence in recent history have included Jews (Abraham Heschel), Hindus (Mahatma Gandhi and Vinoba Bhave), Muslims (Ghaffar Khan and Mohammad Ashafa), Buddhists (the Dalai Lama and Thich Nhat Hanh) and Christians (Martin Luther King Jr., Dorothy Day, Desmond Tutu, Leymah Gbowee and James Wuye).

I quoted Martin King Jr., who said, NonViolent Direct Action seeks to create such a crisis and foster such a tension that a community which has constantly refused to negotiate is forced to confront the issue. It seeks to dramatize the issue so that it can no longer be ignored. We who engage in Nonviolent Direct Action are not the creators of tension. We merely bring to the surface the hidden tension that is already alive. We bring it out in the open, where it can be seen and dealt with. Like a boil that can never be cured so long as it is covered up but must be opened with all its ugliness to the natural medicines of air and light, injustice must be exposed, with all the tension its exposure creates, to the light of human conscience and the air of national opinion before it can be cured.

I said that declaring sanctuary was a classic NonViolent Direct Action, because it seeks to dramatize an issue so that it can no longer be ignored— which is that vulnerable people who are seeking refuge in our country are in danger from the very authorities who have been tasked by our society to protect them from danger. Thus people of faith must take these sacred places and make them safe spaces, where asylum seekers can be protected, as a symbol of resistance against the inhuman treatment of vulnerable people.

I concluded with a sanctuary case study by André Trocmé, a Protestant minister, and Magda Trocmé, a social worker, who moved to Le Chambon, a little village in France, and started a college for refugees who were fleeing from central Europe in 1934. When France was overrun by Germany in 1940 and the Vichy government agreed to handover Jewish refugees to the Nazis, André preached a sermon encouraging all Christians to resist any government demands to hand over refugees. He said, "Tremendous pressure will be put on us to submit passively to a totalitarian ideology. We appeal to all our brothers in Christ to refuse to cooperate with this violence. We shall resist whenever our adversaries demand of us obedience contrary to the orders of the gospel. We shall do so without fear, but also without hate."

I said that Le Chambon became "the safest place in Europe for Jews and should be our role model. I told them how everyone who was asked to hide Jews housed them in homes, on farms, and in public institutions, providing them with a safe haven for as long as they wanted. If asked by the Vichy government about these people living in their homes, the people replied that they were their cousins. People made false identification cards and helped set up an underground railroad that led some 5,000 Jews to safety in Switzerland. Though Le Chambon was eventually raided by the Gestapo, and André's cousin, Daniel, was arrested, sent to a concentration camp, and killed, not a single villager ever turned a Jew over to the police.

After telling this story, I introduced the Love Makes A Way code of conduct for our NonViolent Direct Action campaign. We committed that we would:

> NOT bring weapons.
> NOT use drugs or alcohol.
> NOT hide our identity behind hoods or masks.
> NOT resort to physical violence or verbal abuse.
> NOT misuse facilities or damage any property.
> NOT react if attacked, but respond pro-actively.
> NOT embarrass police, resist arrest or go limp.

We also committed that we would:

Dress neatly and tidily.
Act in an exemplary manner.
Be strong but gentle, calm and constructive.
Use good manners and good humor at all times.
Adopt a dignified, friendly approach towards all.
Work cooperatively with the coordinating group.
Render assistance to asylum seekers any way we can.
Support nonviolent resistance of any attempt by the authorities
to remove asylum seekers who were seeking the sanctuary of
this sacred place.
And, if arrested, treat the authorities politely and respectfully.

Then we formed a team to provide training sessions for all volunteers committed to supporting sanctuary at St. John's so they could deal with their fears of confrontation and develop strategies of physical and nonviolent resistance in order to defend sanctuary against any incursions by the border security force.[94]

A crowd of some thousand supporters gathered at St. John's Cathedral to declare sanctuary. I welcomed those present by saying, "I would like to honour the traditional owners of this land past and present whose representatives have publicly welcomed asylum seekers."

I invited everyone present to take a stand for sanctuary by rendering asylum seekers any assistance we could and joining the congregation of St. John's cathedral in calmly, resolutely and nonviolently resisting any attempt by the border security force to remove any asylum seeker seeking the sanctuary of this sacred place.

Then I invited everyone present to say to our fellow Australians:

Let us rise up against systemic abuse in our name.
Let us rise up against state sanctioned brutality as policy.
Let us rise up against sovereignty at the expense of humanity.
Let this be a turning point in our history when, as a nation,
we choose no longer to take the road much travelled—
that callous closed-minded road of calculating cruelty
that leads only to despair—
but instead we choose to take the road less travelled—
that kind, open-hearted road of generous hospitality,
which is the only hope for any of us.

94. This team was supervised by cathedral staff (Peter Catt, Sue Wilton and Jenny Basham), guided by legal advisors (Phil Hall and Julian Nathan, Jason McLeod) and led by Kenn Baker, Penny Barringham, Peter Branjerdporn, Mike Campbell, Michelle McDonald and myself.

I also invited everyone present to say to those seeking asylum in Australia:

> We will accept you.
> We will respect you.
> We will protect you.
> In this sacred space,
> we will embrace you, open our arms to make space for you,
> we will wrap our arms around you, to comfort you and keep you safe.
> We know it will hard. But we will do it.
> For it is most important to do it when it is most difficult to do.

As the massive crowd cheered each defiant resolve to stand by those seeking asylum, it was a magnificent manifestation of a call and response, where the speaker and listeners are perfectly united in a public demonstration of civil resistance.

The call for sanctuary captured many people's imaginations. As Rev. Dr. Peter Catt said, "This sanctuary movement has grown so much we're in the process of turning the whole of Australia into a sanctuary. The whole nation is on board. I think the fact that the movement has become so public and widely supported gives it a resilience that means we can do this and it will make it very hard for border force and the government to make a move on these people." And I think our campaign helped in some small measure to ensure that none of the 267 asylum seekers who were facing deportation were deported.[95]

The struggle goes on. Even as I write our friends, Andy Paine, Peter Branjerdporn, David Fittell, Mark Delaney and Greg Manning have joined others in a 24-hour-a-day vigil in support of 120 refugees who have been incarcerated in Kangaroo Point Central Apartments.

I was privileged to be able to join these friends in a socially distant vigil for refugees in detention at Kangaroo Point on Sunday evening 15 September 2020. It was organized by Lisa Bridle, starred Martin Arnold, dressed as our own superhero priest, and featured Peter Branjerdporn and I belting out a heartfelt rendition of "Sorry," my strong angry song of grief:

> I was told that we were the good guys - a long time ago.
> I was told that we fought the good fight - from go to woe.
> I was told that we wrote the guidelines - to give a fair go.
> I was told that we'd always do right - by friend and foe.
> Sorry, Aussies, I don't think that no more!

95. Davey, "The whole nation is on board: inside the sanctuary movement to protect asylum seekers."

Sorry, Aussies, I think we're against what we say we're for!

I was told we'd vote for a demagogue - to hit the road.
I was told we'd welcome the underdog - bring 'em home
Sorry, Refugees, I don't think that no more!
Sorry, Refugees, I think we're against what we say we're for!
Sorry. So Sorry. Sorry. I'm Sorry.[96]

Protesting Through Advocating

I've protested the "status quo" by *advocating* for those scapegoated by our society.

On 27 August 2020, the Australian white supremacist terrorist, Brenton Tarrant, was sentenced to life without parole for killing fifty-one and wounding forty more Muslims during Friday prayers in Christchurch, New Zealand, on 15 March 2019.

When I was in Christchurch in 2016 to conduct a series of interfaith conversations, I went to the Masjid Al Noor for Friday prayers, sat at the back on a chair and prayed with the older believers, who were later specially targeted and systematically slaughtered by Brenton Tarrant. While my friend, Hajj Ibrahim Abdelhalim, the Imam of the Linwood Mosque, was not harmed, his dear wife was shot in the arm, along with so many others.

NZ Prime Minister, Jacinda Ardern, was appalled at what she called "an extraordinary and unprecedented act of violence." She went on to say "Many of those who will have been directly affected by this shooting may be migrants to New Zealand, they may even be refugees here. They have chosen to make New Zealand their home, and it is their home. They are us. The person who has perpetuated this violence against us is not. They have no place in New Zealand. There is no place in New Zealand for such acts of extreme and unprecedented violence, which it is clear this act was." [97]

And now we know the NZ Prime Minister was right. The perpetrator was not a New Zealander. He was an Australian. "One of us." And if there is any doubt about Brenton Tarrant, "One of us" in the highest office in our land, leapt to his defence. Shortly after the attack Australian Senator Fraser Anning was quick to blame the victims. He tweeted: "Does anyone still dispute the link between Muslim immigration and violence?" "As always,

96.. From *Songs Of Love And Justice:* www.daveandrews.com.au/media/songs/03_
sorry.mp3

97. https://www.theguardian.com/world/2019/mar/15/one-of-new-zealands
-darkest-days-jacinda-ardern-responds-to-christchurch-shooting

. . . the media will rush to claim that the causes of today's shootings lie with . . . those who hold nationalist views, but this is all clichéd nonsense. The real cause of bloodshed on New Zealand streets today is the immigration program which allowed Muslim fanatics to migrate to New Zealand in the first place."[98]

We Australians must admit there has always been a strains of intolerance and violence lurking just beneath the surface of our civilization that have erupted in breathtaking acts of bigotry and brutality from time to time - whether its killing Aboriginal peoples to take their land or killing Chinese laborers to stop them 'taking our gold' or killing Muslims for daring to immigrate to 'our country'.

Muslims have lived peacefully in Australia for more than two hundred years, but with every act of terror and counter-terror in recent years, ancient memories of the thousand years' conflict between Muslims and Christians have exploded into our public consciousness. Muslims have been repeatedly represented as the precursors of an Islamic invasion and, consequently, "as antisemitism was a unifying factor in the 1910s, 20s and 30s, Islamophobia has become the unifying factor in the early decades of the 21st century."[99]

Australian political parties such as One Nation intentionally promote an anti-Muslim agenda, and Queensland newspapers such as the *Courier Mail* amplify it by quoting blood-curdling statements from the most hair-raising extremists they can find without any regard for how they are misrepresenting the views of the vast majority of our Muslim neighbors. In so doing, these publications are doing the work of the terrorists they quote, frightening us out of our wits, setting neighbor against neighbor and scapegoating the entire Muslim community.

One of my close Muslim friends, Salam, who is "Peace" by both name and nature, is an embodiment of the best of Islam that I have encountered. She and her circle of friends are vital and vibrant, soulful and wise, strong and gentle, gracious and engaged. Salam usually wears a brilliant smile, with her head wrapped in a brightly colored scarf, but I remember when I first met her, there were tears running down her cheeks. One member of her community wearing a *hijab* (scarf) had been attacked in the street; another member of her community wearing a *niqab* (veil) had been stalked and then assaulted in her own home; and Salam herself had been abused by a complete stranger, who had threatened to do her serious harm.

98. https://www.theguardian.com/world/2019/mar/15/australian-senator-fraser-anning-criticised-blaming-new-zealand-attack-on-muslim-immigration

99. Walker and Taylor, "Far right on rise in Europe, says report."

Scapegoating is the singling out of someone—a fall guy, whipping boy, or vulnerable girl, just like Salam and her friends—for unmerited punishment. Scapegoating is an ancient tradition of projecting blame onto an "other," a practice that was first enacted by the people of Israel on the Day of Atonement, when a high priest laid the sins of the people on the head of live goat—literally, a scapegoat—and then sent it, fleeing for its life, into the wilderness.[100] This practice is still with us today.

These days, scapegoating is a strategy that many peoples use to avoid accepting responsibility for our problems, to project that responsibility onto an "other" and to justify venting our frustration and aggression upon them. Many so-called Muslims in the so-called Islamic State are scapegoating Christians, Yazidis and any Muslims who aren't supporters of the Islamic State (IS). Similarly, many people in our country are scapegoating Muslims, such as Salam and her friends, simply because they wear *hijab* or *niqab*, judging them to be guilty by association and to punish them as extremists in retaliation for the violence of IS.

If we continue to practice scapegoating, we will become what we despise. We will develop our own kind of homegrown, gumleaf, jingoistic, ocker extremism. Though we won't cut off anyone's head, we'll graffiti their Mosques, mock their customs, demand they eat *halal* bacon to prove they are Aussies and, as Senator Jacqui Lambie says, run anyone who practices *sharia* out of the country.[101]

One of the most important, powerful, public interfaith demonstrations of advocacy that we were a part of came after we had built low-profile, under-the-radar interpersonal bridges between the Muslim and Christian communities over the course of seven years.

The demonstration was sparked on 13 August 2015, when *The Age* reported:

> . . .ugly scenes are expected at mosques across the country in October, with neo-Nazis and far-right activists planning co-ordinated protests against Muslim migration and Islam. The call to arms was enthusiastically backed by the United Patriots Front, a fringe splinter group of the Reclaim Australia movement, and others. The self-styled "great Aussie patriot" Shermon Burgess, organiser of the UPF, told followers in a video that "the whole world is going to rally against Islam," and called on Australians

100. Lev. 16:7–26.

101. https://www.abc.net.au/news/2014–09–22/jacqui-lambie-renews-attack-on -sharia-law/5761342

to follow suit. "It doesn't matter where you are in the country, find a mosque and you get there."[102]

Concerned about the increasing anti-Muslim hysteria in Australia, my Muslim colleague Nora Amath, the President of Australian Muslim Advocates for the Rights of All Humanity (AMARAH), asked if we could organize Christians leaders to stand in solidarity with Muslims.

In response to her request and to further threats from the United Patriots Front, the Australian Defence League and Reclaim Australia to "rally against Islam," we organized a group of twenty Christian leaders from various denominations around Logan City and South East Queensland to gather at the *Masjid Al Farooq* Mosque in Kuraby and publicly stand in solidarity with the Muslim community.[103] This mosque was often the focus of anti-Muslim outrage and was the first mosque burnt down anywhere in the world after the 9/11 attacks.

The Muslim community breathed a sigh of relief and some wept openly as the Christian leaders who gathered that day said publicly: "We are all people of faith. An attack on any of us because of our religion is an attack on all of us. All of us have the right to feel safe on our streets and in our homes. All of us have the right to practice our faith freely without fear. We appeal to every member of our community: stop this harassment, stop these attacks, stop this climate of suspicion."

We asked all people to commit to the following:

Act in an exemplary manner, being strong but gentle.
Adopt a dignified, friendly, approach towards all.
Respect people regardless of their faith tradition.
Acknowledge similarities and differences between our traditions.
Use our wisdom, knowledge and skills to serve one another.
Discuss any problems we have face to face and solve them peacefully.
Remember that the one thing we all agree on is that we are called to love God unreservedly and to love our neighbours as ourselves.
In this light, we should not judge each other, but encourage each other to judge ourselves according to our call to love God and to love our neighbours.

---

102. http://www.theage.com.au/victoria/authorities-brace-for-ugly-scenes-as -australian-patriots-plan-mosque-protests-20150813-giy69k.html?utm_campaign =echobox&utm_medium=Social&utm_source=Facebook#ixzz3kMauVyzw

103. Participants included representatives from the following denominations: Anglican, Catholic, Orthodox, Lutheran, Quakers, Churches Of Christ, Salvation Army, Uniting Church, Wesleyan Methodist Church and the Waiters Union.

With good media coverage, the message of solidarity rang loud and clear, and the crisis in Kuraby passed without any further threats of "rallies against Islam."

We were part of another protest after many innocent people were killed in Palestine and Israel in 2012. On the Palestinian side, the Palestinians said they fired a thousand rockets into Israel as part of Operation Stones of Baked City, which killed six Israelis, because Israel had blockaded the Gaza Strip and the Israel Defense Force (IDF) had attacked Gaza civilians. The Israelis, on the other hand, blamed Hamas, the al-Qasaam Brigades and the Palestinian Islamic Jihad (PIJ) for Israel's Operation Pillar of Defense, which launched over a thousand strikes on the Gaza Strip and killed a 174 Palestinians. After days of negotiation mediated by Egypt, Israel and Hamas agreed to a ceasefire on 21 November 2012. According to Human Rights Watch, both sides were guilty of violating the laws of war.[104]

Our friend Salam el Merebi, who is married to a Palestinian, asked if we could arrange a meeting to organize a protest against the fighting and killing on both sides. Salam and her Palestinian friends, Rassa Kiswani and Mohamad Alsharufa, were quite clear that even though the death toll was typically asymmetrical (with six Israelis killed compared with 174 Palestinians), they wanted to protest against the violence and tragic loss of life on both sides. They also wanted Christians, Muslims and Jews to come together to be part of this protest.

Christians, Muslims and Jews all came together at the House Centre in West End, where we sat in a large circle and discussed how we could stage an inclusive, creative protest about the loss of life. Salam insisted that we needed to get beyond the binary, us/them, pro-Palestine/ anti-Israeli dynamics that usually define Gaza solidarity protests because "every life matters." Indeed, she said, it is only when we realize our common humanity that we will stop killing each other. The phrase, "every life is worth remembering," resonated with us all, and it became the theme of the protest.

Someone offered to find the names of all the civilians on both sides who were killed. Someone else offered to find a photo of each person. Someone else offered to track down a bio for each person. Someone suggested we buy a thousand white carnations to pass out in their memory, and someone else suggested we make cards, printed with the photos and bios, and tie them to the flowers, and then pass them out in memory of those who were killed on both sides. After all, "every life is worth remembering." Then we set to work.

104. https://en.wikipedia.org/wiki/Operation_Pillar_of_Defense

On the Friday night before the protest, thirty people, many of them from the Indonesian community, spent several hours separating the flowers and tying the cards to them. On Saturday morning, about fifty of us gathered in someone's home to get ready for the protest, which was filled with the fragrance of a thousand fresh carnations.

To prepare our hearts for our inclusive, creative, nonviolent protest against violence, we agreed to pray three prayers together—one Christian, one Muslim and one Jewish.

To start with we prayed a Jewish Prayer:

> For every aspiring ballerina huddled
> scared in a basement bomb shelter
> For every toddler in his mother's arms
> behind rubble of concrete and rebar
> For every child who's learned to distinguish
> "our" bombs from "their" bombs by sound
> For everyone wounded, cowering, frightened
> and everyone furious, planning for vengeance
> For the ones who are tasked with firing shells
> where there are grandmothers and infants
> For the ones who fix a rocket's parabola
> toward children on school playgrounds
> For every official who sees shelling Gaza
> as a matter of "cutting the grass"
> And every official who approves launching projectiles
> from behind preschools or prayer places
> For every kid taught to lob a bomb with pride
> And every kid sickened by explosions
> For every teenager who considers
> 'martyrdom' his best hope for a future:
> May the God of compassion and the God of mercy
> God of justice and God of forgiveness
> God Who shaped creation in Her tender womb
> and nurses us each day with blessing
> God Who suffers the anxiety and pain
> of each of His unique children
> God Who yearns for us to take up
> the work of perfecting creation
> God Who is reflected in those who fight
> and in those who bandage the bleeding—
> May our Father, Mother, Beloved, Creator
> cradle every hurting heart in caring hands.
> Soon may we hear in the hills of Judah

and the streets of Jerusalem
in the olive groves of the West Bank
and the apartment blocks of Gaza City
in the kibbutz fields of the Negev
and the neighborhoods of Nablus
the voice of fighters who have traded weapons
for books and ploughs and bread ovens
the voice of children on swings and on slides
singing nonsense songs, unafraid
the voice of reconciliation and new beginnings
in our day, speedily and soon.
And let us all say: Amen.[105]

Then we prayed a Muslim Prayer:

In the name of God, the Most Gracious, the Most Merciful
Praise be to God, the Cherisher and Sustainer of the worlds
O Lord, we have come together today
from different backgrounds, creeds and religions
so that we may know one another.
Fill us with the reconciling spirit
of your presence so that we may join one another
to do good and build a better humanity.
O Lord, lead us to the path
of hope, compassion, mercy, love and peace.
Let us pray that all living beings realise
that they are all brothers and sisters,
all nourished from the same source of life.
Peace be with you, peace be with you, peace be with you all.
Amen.[106]

Then we prayed a Christian Prayer:

Lord, make me an instrument of Your peace,
Where there is hatred, let me sow love,
Where there is injury, pardon,
Where there is despair, hope,
Where there is darkness, light,
Where there is sadness, joy.
O Divine Master, grant that I may not
So much seek to be consoled, as to console,
To be understood, as to understand,
To be loved, as to love,

105. Barenblatt, "Prayer for the Children of Abraham/Ibrahim."
106.. Nora Amath, unpublished.

For it is in giving that we receive,
It is in pardoning that we are pardoned,
And it is dying that we are born to eternal life.[107]

Then we finished by saying a Buddhist mantra together mindfully three times:

Hatred never ceases by hatred,
but by love alone is healed.[108]

We went out in mixed teams of three—one Christian, one Muslim and one Jew—to show our solidarity with humanity across all traditional religious divisions, now visibly united against violence on all sides. We visited three places—Brisbane City Mall, King George Square and the West End Markets—passing out the flowers with the cards, saying, "every life is worth remembering." We only engaged in conversation when invited. If anyone wanted to talk about the issues in the conflict between Israel and Palestine, we referred them to a team of experts in each location. If anyone was abusive, we just said, "G'day," and walked on.

The general public responded well to the beautiful peaceful commemoration, saying it invited conversation rather than alienating people through clenched fists and angry voices. People welcomed the gift of flowers, and many stopped to talk with the nonthreatening experts about the conflict between Israel and Palestinians.

My dear Palestinian friend Mohamad Alsharufa told me that his involvement with the protest was transformative. "Up until today I wanted to believe that there must be some Jews somewhere who cared for Muslims like me. But it was my hope, not my experience. However, today," he said with tears in his eyes, "I actually met one!" For Mohamad, in that meeting, nothing changed, and yet everything changed.

On July 1, 2020, I joined a Global Coalition of Christians Issuing a Call for Palestinian Justice. I said I would support Kairos Palestine in their Call To Decisive Action

I appreciate the spirit of Kairos Palestine who seek to see "enemies today and human beings tomorrow, vested with the grace of God, moving forth to build together, to wipe off sins committed against human rights, to regenerate and care for new generations of Palestinians and Israelis, to develop the earth where God wants us to continue God's work."

---

107. Francis of Assisi. https://www.loyolapress.com/catholic-resources/prayer/traditional-catholic-prayers/saints-prayers/peace-prayer-of-saint-francis/

108. Kornfield, "Siddartha," in *The Art Of Forgiveness*, 5.

I promised to call on fellow Christians "to engage in a process of study, reflection and confession concerning the historic and systemic deprivation of the rights of the Palestinian people, and the use of the Bible by many to justify and support this oppression."

At the same time I promised to "oppose anti-Semitism by working for justice against anti-Judaism, racism and xenophobia; oppose the equating of criticism of Israel's unjust actions with anti-Semitism."

And I promised to continue to "support initiatives between Israelis and Palestinians and interfaith partnerships that combat apartheid and occupation and create opportunities to work together for a common future of mutual respect and dignity." [109]

I have also advocated for other religious minorities, including Hindus, Buddhists and Jains. In September 2017, a television commercial run by Meat and Livestock Australia (MLA) sparked national controversy for depicting a number of deities sharing a yarn over a plate of lamb. Members of Australia's Hindu community were particularly upset, as many felt the depiction of Ganesha, the beloved Elephant-headed Indian God of Good Fortune, was offensive, since he is a vegetarian. There were also objections to the line about Ganesha being "the elephant in the room." The Indian High Commission even lodged an official complaint with the Department of Foreign Affairs and Trade.[110]

My dear Hindu friend Palani Palanichamy O Thevar, advisor and past president of the Federation of Indian Communities of Queensland, called me to express his outrage and to ask me if I could join his community in a protest they had organized outside Parliament House on 22 September. I said I would be happy to support them.

At the protest, I stood up in front of everyone and said that as a Christian, I wanted to stand in solidarity with my Hindu, Buddhist and Jain friends to protest against the Meat and Livestock Australia ad for lamb. Referring to the controversial line about "the elephant in the room," I said that I didn't like the way the ad was employing Ganesha, a prominent Hindu deity, "to promote eating flesh, since most Hindus, Buddhists and Jains have a long, strong, sacred tradition of practicing *ahimsa*—and not eating meat at all!"

I went on to say that the group marketing manager at Meat and Livestock Australia, Andrew Howie, had displayed "gobsmacking ignorance and blatant disregard for the sensitivities of more than a billion of our Hindu,

109.. *A Cry For Hope – A Call For Decisive Action* https://bit.ly/3eR6Gvw

110. https://junkee.com/lamb-ad-controversy-banned/136480

Buddhist and Jain neighbours" by saying, "In this latest campaign we are showing no matter your beliefs, background or persuasion, the one thing we can all come together and unite over is lamb."

I said that I wanted to stand in solidarity with my Hindu, Buddhist and Jain friends because I also felt terrible anguish in my heart when my religion was cynically used to promote the opposite of what I believed for profit. The *Brisbane Indian Times* wrote that even "Dave Andrews, Christian, and meat-eater," supported the protest. Two months later, after a sustained campaign against the ad, thankfully it was banned.

Protesting Through Dissenting

I've protested the "status quo" by *dissenting* from my country's commitment to war.

On 16 February 2003, I took part in a public embodiment of dissent by marching with a hundred thousand people in Brisbane as one of many coordinated protests in more than six hundred cities in sixty countries around the world to express our collective global opposition to the imminent Iraq War being launched by U.S. President George W. Bush and an international coalition of armed forces. Though Saddam Hussein, the Iraqi president, did not have any weapons of mass destruction or anything to do with 9/11 attacks on the U.S. in 2001, he had reportedly tried to kill Bush senior. Bush junior, who claimed to be a devout born-again, Bible-believing Christian, exclaimed, "God told me to strike al-Qaeda and I struck them, and then he instructed me to strike at Saddam, which I did."[111]

Social researchers described the February protests as "the largest protest event in human history." According to BBC News, "between 6 and 11 million people took part over the weekend of the 15th and 16th of February." Our elected leaders totally ignored us.[112] So some of our friends, including Donna Mulhearn, joined a Human Shield mission in Baghdad. Human Shield is an international movement that courageously used nonviolent means to protect civilian infrastructure (public hospitals, water treatment plants and wheat grain silos) in face of the impending war. Upon Donna's return to Australia, instead of being awarded a medal for bravery, she was misleadingly branded a "traitor" by the prime minister for "supporting Saddam Hussein."[113]

---

111. Austin et al., *God and War*.

112. https://en.wikipedia.org/wiki/15_February_2003_anti-war_protests#Australia

113. Mulhearn, *Ordinary Courage*.

The U.S. invasion of Iraq was an unjustifiable illegal war of aggression. We all remember with horror reports of the allied "Shock and Awe Campaign." Since the invasion in 2003, over a hundred thousand innocent Iraqi civilians have been killed—and we are still counting. Thousands more have lost limbs, often from unexploded allied cluster bombs, which then become crippling land mines. The American military has attacked hospitals to prevent them from giving out casualty figures of allied attacks that contradicted official figures.

The names Hafitha, Samarra and Ramadi will live in infamy because of the wanton destruction, murder and assaults they committed upon human beings and human rights. Our friend Donna described how allied forces broke into numerous homes, took away the men, humiliated the women, and traumatized the children in Fallujah.[114] Since the invasion, over fifty thousand Iraqis were imprisoned by U.S. forces, but only a tiny portion have been convicted of any crime. The gulags run by the U.S. and the new Iraqi government feature a wide variety of torture and degrading abuses that lead prisoners to psychological breakdown, death and suicide. There is no doubt that this war of aggression completely undermined international law and contributed to the rise of terrorism in the Middle East.[115]

I wrote an open letter to the Aussie armed forces, asking them to refuse to fight this war. I said that "Aussies have always been proud of our diggers. And no nation could have been prouder of their troops than when the ADF went to the aid of the people of East Timor." Then I noted how "this war does not have the support of the UN, the world community, or the majority of the Australian people." I asked why this might be so and said that the CIA could not make a link between Al Qaeda and Iraq. While I acknowledged that "Saddam is a butcher," I said that "killing more innocent Iraqis is no solution. We are told Iraq has weapons of mass destruction. But so does Israel. And no one is saying we should invade Israel." Then I noted how most of the world "sees this war as immoral, illegal, and ill-advised." I identified it as "U.S. aggression, in contravention of the UN," and said that it would "only serve to create more ill will—even if it succeeds in regime change." I begged the Australian troops, "in the great Aussie tradition, to disobey all orders that defy common sense and common decency—and refuse to fight in this war." In conclusion, I said that we would "of course support you as people whatever you decide to do."

114. Hill and Mulhearn *The Sacking of Fallujah.*

115. William Blum, "Great Moments in the History of Imperialism," Information Clearing House (23 June 2006), http://www.informationclearinghouse.info/article13719.htm

Interestingly enough, on 14 March 2004, I noticed a report in the Sydney *Sun-Herald,* which revealed that "during the course of the Iraq war, Australian fighter pilots aborted over 40 missions, refusing to drop bombs on targets assigned to them by US field commanders" [116] because they felt they would endanger the lives of civilians. [117]

After writing my letter of dissent, I wanted to find a way to flesh out my dissent publicly, and so I looked around for people who shared my Quaker-like approach to protest, with whom I could demonstrate my opposition to the war assertively but not aggressively. During this time, I providentially met Edmund Cocksedge, who was a member of a local intentional Christian community called the House of Freedom in Brisbane and was committed to a simple lifestyle, servant leadership, common purse and direct nonviolent action.

Edmund was born in 1915 in England just after the outbreak of World War I. He was brought up in the cathedral city of Canterbury in a devout, nonconformist Congregational family. While still a young man, Edmund moved to London, where he got involved with the Bloomsbury Baptist Church. Through them, he began to help young people who were "doing it tough" on the council social housing estates. He also got involved with the Tramp Preachers, who preached radical identification with the poor, and the Peace Pledge Union, which practiced revolutionary, nonviolent intervention in times of conflict in the hope of securing peace.

At the age of twenty-one, as war was looming with Germany, Edmund decided to go to Germany to make contact with the Bruderhof, a community of passionate anti-Nazi pacifists, who were being persecuted by the Nazis for their implacable opposition to militarism. It was hard for the young Edmund to go to Germany at that time, because some of his closest family and friends were quite bitter about it and "argued against the concepts I expressed." It was even harder for Edmund when he got to Germany, because the Bruderhof were suffering for their stand against the state and were very

116. Terry Cook, "Australian pilots aborted US-assigned bombing raids during Iraq war."

117. Sadly, since writing this book, Maj Gen Justice Paul Brereton has released a report, which found "Australian special forces were allegedly involved in the murder of 39 Afghan civilians, in some cases executing prisoners to 'blood' junior soldiers before inventing cover stories and planting weapons on corpses. . .. A small group within the elite Special Air Services and commandos regiments killed and brutalised Afghan civilians, in some cases allegedly slitting throats, gloating about their actions, keeping kill counts, and photographing bodies with planted phones and weapons to justify their actions." https://www.theguardian.com/australia-news/2020/nov/19/australian-special-forces-involved-in-of-39-afghan-civilians-war-crimes-report-alleges

poor and under constant surveillance by the Gestapo, who conducted random raids of the community to command compliance and then confiscated property when that compliance was not forthcoming.

Edmund returned to England an older and wiser man, committed more than ever to simplicity, solidarity, community and nonviolence. He established connections with the anarchists in Spain, supporting their struggle against fascism, but "experienced great tension" when he criticized the atrocities committed by both sides in the Spanish Civil War. He also linked up with the nonviolent activists, or *satyagrahis,* in India, supporting their struggle against the imperialism of his own country while risking being branded a traitor for his advocacy of the Indian Independence Movement. Meanwhile, against the background of the build-up for war against Germany, Edmund and his friends in the Peace Pledge Union decided to go on a peace trek round England, encouraging conscientious objection. Later Edmund moved to Australia.

At the age of sixty, Edmund was still an indefatigable campaigner when it came to "witnessing for peace and justice" through direct nonviolent action. Edmund was arrested many times in Australia for his anti-war activities, one of the most notable being when he was arrested at St. John's, the Anglican Cathedral, for protesting the complicity of the church with the state over the Vietnam War.[118]

Edmund's approach to protest was also shaped by the Quakers, whose founder, George Fox—like Gandhi—based his approach on the Sermon on the Mount. At the age of eighty-eight, Edmund used to join with Brisbane Friends in King George Square, opposite the City Hall, in the evening after work every week during the Iraq war to demonstrate dissent by steadfastly and silently standing in a line, single file, facing the oncoming crowds of workers making their way home, holding up posters saying, "Iraq—Bush's War For Oil," "Say No To The War In Iraq," "War Is Terrorism," and "Make Tea Not War."

I remember standing shoulder to shoulder with Edmund and the Brisbane Friends.

However there were other protests by other dear friends I felt I could not support.

For example, some of my good friends, citing Pope Francis's New Year's peace message, which said, "the name of God cannot be used to justify violence," decided that on Ash Wednesday, the first day of Lent, they would remove the sword from the crucifix on the war memorial at the gates

118. Andrews, *Christi-Anarchy* 134–135.

of Toowong cemetery, saying that using a sword as a crucifix was an act of blasphemy. Jim Dowling removed the metal sword from the cement crucifix while Tim Webb placed the sword on an anvil and reshaped it into a garden hoe, enacting the biblical prophecies of Micah and Isaiah that "They will beat their swords into ploughshares and their spears into pruning hooks. Nation will not take up sword against nation, nor will they train for war anymore."

My friends knew full well about my commitment to follow the nonviolent Jesus and asked me if I would publicly support their symbolic action. I thought about it overnight, then wrote the following post the next day. "What can I say to my friends who removed the sword from a war memorial crucifix? I agree with your analysis. It is blasphemous to combine a cross with a sword; it is sacrilegious to allow the ultimate symbol of suffering violence to be co-opted by the universal symbol for inflicting violence; and it is dangerous to sacralise an unethical pre-emptive strike, such as ANZAC, that rationalises an illegal invasion and the slaughter of 87,000 Turks at Gallipoli. But I disagree with your action. Desecrating a war memorial adds only insult to the injury of the sorrow felt by those whose loved ones are memorialised there. It distorts the message of peace that you preach and distracts from the important point, which you have taken great pains to make." [119]

Sometimes I needed to demonstrate my dissent against war and the machinery of war on my own, all by myself, as I did at Easterfest, Australia's largest Easter festival. As the promo on the websites says, Easterfest is "not just AT Easter, but ABOUT Easter!" Easterfest used to draw tens of thousands of people from across Australia, who made the pilgrimage up the mountain range to the beautiful regional garden city of Toowoomba.

For four days, "some 200 artists from across the world perform on stages in Queen's Park, as well as cafes, restaurants, pubs, theatres, shopping centres and churches, with music of every kind. From jazz to heavy metal, from acoustic folk to indie pop, from blues, funk and soul to good old rock and roll." Interspersed throughout these performances, there were presentations by high-profile Christian speakers sponsored by the Bible Society.

In 2008 the Bible Society asked me to present my Plan Be campaign for a Blessed Be-Attitude Revolution, which I did. Then in 2009 I returned to Easterfest with no plan to play an upfront role, as I was there to support Ange by being her backup while she was hosting her Lastfirst Fair-Trade/Fair-Go stall.

119. 3 March 2017, https://bit.ly/2Kd4Sz2

After helping Ange set up her stall, I decided to go for a stroll around the festival to see what other organizations, such as Compassion, Destiny Rescue and Just Motivation, were doing to bring a focus on social justice issues, something Easterfest organizers said "cannot be separated from the message of Easter."

As I was wandering around, I came across a military tent with a tank parked outside. Not a water tank—which are common in our parched part of the world—but a war tank, a heavily armored, ironclad fighting vehicle designed for frontline combat, mounted on all terrain tracks, carrying a large-calibre machine gun. I was shocked to see a big, brutal, firepower, fighting vehicle on display at an event that was "not just AT Easter, but ABOUT Easter!" and so struck up a conversation with the man in uniform who was in charge of the display. "G'day mate, I said. "Could you tell me why you have a tank on display here?"

"The Easterfest organizers invited me to put it on display," he said, "as it's an instantly recognizable, eye-catching symbol of ANZAC, and the AN-ZAC story powerfully illustrates the Easter story of sacrifice."

I was gobsmacked. How could anyone think that the ANZAC story and the Easter story were the same? But rather than react, I accepted his invitation to watch a documentary about ANZAC, which stands for Australian and New Zealand Army Corps, whose soldiers were known as "Anzacs."

The documentary recounted the story about how when World War I broke out in 1914, the Anzacs went to Europe to support the British Empire. "In 1915, Australian and New Zealand soldiers formed part of an Allied expedition that set out to capture the Gallipoli Peninsula, according to a plan by Winston Churchill, to open the way to the Black Sea for the Allied navies. The ANZAC force landed at Gallipoli on 25 April, meeting fierce resistance from the Ottoman Army commanded by Mustafa Kemal (later known as Atatürk)."[120] But what had been planned as a bold strike became a stalemate, and the campaign dragged on for eight months. The finally,

> . . .at the end of 1915, the Allied forces were evacuated after both sides had suffered heavy casualties and endured great hard-ships. The Allied casualties included 21,255 from the United Kingdom, an estimated 10,000 dead soldiers from France, 8,709 from Australia and 2,721 from New Zealand. News of the land-ing at Gallipoli made a profound impact on Australians and New Zealanders at home, and 25 April quickly became the day on which they remembered the sacrifice of those who had died

120. http://en.wikipedia.org/wiki/Anzac_Day

in the war. The creation of what became known as an "Anzac legend" became an important part of our national identity.[121]

I had lots of problems with the way the story was told. First, it glossed over the fact that the imperial war was one in which we should not have had any part. Second, our participation involved us in an unethical preemptive strike and therefore implicated us in the illegal invasion of another country, where we slaughtered eighty-seven thousand Turks at Gallipoli. Nonetheless I appreciated the fact that in the midst of the slaughter, there were many examples of heroic self-sacrifice—such as the famous story about Simpson.

So I said to the attendant, "I'm sure there were many examples of heroic self-sacrifice at ANZAC cove. But if it is sacrifice, not slaughter, that you want to commemorate, wouldn't it be better to have a statue of Simpson and his donkey rather than that bloody tank? After all, Simpson—a stretcher bearer, who commandeered a donkey, wrapped a red cross around its muzzle and rescued wounded diggers under fire for three and a half weeks until he was killed—was a real Christ-figure at ANZAC cove."

"Maybe you're right," he said. "But I was asked to bring the tank, so I brought the tank."

I thanked the attendant and returned to Ange's stall to bring her a coffee and have a chat about what I should do about the tank. I was deeply disturbed that the organizers thought that a heavily armored, ironclad, combat machine, which was designed to kill people—not to give life, but to take life—was a suitable symbol for Easter, one that would somehow communicate the message of Easter.

That night I wrote a short flyer expressing my concerns about having the tank at Easterfest. The next day I handed out my flyers and invited people with similar concerns to gather around the tank early Easter Sunday morning to reflect on the significance of the tank as distinct from the cross as a symbol of Easter.

Most people ignored me. Not many wanted to engage in conversation about the tank. They were too busy enjoying themselves, which was to be expected. After all, it was a music festival, not a semiotics seminar. A few people took the flyers, and some said they'd come on Sunday, but most people hurried on to the next gig.

Though my actions didn't get much attention, my "potentially disruptive activities" must have been reported to the management, because it wasn't long before a couple of broad-shouldered security guards showed up, ordered me to desist and directed me to come with them to the main office.

121. http://en.wikipedia.org/wiki/Anzac_Day

The manager, Isaac Moody, introduced himself and asked me to sit down. Then, very politely, he asked why I was trying to "make trouble." I assured him that I wasn't trying to "make trouble." If I wanted to "make trouble," I told him, I could do a much better job. He said, "But you're organizing a demonstration." I said, "No, I am only organizing a conversation about the presence of a tank at Easterfest." He said, "But you're causing division." I said, "No, in point of fact, you are causing division, because you arranged for the tank to be an exhibit at Easterfest even though the military man warned you that it would be contentious."

"Okay," Isaac conceded, "you may have a point. But since it is contentious, and a public debate about the presence of the tank at Easterfest has the potential to ferment a significant level of discontent—if not a completely unprecedented level of disruption—I'd appreciate it if you held the conversation off-site, rather than on-site." I told him that I would be very happy to do that on one condition: that he would agree to meet with me after the festival to discuss the matter face to face. He agreed.

So I conducted the public discussion about the tank that Easter Sunday in a local public bar. I asked people what they thought about the significance of the tank, as compared to the cross, as a symbol for Easter. On the one hand, some people thought it was blasphemous, because the tank stood for slaughter and the killing of enemies, whereas the cross stood for sacrifice and a willingness to die to save friend and foe alike. People also thought it was outrageous for Christians to confuse the two and mistake one for the other, as if the inherent violence of the one was the same as the inherent nonviolence of the other. On the other hand, some people thought it was ironic, because even though the cross was once a sign of Christ's commitment to nonviolence and sacrifice, Christians since Constantine have taken the cross and used it has a bloodthirsty battle-banner under which they send in the troops (in recent wars accompanied by tanks) to perpetrate terrible acts of violence and slaughter.

People also thought it was tragic, because by confusing Easter with ANZAC, Christians were supporting the allied invasion of Iraq, even though it was clearly an illegal and unjust war, which was based on a lie, and had led to the deaths of over half a million Iraqis.[122]

A month or two later I met with Isaac Moody to talk about the tank and the cross. He acknowledged the validity our concerns and said he was open to suggestions about how he might progress further discussions at Easterfest. But in spite of the many creative suggestions that we gave him to help punters at Easterfest engage with the nonviolent message of the Easter

122. Andrews, *Crux*.

event, nothing was ever forthcoming. After a couple of years, the festival closed.

Protesting Through Disrupting

I've protested the "status quo" by *disrupting* ecclesiastical business as usual.

Yvonne Sherwood, a professor of religious studies at the University of Kent, contrasts "Wisdom" with "not-so-wise" prophetic traditions in the Bible:

> Whereas Wisdom uses phrases such as "a word fitly spoken is like apples of gold in a setting of silver" (Prov. 25:11), the prophet does not choose which words to use but is governed by the word they are compelled to give. Moreover, they do not just *say* the word, they *do* the word. Like Performance Artists who aim for sensation or the destruction of convention, prophets seem to have an aim of shocking their audience. Frequently their acts are contrary to acceptable behaviour, social convention, and religious sensibilities. In this regard the prophets allow themselves to become extremely vulnerable: open to ridicule, accusations, rejection and dismissal of their message. Indeed, they were often told to expect such rejection, and at times they were imprisoned or physically punished by the community they were seeking to influence.[123]

Before people got to know me well, I remember going to a church, where I was booked to preach, a week before they expected me, dressed like a tramp in dirty, daggy, ragged clothes. I waited on the doorstep to observe the kind of welcome I might receive. No one would talk to me. When I begged for help, a few people referred me for welfare to a pastor, who wasn't there at the time, but would be back soon. I was disgusted and felt I had to disrupt their script. So when I returned the next week, suitably attired for the occasion, I stood in the pulpit and "disturbed them with the word," quoting Jesus, who said, "in as much as you did it to the least of these you did it to me!" (Matt. 25:40). As people got to know me better, they were more cautious about inviting me to preach.

Another time that I remember disrupting the script, I was teaching students at a Bible college about what Jesus said in his parable of the Sheep and the goats in Matthew 25:31–46. Following is my adapted version of the parable:

123. Sherwood, "Prophetic Performance Art," 1.1.

When the Human One comes, all the nations will be gathered before him, and he will separate the people one from another as a shepherd
separates the sheep from the goats. He will put the sheep—who have done
right—on his right, and the goats—who haven't—on his left. Then the True
Leader will say to those on his right, "Come, join the party. For I was hungry
and you gave me feed. I was thirsty and you gave me a drink. I just arrived
in town and you took me into your home. My clothes were in tatters and
you gave me your own outfit. I was sick in bed and you came and spent time
with me. I was stuck in prison and you were there for me and my family."
Stunned, the people on the right will say to him, "When on earth did we see
you hungry and give you a feed, or thirsty and give you a drink? When did
we meet you after you had just arrived in town and give you a bed for the
night? When were you sick in bed and we spent time with you? When were
you stuck in prison and we were there for you and your family?" The True
Leader will say, "Whenever you did the right thing by those whom most
consider least, you did the right thing by me!" Then, turning to those that
are left, the True Leader will say, "Get out. You can go to hell with everyone
else who has made life hell for others. I was hungry and you never gave me
a feed; thirsty and you never gave me a drink; lonely, without a friend, and
you walked by; half-naked and you didn't give me any clothes; sick in bed,
and stuck in jail, and you didn't even visit." And those who are left will be
bewildered, and say, "When did we see you hungry or thirsty? When did we
see you without a friend or without clothes? When did we see you sick in
bed or stuck in prison?" And the True Leader will say to them, "Whenever
you did not do the right thing by those whom most consider least, you did
not do the right thing by me!"

I explained to the students that the story of the sheep and the goats
is a classic Christ story in the way that it lures an audience into listening
to a harmless narrative, only to be led, slowly but surely, into a shocking
encounter with a truth, which is so frightening that they have been trying to
avoid it all of their lives.

I pointed out how the shock in the story for the people in Christ's
time—and for most Christians today—is that he insists that we will not be
judged on the basis of whether we have subscribed to the right set of doc-
trines or obeyed the right code of behavior; rather, we will be judged on the
basis of whether or not we have done the right thing by those whom most
people consider to be the least!

In spite of picking up on their strong, but as yet unspoken, evangelical
reservations, I pressed on, saying that some Christians argue that Christ
can't be saying what he seems to be saying, which is that we will be judged
on the basis of the justice that we do, or do not do, for the disadvantaged.

These Christians insist that we are saved by our relationship to Christ, not by our response to disadvantaged people. But the whole point of the parable is that the *true* nature of our relationship to Christ is demonstrated by our response to disadvantaged people. We may claim to love Christ, which is fine, fantastic, but, in this parable, Christ says loudly and clearly that the only way that any of us can *prove* it is through our love for the poor.

At this point, the class erupted, denouncing me as a defector from the true faith. Didn't I know that "we are not saved by works, but by faith alone!"[124]

Rather than argue, trading an endless exchange of Bible quotes, I picked up my Bible, held it up so all could see it, ripped out the pages containing Matthew 25:31–46, crumpled them in a ball, and threw them in the rubbish bin.

If they were angry before, now they were enraged, abusing me for my ungodly act of tearing pages from the Holy Bible and throwing them in the rubbish bin!

Shouting over the abuse they hurled at me, I said, "What is more ungodly, ripping out pages from the Holy Bible and throwing them in the rubbish bin? Or totally rubbishing the teaching of Jesus because it confronts us and doesn't fit our theology?"

Unsurprisingly, the college later instituted an inquiry about me, decided that my conduct was not appropriate for a lecturer in a Bible college and sacked me on the spot.

I remember another time that I disrupted the script, when I was talking to students in a Christian fellowship—which I had also been a part of back when I attended the University of Queensland—about Christ's commitment to the poor. After I finished speaking, the students took me to task for preaching what they sarcastically called a "social gospel."

I replied that as far as Christ was concerned, the gospel was meant to be "good news to the poor" (Luke 4:18), so if the gospel they preached wasn't "good news to the poor," it could not be the gospel of Christ.

This upset them and they expressed their disgust with my "liberal theology."

In that moment I recalled Tony Compolo's famous retort to evangelical students and thought I'd give it a try myself: "You care more about your theology than the poor. You really couldn't give a shit about the poor. And now you are more outraged that I swore than I challenged your commitment to the poor."

124. Galatians. 2:16.

And so it proved to be. Word quickly got around the Christian fellowship that I had said "shit" in their consecrated chapel service, and from then on, I was never invited again.

Years later I was chatting with a member of parliament and learned he had attended that same Christian fellowship. He said, "I was there that day you swore!"

I asked him, "Do you recall what I was talking about and why I said what I did?"

He said, "No. All I recall is that you said 'shit'!"

This sadly proved the very point I had been making. He recalled I said "shit" because he was more outraged that I had sworn than for challenging his commitment to the poor.

And no, he didn't invite me to speak at the next parliamentary prayer breakfast.

Of all the disturbing disruptions I have participated in, the most disturbing was with YWAM.[125]

For the uninitiated, YWAM, which is pronounced *Why? Wham!*, stands for Youth With A Mission, which, with its vast army of thousands of gung-ho, voluntary, young evangelists, is not only one of the biggest, but also one of the most energetic, mission agencies in the world today.

Ange and I first encountered YWAM when we, along with a whole generation of flower-power Jesus freaks, were checking out alternative communities, and we came across this up-and-coming group.

However, right from the start, Ange and I knew that YWAM was not for us. We found YWAM to be an extraordinary, larger-than-life, high-flying, fast-moving, do-anything, go-anywhere, global evangelistic agency, and we were really looking for a more ordinary, small-is-beautiful, low-profile, long-term, hands-on, grassroots, local community ministry.

Ironically enough, even though we didn't find what we were looking for in YWAM, we did find what we were looking for *through* YWAM, because through YWAM, we met an ex-YWAMer named Floyd McClung. Courtesy of this lovable, lanky, long-haired, full-bearded, 6' 7" gentle giant, we were introduced to a community called "Dilaram: The House of the Peaceful Heart," which was to become our future home.

Floyd and Sally had set up the first Dilaram Community in Kabul, Afghanistan. Then Harry and Rosie started the second Dilaram Community in Kathmandu, Nepal. Then Ange and I started the third Dilaram

125. The following paragraphs are excerpts from Prologue to Andrews, *Christi-Anarchy*, 1–9.

Community in Delhi, India, along with Steve and Kathy Aram. We got on a bit of a roll, and it only took a few years for us to establish a dozen different Dilaram Communities in half a dozen different countries around the world. During this time, YWAM also offered Dilaram the use of some houseboats in Amsterdam to establish a community in the Netherlands.

Our time in the House of the Peaceful Heart was a dream come true, for we saw a dearly held vision that our generation had for society become a reality. In Dilaram, we experienced people simply living together in beautiful, peaceful, compassionate, therapeutic communities. When word got out about Dilaram, crowds of young people from all over the world made their way to join us in our quiet little revolution, and so the movement began to gather some momentum.

Thus our next memorable encounter with YWAM was when, believe it or not, they proposed a "marriage" with Dilaram. Loren Cunningham, the Director of YWAM at the time, decided to use this proposed merger or cooperative venture as an opportunity to resolve a conflict that he'd had with Floyd a few years earlier, which had caused Floyd to leave. As time went by, it became clear that Loren Cunningham had much more on his mind than conflict resolution, for he was so impressed with the job Floyd had done with Dilaram that he not only wanted Floyd to come back to YWAM, he also wanted Floyd to take over his role as the Director of YWAM.

From the very moment that the idea of a merger between YWAM and Dilaram was mooted, I had some very serious reservations. Ange and I, like many others, had joined Dilaram—not YWAM—because we wanted to be a part of Dilaram—not YWAM.

We feared that if we entered into this so-called "marriage" (in what appeared to us to be a very patriarchal approach), Dilaram would inevitably be expected to play a subordinate role to YWAM. We were also scared that, in the process of subordination, the culture of Dilaram as a movement would be subsumed into the culture and structure of YWAM as an organization.

Our concerns were validated when we were told that people would be expected to go through a YWAM orientation course before being allowed to join a Dilaram Community. Furthermore, Dilaram leaders were expected to attend conferences for YWAM leaders and to lead their communities in the more directive YWAM style that was modeled at those conferences. The incentives for Dilaram leaders to take on the YWAM style were really attractive: a higher position, a wider reputation, greater privileges and bigger perks—which they called "love gifts."

So I decided to protest and to embody my personal protest by speaking out publicly against the YWAMization of Dilaram.

Little did I know that, even then, it was already too late. At one stage, in the middle of the debate about the future of Dilaram, I was sent to consult with some of the other communities. While I was away, Loren Cunningham, the director of YWAM, turned up at my community. In my absence, he did his best to portray my criticism of Floyd's position on the YWAMization of Dilaram as nothing but a devious, underhanded attempt to undermine Floyd's leadership. Before he left, Loren melodramatically made it a point to pronounce woe upon those "who would dare to touch the Lord's anointed."

Now I don't know a lot about pronouncing "woes" on others, but I can tell you that the particular woe Loren had in mind for me hit me like a hammer. As I was preparing to return from my trip consulting with other communities, Floyd called me and said it would probably be better if I met him at the airport rather than coming back to my community. When I arrived at the airport, I was met by Floyd and some members of the International Council of YWAM, who had flown in from the four corners of the compass to help Floyd deal with me.

These members of the International Council of YWAM proceeded to take me apart. They said I was a rebel and, as an unrepentant rebel, I would be summarily excommunicated. I said that they misunderstood me: though I opposed the YWAM takeover of Dilaram that Floyd and Loren had proposed, I had never intended to oppose Floyd himself. "Look," I said, "to prove to you that I have absolutely no interest at all in expanding my power base in Dilaram, especially at my friend Floyd's expense, I would be more than willing to take a vow of silence for the next six months, during which time I will take on the job of cleaning the toilets in any Dilaram Community you want to choose—on the condition that at the end of the six months, you bring me before an assembly of Dilaram communities, where you can state your view, I can state mine, and we can allow the assembly to settle this matter once and for all."

They sat there for a while, saying nothing. Then they said something I will never forget. They said that it didn't matter what I said, there would be no deal, because the Lord had shown them that I was a rebel, and the only thing that the Lord would have them do with a rebel like me was to excommunicate me. So they did—right there, right then, in the restaurant at the airport.

From that moment on, I was no longer allowed to be part of the community that, up until then, had been my whole life. I was literally put out of my home—and not permitted to return, not even to pick up my luggage, lest anyone talk to me. Everyone was forbidden to talk with me or offer me any help at all, and those who did so risked the same treatment—so very few did. In the ensuing days I tried to talk with people, but when people who had been my friends saw me coming down the street, they would turn their back on me and walk away.

I was devastated that people I respected wouldn't even give me the time of day, but would precipitously pitch me and my family out of our home, dump us out in the street and then ban everybody—on pain of ex-communication—from helping us, all in "the name of the Lord."

I desperately tried to make some sense of the tragic sequence of events that had turned my greatest dream into my worst nightmare and had reduced me to complete and utter despair.

As I reflected on what I could of done to make them so mad at me, I thought about the part that I had played in the catastrophe myself. At the time I couldn't recollect anything that I'd done wrong. I could only remember the things that I'd done right. I'd stood by my commitment to my community and consequently taken a strong stand against a corporate takeover that threatened to destroy that community. I'd listened to a lot of little people who were being hurt in the process, and I'd spoken up on their behalf to the big people, who were trampling their feelings underfoot. I'd resisted the inducements that were secretly offered to me in a bid to buy me off, and I'd fought a gallant fight in a losing battle for the sake of the liberty and the equality in which I believed.

In hindsight, some of my actions were rather less than heroic. No doubt my words and my deeds were well intentioned, but in the heat of the debate, when my blood was up, many of the things that I said and did must have been insensitive and unnecessarily hurtful. So, although it was never my intention to cause Floyd any grief, to be fair to Loren, I must confess that by coming to blows with Floyd over the future of Dilaram in the way I did, it made it easy for someone like Loren, who didn't really know me, to think that I was simply a rebellious.

But in hindsight I also needed to answer the question of why YWAM acted the way they did. At one level, that question can be answered in personal terms. Loren wanted Floyd as his successor and, as a man of faith, he was prepared to move heaven and earth to get what he wanted. Floyd was more than willing to go along with what Loren wanted because, by becoming the Director of YWAM, he could become one of the most significant mission leaders in modern times.

At another level, that question can be answered in organizational terms. YWAM needed more energetic leadership, and Floyd undoubtedly fit the bill: he was as fine a capable young charismatic leader as you could find. Maybe YWAM wanted Dilaram, or maybe YWAM just wanted Floyd. I don't know, but if Dilaram was what it took to get Floyd, YWAM seemed determined to take it over, come hell or high water. So when I stood like King Canute, trying to stop the YWAM tide from taking over Dilaram, I was doomed from the start. YWAM didn't really have anything against me as a person. YWAM as an organization simply swept me out of their way in pursuit of their corporate plans.

But at another level, this question can be answered in theological terms. In fact, YWAM themselves chose to justify their actions in these terms. When people questioned YWAM about why they did what they did, the answer they gave was always, "It was the Lord." It was "the Lord" who told them to excommunicate me as an unrepentant rebel. It was "the Lord" who told them I ought to be put out of my home and never permitted to return, not even to pick up my luggage, because nobody should be able to relate to me at all. It was "the Lord" who told them that anybody who helped a rebel like me should be treated as a rebel themselves and be summarily excommunicated. Thus the greatest injustice that I had ever experienced in my entire life to that point was justified—signed, sealed and delivered—in "the name of the Lord."

To my great regret, everything that I said would happen if YWAM took over Dilaram played out as I predicted. Within five years, Dilaram was totally co-opted and controlled by YWAM, and its charism as a community completely disappeared.

It took me a long time to recover from my excommunication from Dilaram by YWAM. For months I had a physical pain in my chest that expressed the personal heartbreak I felt after being so rejected and disregarded. Moreover, whenever I bumped into somebody from YWAM—even if they had absolutely nothing to do with the ban—I relived the trauma and would begin to tremble. In my mind, again and again, I heard the words of banishment from the leaders, and over and over again, I watched many friends turn their backs on me and walk away. During this time, I seriously considered suicide.

For some time, Ange and I withdrew, and it was by taking refuge in the love of God that I gradually began to heal. It was very difficult to begin with because "God" and "God language" had been used to denounce me and destroy my life. That being so, it was very hard to pray or to read the Scripture, but I still trusted that the love of God was big enough and good enough to bring me through.

As Ange and I withdrew, we also tried to commit ourselves to a constructive course of action. Like Gandhi, we tried to be proactive and to avoid being reactive. We wholeheartedly committed ourselves to continue to follow through with the things we believed in, trusting that somehow in the process we would be healed. Over a period of five years, we experienced a profound level of healing. The pain in my chest eased, and I stopped shaking every time I met someone from YWAM.

We also actively sought reconciliation with Floyd, meeting him in Europe, Asia and Australia. As a result of our meetings, YWAM eventually decided to drop the charges against me, withdraw my excommunication and extend an invitation for me to "join YWAM" because they "needed people who would challenge them." I told them I appreciated the offer, would be happy to help them as I could, but I had never wanted to join YWAM and was extremely apprehensive about "joining" them and trying to "challenge" them as a member of YWAM myself.

Over the next twenty-five years, I did end up working to help reform YWAM with my friend Jeff Fountain, the European Director of YWAM and a member of the International Council of YWAM, who shared my concerns. I advocated for changing YWAM by raising issues about the organization from the outside, while Jeff advocated for changing YWAM from the inside. Unfortunately, neither of us saw the major changes for which we hoped.

Because I believed that it was important to forgive, but not forget, I sought to wrest as many lessons as I could from my unfortunate and painful experiences with YWAM.

The first lesson I learned was that I had, up until then, lived a life of faith based on success, and I needed to learn to live a life of faith grounded in failure—a life of faith that was truly disillusioned, meaning without any illusions about myself and my capacity to make the dream of community a reality by myself.

The second lesson I learned was that I needed to enter into solidarity with others who, like me, had tried their very best and yet failed to make their dream a reality. I needed to learn to enter into a deep, compassionate comradeship with all who had fought for love and justice on multiple fronts simultaneously, had lost many battles, but had never lost hope in the eventual triumph of good over evil.

The third lesson I learned was that if we were ever going to nurture the culture of a community committed to love and justice effectively, we needed to learn to be "in the system," but not "of the system" by intentionally creating radically empowering, participatory, reciprocal structures while deliberately subverting traditionally dominant and dominating, disempowering, hierarchical structures.

By choosing to be "in the system," but refusing to be "of the system," I have been scolded, censured and sacked, blacklisted, banned and excommunicated, dressed down, beaten up and tossed out of at least a dozen so-called

Christian mission and ministry organizations since YWAM. Interestingly enough, after those organizations have had time to reflect on the issues that I raised, most of them, like YWAM, have invited me back.

My biggest challenge has been to do my inner work by dealing with negativity so that when I am invited back, I can respond positively. It is a great joy to find within me a readiness to aid the very people who have tried to destroy me.

Interestingly enough, almost thirty years after I was excommunicated by YWAM, I took the opportunity to visit the *International YWAMer* office in Colorado, U.S. My friend Paul Filidis, the director of YWAM International Communications, and Bryan Bishop, the editor of the *International YWAMer,* kindly invited me to reflect on what I had learned from my painful experiences with YWAM about leadership, particularly about "hearing" and "speaking" the "word of the Lord." They generously published the interview for YWAMers around the world to read.[126] The following paragraphs are excerpted (and slightly edited) from that interview, "Leaving Room for Doubt."

> Bryan: It seems to me that one of the difficulties with leadership is when there's disagreement. If as a leader you feel that you have heard from God and then others don't agree with you, how do you deal with that?
>
> Dave: I believe too that we can "hear from God," but I believe none of us can be sure that we hear correctly. I love the example of the gathering in Acts, where after days of meeting in Jerusalem, the apostles say, "It seemed good to us and the Holy Spirit not to burden you" (Acts 15:28). It "seemed good to us." Now, that humility to me makes all the difference. This is what we think God is saying, but we're not sure. If we have the humility to say, "I think I'm right, but I'm not quite sure," then there's still a place for listening to the voice of God, but there's also a discussion about whether this is what God is really saying. And you involve the very people that you are in partnership with in that process.
>
> Paul: It needs that preamble, "it seems to me, I think that. . ."
>
> Dave: I can remember when those guys [some members of the International Council of YWAM] flew into Amsterdam to prophesy against me. They were all so sure. I tried to say, "I don't think that's so." They said, "You're arrogant.

126. Andrews, "Leaving Room For Doubt," 4–7.

You keep on using the word 'I,' when we've got 'the word of the Lord.'" I was trying to fight for a space for dialogue, for some discussion. After all, Frederick Buechner says, "Where there is no room for doubt, there is no room for me."

Paul: But we believe in the culture that YWAM is in, if God is personal, if God is close, if I can know God, it almost demands that kind of certainty.

Dave: Just because God is absolute doesn't mean we know the absolute absolutely. We can only know the absolute relatively. We come to God from our limited backgrounds, experiences, prejudices, and therefore even when we do "hear the voice of God," chances are we warp it, we twist it to our own interests. And that's in fact why I believe it's not enough to have hierarchical accountability. We need mutual accountability. The problem with top-down unilateral accountability is everybody is accountable, except for the person at the top. Whereas side-by-side reciprocal accountability means everybody is accountable to each other.[127] We need to bring the question about what we say when we say, "it seems to us thus," into a space for dialogue, so the very person who is saying, "it seems to us thus," is actually accountable to others.

Bryan: Do you think leaders have spiritual authority over the people that follow them?

Dave: I believe that at any one time, a person can be open to the Spirit, taking an initiative that should inspire people to respond to what God is saying, but in order to be healthy, that initiative-taking needs to happen with different people at different times. I think it is unhealthy for any person to get stuck in the "leadership role," and it's unhealthy for people to get stuck in their relating to a person in terms of that "leadership role." Because then the leader can develop the illusion that he or she is the (only) one through whom the voice of God speaks when, in fact, God can speak to all of us.

Bryan: So a person could have a certain function of management, but not see himself or herself as always the leader.

127. This portion has been edited.

Dave: That's right. And you always need to be open to "the least" being the ones through whom God speaks. That's a biblical principle.

Paul: Why do people submit themselves to abusive leadership? Why do people almost seek it out, or don't confront it when they are under it?

Dave: Well, I think generally, we want to love and be loved. I think we want to get along with people and we want them to think well of us. And I think that's true of leaders as well as anybody else. We want [their] acceptance, we want [their] respect—and in a society where people treat each other justly, that would not be damaging or destructive, but the reality is we live in a world where people often misuse their power, and our desire to please [leaders] is now turned against us and can destroy us.

Paul: And conversely, why are there bad leaders who end up manipulating their followers?

Dave: Why am I tempted to manipulate people and exploit people? Because of my ambition. I want recognition. And in my culture, recognition comes from success. If I can manipulate people or exploit people in order to achieve and accomplish goals that reflect well on me, I'm tempted to go down that route. The only way that I'm free to give up those ambitions is to find a sense of my value apart from my accomplishments. It's only in experiencing existentially the love of Christ for me regardless of my performance that I can then be free not to manipulate and exploit people to perform for my benefit.

Paul: Now, the influential leader, the charismatic leader, the leader who has the gift of persuasion, how can he or she safeguard that from going wrong?

Dave: I believe we need to create structures in which we need to make decisions by consensus or consent. The difference between consensus and consent: consensus is where we all come to agreement, whereas consent is where people express disagreement but give us permission to move ahead. There may be a timeframe that needs to be met. Rather than just ride roughshod over people, we say, "Look, I know you don't agree with this. Most of us do agree. Would you give us permission to go ahead under these circumstances?" Now, what that does, it locates any decision about any activity that may be promoted by a charismatic figure, it locates that within dialogue and discussion, where the leader needs to seek the permission of other people. Even then, the problem is that the leader may be more persuasive than others and might silence others, so I believe that charismatic leaders should speak less than the average person in their communities, not more, so that they redress the imbalance of power that they know they create.

Bryan: Is there anything you'd like to say in general to YWAM?

Dave: All I can say is, I know from my own personal struggles that I think all of us need to be more humble and more modest and more gentle with ourselves and with others, and all of us need to be aware that when we most think we are right that we could be wrong. And all of us need to cherish not only those who agree with us, but also cherish those who disagree with us. We should realize that we will never know the fullness of who God is, and what God wants us to do, without working things out together, particularly with the people who oppose us. I think we're not only called to love our enemies for their benefit. We're called to love them for our own.

The Prophetic Practitioner

Richard Rohr says "True prophets are not part of the authority structure of their society or their religious institution. Unlike priests . . . prophets are never appointed, ordained, or anointed by the religious establishment." He says "This leads inevitably to tension and even some measure of conflict between the prophet and the establishment."[128]

The role of the prophetic practitioner is like a performer who "energizes" people to get "back on track"—not just "on script," but "in touch" with the "Spirit behind the script"—by creatively "visualizing" their inspired passion and compassion through symbols, dramas and demonstrations that embody the possibilities of a new reality.[129] Prophetic practitioners seek to demonstrate "that God *can*, and *is*, breaking in and radically altering the present state of reality; [to] provide a tangible, visual illustration of [the Spirit's] presence and activity 'among us' . . . [so people can see] that another

---

128.. Rohr "Disciples Prophets and Mystics," adapted from Rohr, *Way of the Prophet*.

129. All quotes in this paragraph are from Catchim, *The Prophetic Ministry*, Part 2.

world is possible."[130] Prophetic practitioners are painfully aware of the "the gap" that exists between God's will and ours, but we actively seek to "stand in the gap" and demonstrate—as best we can—what God's values might look like if they were lived out in our context.

Practicing Radical Hospitality

I've tried to practice "the Spirit behind the script" in terms of *radical hospitality.*

My friend Keith Hebden, a minister, writer and activist, notes that "authentic prophecy is rarely experienced outside a prophetic community experiencing being in the forgotten places of the empire."[131] So it's not surprising that, as Catchim says, "some prophets can have a bohemian, socially deviant look about them. They opt out of the mainstream and subvert the dominant culture through visible protests, whether it be fashion, eccentric lifestyles, or just plain eccentric behaviour. Refusal to 'buy in' to the dominant culture helps them stay connected to an alternative outlook on life."[132]

Early in 1973, about a year after we were married, Ange and I set out for Kabul, Afghanistan to join Floyd and Sally McClung, who had set up an intentional Christian community there to provide hospitality and short-term support for world travelers who got into trouble on the "hippy trail." After selling most of our belongings, we bundled ourselves into an old Ford Transit van, along with Peter Grushka and a few friends, and drove overland from Germany to Afghanistan, just as thousands of other travelers had done before us.

Kabul was known as "the crossroads of Asia," and as Floyd writes in his memoir *Living on the Devil's Doorstep: From Kabul to Amsterdam,* "The city had heaps of rundown hotels full of hippies. Drugs were plentiful—pharmacists sold morphine shots over the counter for a pennies. The best hashish in the East could be had for less than twenty-five *afghanis,* the price of a bar of chocolate in the West."[133] As Floyd describes it,

> Some travelers were thrown into jail and stayed there for months, even years. The award-winning movie, Midnight Express, about the experiences in a Turkish jail of Billy Bums, an American

130. Catchim, *The Prophetic Ministry,* part 2
131. Hebden, *Seeking Justice.*
132. http://5qcentral.com/prophetic-catchim/.
133. McClung, *Living on the Devil's Doorstep,* Kindle location 419.

youngster arrested for trying to smuggle drugs, paints a grimly realistic picture of what was in store for those who were caught, . . . [such as] having to share a dirty cell with up to ten other people—murderers and rapists among them.[134]

When Floyd first visited Kabul, he felt like he'd found the "lost children of my generation: the idealists who had found only painful, punishing reality."[135] So he talked to Dr. Christy Wilson, the Pastor of Kabul Community Christian Church, about what he could do. "'Stay here in Kabul,' he urged. 'Set up a house that will provide help for them, and my congregation will support you.'"[136]

To begin, Floyd and Sally took up digs in the Olfat Hotel, which "was located just off Chicken Street, a long narrow thoroughfare that was the main route of the hippy district. All along Chicken Street were small shops that sold clothes, incense, drugs, food, and—as you may guess—lots of chickens."[137] As Floyd describes the Olfat, it "was more of a shabby warehouse than a hotel. The 'bedrooms' consisted simply of a small, bare chamber occupied by just a rough *charpai*, a wooden frame held together by rope, with a blanket thrown on top to act as a mattress."[138]

Floyd and Sally's approach was to operate a *chai* house in the evenings, giving them a chance to come alongside the young travelers. It soon became "abundantly clear," from talking to people who came for chai and conversation, that the travelers were in urgent need of a medical clinic. So when a qualified doctor turned up, they opened up a clinic in an empty storeroom at the Olfat.[139] "Many travelers came in basically because they were sick enough to seek help anywhere, and once they got to us, they stayed."[140]

Because of the large number of travelers who needed a place to stay to recover, Floyd and Sally wanted to find "a house with more room, preferably well out of the downtown hippy district. It needed to be big, inexpensive, and close to the bus route into town."[141] They found a house "about four miles from the Olfat area of Kabul and only two blocks from a bus stop. There were twenty-three rooms in the building, and it had a high stonewall

134. McClung, *Living on the Devil's Doorstep*, location 356, 366.

135. McClung, *Living on the Devil's Doorstep*, location 186.

136. McClung, *Living on the Devil's Doorstep*, location 438.

137. McClung, *Living on the Devil's Doorstep*, location 475.

138. McClung, *Living on the Devil's Doorstep*, location 463

139. McClung, *Living on the Devil's Doorstep*, location 701.

140. McClung, *Living on the Devil's Doorstep*, location 714.

141. McClung, *Living on the Devil's Doorstep*, location 920.

around the yard plus a private well." [142] They called the house "Dilaram House," because *dil-aram* means "a peaceful heart" in the Farsi language.[143]

By the time Ange and I arrived in Kabul, Dilaram House had developed a distinctive culture of radical hospitality that Ange and I happily embraced ourselves. As we worked with the so-called "hippies," "junkies" and "freaks"[144] who found their way to Dilaram, we developed a decidedly "bohemian" and "deviant look" and an "alternative outlook," as Catchim describes those who take on the role of a prophetic practitioner in society.[145] Between twenty and forty of us lived together in Dilaram House, and most of us dressed in the same hippy attire as the people we had come to help: the men had long hair and beards and wore long cotton *kurta* shirts and loose cotton *pyjama* pants, and the women had long hair and beads and wore bright and colorful handmade tribal *kuchi* clothes. Though we looked like any other hippy community, we were a uniquely friendly and healthy drug-free hippy community, making us an ideal community for the troubled travelers.

Everyone who lived in Dilaram had responsibility for running the house and making decisions about the house, including house rules. All drugs were proscribed, and all drug addicts were encouraged to participate in the rehabilitation program that Dilaram offered. Everyone was expected to participate in the daily rhythms in the house, which wasn't run on a tight schedule, but had a loose routine that involved domestic chores, study sessions and community meals, around which we had long conversations with the guest travelers about their searchings and longings. Many of those conversations inevitably turned toward spirituality, but we did our best not to be "religious propagandists," whom the travelers abhorred.[146]

Shortly after Ange and I arrived, we discovered that there was a lot more to extending radical hospitality than we had anticipated. We were asked to care for a young man I'll call "Carlo," an Italian drug addict with advanced tuberculosis, who was at death's door. Carlo's hair was matted, filthy and full of fleas. Ange was asked to wash his hair and brush out the fleas. Though she was happy to help, as she brushed the fleas out of Carlo's hair, they all migrated to her hair. Carlo was an addict, and as drugs were

---

142. McClung, *Living on the Devil's Doorstep*, location 923.

143. McClung, *Living on the Devil's Doorstep*, location 932.

144.. Some of these terms are now considered pejorative, but at that time we all used these terms happily.

145. Catchim, *The Prophetic Ministry*, Part 2.

146. McClung, *Living on the Devil's Doorstep*, location 833.

forbidden in the house, he normally would have been expected to stop taking drugs—even if it meant going "cold turkey," an abrupt withdrawal that usually involved an unpleasant or sometimes violent reaction. But Carlo was too sick to go "cold turkey," and so I was asked to go to Chicken Street to buy some morphine for him so he could continue to get a fix until he was well enough to go "cold turkey." You can imagine how strange I felt, coming to a drug-free community, to be asked to go and buy drugs for a guest. But under the circumstances, it made perfect sense to me.

Ange loved the culture of radical hospitality in Dilaram, for as she says, "The thing I have held most dear through the years is a vision of hospitality as a way of life." She believes it is the legacy of Jesus, which she has always tried to nurture in herself and others. But Ange will also tell you that in Dilaram, her understanding of hospitality was given a whole new dimension. A young German woman I'll call "Camilla" was brought to the house after she ate magic mushrooms and lost her mind, and Ange was asked to care for her. This was extremely challenging, since Camilla had to be locked in a room, and from outside the bolted door, you could hear her throwing herself from one side of the room to the other, crashing against the walls and screaming at the top of her voice. No one had any idea what to do, but Ange rose to the challenge.

She went to the kitchen, made a cup of tea, put a teapot, two cups and two saucers on a tray with a plate of biscuits, and asked us to unbolt the door. She stepped into the insanity as naturally and normally as she could and then sat there calmly and quietly pouring the tea while Camilla continued to throw herself from one side of the room to other, crashing and screaming. After some time Camilla tired herself out from her exertions, and Ange asked her to sit with her and have a cup of tea. Eventually, after what seemed to be an excruciatingly long time to those of us who were listening anxiously but safely on the other side of bolted door, Camilla sat down with Ange and had a cup of tea. From that moment, Ange and Camilla became close friends. As Camilla slowly came to her senses, Ange helped her sort out the underlying problems in her life. Ange and Camilla both had a great love of beauty, and Ange was very pleased when Camilla eventually retuned to Germany and set up a flower shop.

Through Dilaram, we got to know another Australian couple named Pete and Kate Fitzgerald. Pete and Kate had been traveling overland when Pete became seriously ill. When they got to Kabul, Kate left Pete in a desperate plight, lying on a *charpai* in a cheap hotel, while she went to look for help. Kate met someone from Dilaram, who invited the couple to stay in the house until Pete could be nursed back to health. While staying at Dilaram, Kate became a Christian, but Pete remained skeptical, but then Pete met Dr.

Herb Friesen, who offered his services to people in the house for free. Pete was so impressed with Herb's Christlike compassion that Pete eventually decided to become a Christian.

In July 1973, about six months after we arrived in Kabul, there was a revolution in Afghanistan. I remember the planes flying overhead, the tanks rumbling in the streets and hiding out in a friend's house during the coup, eating tins of smoked oysters and listening to the reports of the events on the BBC. The police suggested that some of us in Dilaram should leave the country, and the community decided that Steve Aram, Kathy Hambach, Carol Wald, Ange and I should go to India to establish another Dilaram in New Delhi.

The journey from Kabul via the Khyber Pass through the lawless North West Frontier Province to Peshawar is one of the most legendary journeys in the world. But the most significant part of the trip for me was when we arrived in Peshawar. As I was stepping off the bus, a man grabbed me by the balls and said, "Welcome to Pakistan." I was, as you can imagine, surprised and nonplussed. While I was adjusting to this unexpected greeting and distracted by the unusual sensation of my testicles being clutched by a stranger, the stranger's accomplice ran off with my briefcase, which had all our currency in it.

Years later, while I was in speaking at a conference in Pakistan, I told the audience the story, and I thanked the people of Pakistan for helping me involuntarily redistribute the rest of the money that was leftover from selling our house. Everyone laughed, but at the time, it was no laughing matter. Ange and I had to travel on through Lahore to Delhi and arrive in India with no money. Thankfully, we weren't traveling on our own, as Steve, Kathy and Carol helped us.

When we arrived in Delhi, we found the home of Colin and Gladys Blair, whose name and address we had been given in Kabul. Colin and Gladys were kind enough to let us stay at their place till we found a place of our own. Through Colin and Gladys, we met Ray and Gwen Windsor, who adopted us into their wonderful extended family, supporting us as we settled into the city and providing help whenever we needed it. Ray and Gwen became our mentors in Delhi, just as Charles and Rita had been our mentors in Brisbane. Ray helped us find our first house, which would become the initial base for Dilaram in New Delhi: 27a Friends Colony.

27a Friends Colony was a huge pink house with six bedrooms, an office and a garage with a lovely garden, with two majestic gum trees at the driveway entrance, which was particularly special for Ange and I, as it was a reminder of Australia. How we managed to get a lease when we had next to no money between us was a miracle, but it wasn't long before we moved in and established home. At first, we had no furniture, and so we sat on mats on the floor during the day and slept on cheap, thin cotton mattresses at night, which were so thin that when you turned over, your hips felt the cold hard concrete floor. We cooked our meals on a small portable gas stove and, because we had only a few pots and pans, we ate our food off the saucepan lids with our hands. In spite of our meager resources, we reached out to the travelers we met in the streets, prisons, and hospitals, inviting them to stay with us.

One day a lady from USAID came to our house and said she had heard how we had set up a home for young travelers in trouble and didn't have any furniture. She told us that USAID had stopped renting a number of residences, and if we came to their warehouse, we could take as many household goods as we needed—for free. They gave us kitchen equipment, a fridge, a stove, tables, chairs, cupboards and beds, which was answer to prayer!

Now that we had more resources, we were able to invite a lot more people to come and stay with us. In fact, at one time, we had up to fifty people staying at Dilaram. Ange volunteered to contact the travelers living in Paharganj, a crowded enclave in the centre of town near the New Delhi railway station, which was full of freak hotels, rooftop restaurants and tiny shops selling hippie clothes, incense sticks and cheap hash. Ange got a room in a freak hotel, where a bunch of hard-core junkies were staying, so she could get close to them, make friends with them and invite them home. This was remarkable, because Ange, who was known as a nervous person, was taking a big risk in going to live among heavy-duty addicts in the mean streets of the city.

Among many others, Ange met a young Austrian junkie named Gerhard, who had left Austria to come to India because he wanted to find God and the meaning of life. On the way, he experimented with drugs and became addicted to morphine. By the time Ange met him, Gerhard was sick, scrawny and desperate to kick the habit. He happily agreed to accompany Ange to our house, where he could go through rehab. Over the next few days, Gerhard went cold turkey. The expression "cold turkey" refers to the goosebumps that some junkies get as they go through withdrawal, along with terribly unpleasant (but not life-threatening) stomach muscle spasms and agony in the bowels. A team of people led by Ange took two-hour turns sitting with Gerhard and praying for him. After he got over his withdrawal, Gerhard began to recover, regain his strength and think about what he was going to do with his life. Gerhard had come to the house with concrete questions about Jesus, and he felt he had been able to get substantive answers during his stay, so he decided that he wanted to follow the way of Jesus just as we did. He said he knew that if he followed Jesus, he would have to do a fearless inventory of the wrongs he had done and seek to make them right.

So Gerhard confessed to the Austrian authorities that he had forged his passport, and he told the Indian authorities that he had overstayed his visa. To our surprise—and to Gerhard's long-term advantage—rather than punishing him straightaway, the Indian authorities allowed Gerhard to stay in the community for five months, which gave him a chance to consolidate his newfound way of life before he had to go to the infamous maximum security Tihar Jail near Janakpuri. Once Gerhard returned to Austria, he had to face charges for an earlier drug offense, and so he had to do more prison time. When Gerhard finally got out of prison, he was expected to do military service, but because he was now a follower of the nonviolent Jesus, he refused, but offered to do community service instead. He was assigned to sweep streets of Graz for eight months. During this time, he met and married Anita, who was from Sweden and worked for a Baptist Church. After his community service was over, Gerhard decided to study to become a minister, and so he and Anita moved to Sweden. After completing his studies, Gerhard, Anita and their daughter returned to Austria, where they continue to live and work for the church, and Gerhard works with at-risk young people as a life coach.

While Gerhard was living in Dilaram, a young English boy named Adrian Reith came to join us for his gap year. Adrian had an interest in media and asked if he could try to make a slide show about the house and the people who had come to live there and had found solace for their souls. Adrian made "Dilaram Freaks," a beautiful, lovingly crafted, still-shot documentary, which is the only artistic photographic account of those days. Though much of it is cringe-worthy now, it features a lot of the people who lived with us and celebrates the life we lived together.[147]

We also got to know five legendary Germans who did rehabilitation in Dilaram at different times: Uli Köhler, Nick Tschenk, Dieter Bofinger, Wolfgang Altvater and Wolfgang Striebinger. Uli Köhler went on to facilitate harm-minimization projects in South and Southeast Asia, particularly in his much-loved Afghanistan. These projects were funded by the European Union. Nick Tschenk went on to serve as a member of the state parliament of Baden-Württemberg from Stuttgart for the Green Party and then served as an assistant to the secretary of traffic and transportation, managing the changeover to sustainable energy sources and climate-friendly transport

147. You can check out *Dilaram Freaks* Parts 1 and 2 online.

alternatives in Baden-Württemberg. Dieter Bofinger and Wolfgang Altvater both studied at the University of Tübingen and then went on to minister for the rest of their lives as Lutheran pastors in Germany. Wolfgang Striebinger went on to labor as a community chaplain with homeless people in the heart of Raval's infamous red-light, multi-cultural district in Barcelona, Catalonia for over twenty years.

Some of the people who came to Dilaram didn't need rehab, but were seeking a free meal, a place of refuge, or the possibility of a new beginning. John Herbert had been on a spiritual search and was looking for a community of faith and came to Dilaram hoping that we could help him explore what it would mean for him to follow Jesus. One of John's fellow travelers was caught with drugs by the police and put into the Tihar Jail. When John arrived at Dilaram, he was surprised to meet a guy we'll call "Sanjay," who had befriended John in Goa on the western coast of India. John had fallen off a cliff while walking from Baga beach to Anjuna beach, and Sanjay had dressed his wounds and given him shelter. When John told Sanjay about his traveling companion who was in prison, Sanjay, who was a resourceful gangster with a serious criminal record, offered to break his friend out of prison if John agreed to join Sanjay's gang, an Indian crime syndicate. The gang was looking for a traveler who would pretend to be a British aristocrat to front their operation of cashing stolen traveler's checks. John said he was more than happy to go along with the deal, since it not only provided a way to get his friend out of prison, but also promised him an exotic and glamorous lifestyle, full of helicopter flights, fast cars and beautiful women, along with an exhilarating dash of danger.

When John joined the gang, Sanjay was assigned as his bodyguard. John enjoyed himself until he realized that he was absolutely useless as a con man. When he tried to quit, Sanjay told John that he was not there to protect him, but to protect the syndicate's investment in him, which meant that if John threatened to quit, Sanjay was expected to execute him. John knew he was in big trouble, and he couldn't go to the police, as he was convinced the police were in the pay of the powerful crime organization. So John and Sanjay told us the story and asked for our help. While they were telling us the story, suspicious characters who were hidden behind tinted windows in classic Ambassador cars were threateningly circling our block. We discussed John's options, and it seemed obvious that he couldn't go to the cops, but also that he couldn't quit and run. What to do?

As was our practice, we all gathered as a group to pray about how to respond—all except Ange, who had run into the bathroom and was hiding behind the locked door. As we prayed, we came to the conclusion that the only option John had was to go back to the gang, tell them he wanted to leave, but that he wouldn't turn witness against them, and he would give them any traveler's checks he had that could be used as evidence against them in order to dispel any fear that he might betray them. To give him a better chance of surviving, Sanjay said he that he would stay with the gang and offer his life as a guarantee that could John be trusted. This was a wonderful offer, but we were still nervous that the gang might kill John, so we decided that one of us needed to go with John and Sanjay as a neutral observer to encourage the gang to think hard before resorting to any impulsive violence. To our surprise, Bill, one of the most quiet, modest, humble and unassuming members of the household, offered to risk his life and accompany John and Sanjay.

When the three finally returned, Bill said that Sanjay had stood up for John, and the gang had decided to let them go. About three weeks later, when John went to the center of Delhi on a Harley-Davidson taxi trike, someone from the gang boarded the Harley, sat down opposite him, and plonked down his suitcase, which he had left behind when he and Sanjay had made their hasty escape. He knew that this was a sign that he was still under observation, but the gang had no ill will towards him. John stayed in Dilaram, working as a gardener, and then eventually moved back to Wales after his father died. After taking over the family property, he sought to use one of the main buildings as a center for prayer and some of the lands to build houses to offer affordable accommodations for low-income families.

Most of our time at Dilaram was not as melodramatic as these stories might suggest. Most of our time, we participated in the daily rhythms, doing domestic chores, participating in study sessions and sharing community meals, around which we had long conversations, discussion and debates about everything from *dal, chawal, chapatti* and *achaar* to *Yeshu, yoga, dvaita,* and *advaita Vedanta.*[148]

Many of our meals together were prepared by George Peters, who moved into the Dilaram House in Friends Colony with his family to be our *khansama.*[149] When we first met George and his wife, Grace, they were living in a *jhuggi*[150] hut made from plastic, cardboard and sheets of iron beside a busy railway line. George worked miracles to provide plentiful beautiful food for up to fifty hungry young people at a time with a limited budget and minimal resources.

---

148. *dal* (split pulses), *chawal* (cooked rice), *chapatti* (flat bread), *achaar* (spicy pickle), *Yeshu* (Jesus Christ), *yoga* (spiritual exercises), *dvaita* (dualist), *advaita* (non-dualist), *Vedanta* (Hindu philosophy)

149. *khansama* (household cook)

150. *jhuggi* (slum dwelling)

As a result of these beautiful, deep and meaningful interactions, we developed special relationships with one another, and some of these led to romance and marriage. When Steve Aram and Kathy Hambach, who had come with us from Kabul, got married, it was a wonderful celebration of the flowering of our life together. They were both mature, modest and esteemed members of the community, and their do-it-yourself wedding represented us at our best. It was held in our garden, and everyone in the community attended, wearing colorful clothes made of recycled curtains.

Shortly after the wedding, I came down with hepatitis, and it was serious enough that I was advised to return to Australia to recuperate. Ange was pregnant at the time, and while we were back in Brisbane, Ange gave birth to our daughter, Evonne. Much to our family's consternation, we returned to Delhi when Evonne was just ten days old. But we were confident that we could happily raise her in India, and we were committed to raising her in Dilaram's culture of inclusive, caring hospitality so that she would learn inclusive, caring hospitality as a way of life. Ange has so often said,

> The thing I have held most dear through the years is a vision of hospitality as a way of life. It is a vision I have nurtured in myself, in my nuclear family and in my extended family. I believe it is the legacy of Jesus, which I want to pass on to my children and to my children's children. As you can imagine many of my rels [relatives] would . . . ask me, "Angie why are you doing this? After all, you are a mother, with your own children, and you should be caring for your own children." "That's exactly the point," I would say. "I believe God wants us to care for our children and to teach them to care for others just like their own relatives.[151]

Anyone who knows Evonne knows that she does.

In 1975, two years after we arrived in India, we moved from 27a Friends Colony in the southeast of New Delhi to F9/4 Vasant Vihar in the southwest, an area that was close to the center of the city, but on the other side of the Ring Road that encircled the city, so that our house would be accessible, but affordable.

As one visitor described the Dilaram house in Vasant Vihar, "It looks like any other house. From the gate one sees a well-tended garden."[152] Previously used as a guesthouse, F9/4 was a two-story house that had multiple bedrooms and bathrooms and was large enough to provide living facilities for twenty-five to thirty people. There were three women's bedrooms on the

151. Andrews and Beazley, *Learnings*, 11–13.

152. Parambi, *Dilaram*, 34–36.

ground flour, along with the library, living / dining room, kitchen and guest bathroom. Upstairs, there were three men's bedrooms. The *barsati*[153] on the terrace was kept open for those who wanted to study or write in privacy. A broad driveway led to two garages, formally servants' quarters. The garages were used for additional men's bedrooms. While our family lived in the servants' quarters.

Even though the location of our community changed, our mission remained the same. We continued to focus on meeting and supporting travelers, and so the overwhelming majority of the people in our community were expatriates. However, from the very beginning, more young people from India became interested and involved in the community.

Over the years, we cared for hundreds of people, and scores of people were radically changed by the faith and love that we shared with them. The embassies politely recorded their appreciation for our work, and people from local Indian church groups became curious about what we were doing and so began to visit and see for themselves whether the rumors of strange happenings amongst these strange people were true. Some of these Indian visitors included Vijay Masih, Nimmi Parambi, Susie Mathai and Raj Bhujbal.

The first, Vijay Masih, did not visit from curiosity, for he was sent by the police to check up on what was happening and was paid 100 rupees a day to spy on us. Though there were many drug users in Dilaram House, he reported that they were not being supplied drugs from within the house, but being helped by people in the house to overcome their addictions. After receiving this report, the police showed no further interest in Dilaram, but Vijay did, returning again and again—though not to report to the police. He wanted to be part of Dilaram himself.

As word about Dilaram House spread, other Indian young people came to check us out, including a group of university students who organized a retreat with us. One of the students who came for the retreat was Nimmi Parambi, a Catholic who was studying psychology at Delhi University and was impressed with the concept of a community that combined spirituality and therapy. She began to visit regularly and brought along her sister, Priya, and her friends. One friend, Susie Mathai, was a Marthomite[154] who was studying social work at the university, and she was also impressed with the concept of a community that combined spirituality and social work. Then Raj Bhujbal, a Nazarene who had studied philosophy at the University of

153. *barsati* is a rain shelter on the roof of a building

154. The Mar Thoma Church, also known as the Malankara Mar Thoma Syrian Church, is an autonomous Oriental Indian church, based in Kerala, India.

Pune in Maharashtra and then studied philosophy at L'Abri in Switzerland, decided to move into Dilaram as an unofficial philosopher in residence to help us critically reflect on our philosophy of spirituality and community.

In 1976, about a year after we moved to F9/4 Vasant Vihar, Nimmi began her dissertation for Delhi University on Dilaram House as a therapeutic community. Another thesis about Dilaram House entitled *Dilaram: A Further to Reality Therapy* by Ian Bainbridge observes that in Dilaram, "therapy is not seen as a transaction occurring during particular sessions with a specialist but as part of the lifestyle of the community."[155] This lifestyle encourages people to: 1) be responsible in making decisions for themselves, 2) be answerable to others who are impacted by the decisions that they make, 3) act according to their conscience or their internalized set of ethical values, 4) acknowledge their contradictions (or the times they have acted contrary to their conscience) to themselves, 5) openly admit their contradictions to significant others, whom they can trust with their vulnerability, 6) make amends to those who are impacted adversely by the decisions they have made when they have acted contrary to their conscience, 7) use the opportunity provided by the community to learn to act with integrity and to help others act with integrity according to their conscience,[156] and 8) constantly sensitize their conscience by critically reflecting on their internalized set of ethical values in light of the "myth" of the radical, nonviolent, inclusive love of Jesus.[157]

Nimmi was particularly impressed with the case of a young Indian man, whom I'll call "Krishna Sharma," who was referred to Dilaram House for rehabilitation. As a *brahmin*, Krishna was in the highest Hindu caste, but he had failed medical college, dropped out on dope and was eking out an existence in the tombs at Haus Khas. When Krishna arrived at Dilaram, he was angry and full of threats of violence, but gradually he became more tranquil and managed to cope with his feelings of stress without using drugs. He even became willing to work with his hands. After a while, he earned a reputation for responsibility and reliability and got a job in the Leprosy Mission, where he was trained as a paramedical worker, and proved to be a source of tremendous compassion to the lepers in the district of Barabanki. Through his songs, he shared the joy that he had experienced through his changed life. The change he sang about not only affected Krishna and his relationship with the lepers of Barabanki, but also Nimmi and her friend Susie Mathai. The changes in Krishna's life proved that a community such as Dilaram was

---

155. Quoted in Parambi, *Dilaram*, 60.

156. Parambi, *Dilaram*, 62.

157. Parambi, *Dilaram*, 37.

relevant to Indian young people, and Nimmi concluded that "the solution to the problems of the average Indian student was in dealing psychotherapeutically with each individual in the context of a unified therapeutic culture," one similar to the "integrated therapeutic culture of Dilaram."[158]

After Nimmi completed her dissertation, she asked Ange and I to leave Dilaram and help her and Susie set up an intentional community in Delhi that would be specifically dedicated to Indian young people. When Ange and I were kicked out of Dilaram by YWAM, we responded to her suggestion and agreed to help them set up an intentional community with and for Indian young people, which I'll talk more about in the next section.

Practicing Revolutionary Solidarity

I tried to practice "the Spirit behind the script" in terms of *revolutionary solidarity.*

C.B. Samuel, who also visited Dilaram in Delhi in the mid-1970s, later completed a course of study at Union Biblical Seminary in Yavatmal. In 1978, he completed his dissertation, which expanded Nimmi's concept of community as an "integrated therapeutic culture" to include the concept of community as "a counterculture—an alternative culture in conflict with a surrounding culture based upon injustice."[159] Both Nimmi's and C.B.'s vision of community had a spiritual center, but Nimmi emphasized the potential *therapeutic* effect of radical hospitality as it is practiced by a *community on individuals,* whereas C.B. emphasized the potential *political* effect of revolutionary solidarity as it is practiced by *communes on the institutions of society.*

C.B. had been talking to us about communes for years and he published his manifesto on communes in his dissertation:

> Communes are made up of people who have understood there is much more to life than just making money and pursuing status.... Communes are made up of people who have realized the vitality of living and are aware of their own and others' value and are not willing to sacrifice human dignity and the right to live on the altar of dehumanizing structures. Communes are made up of people who are willing to dirty their hands for the sake of lifting humanity.... Communes are made up of people who see new meaning in one another and respect one another, irrespective of caste, sex, colour or creed! Communes are people who

158. Parambi, *Dilaram,* 127.

159. Samuel, *An Evaluation of the Concept of Communes and its Scope for Application in Youth Ministry in Urban India*

demonstrate to the world the kingdom of God through their work and words.[160]

In 1978, at the same time as C.B. was completing his dissertation, we accepted C.B.'s challenge and decided to try to make such a commune a reality in the context of urban India by joining Nimmi and Susie and starting *Aashiana*, which literally means "nest."[161] During those early months of 1978, Ange and I lived at 9B Mathura Road in Nizamuddin, a suburb in the south-east of New Delhi, and. We got together regularly with Nimmi and Susie regularly. We tried to maintaining daily contact with each other when possible. When it was not possible for us to visit one another, we would talk on the telephone each other. We were determined to develop our common life and we believed that community was based on communication and communion, and the object of community, which Nimmi said was the "'promise of the open heart [that] only hearts kept open to one another could keep.'"

Another Australian, Neil Hockey, joined Ange and I in 9B Mathura Road, Nizamuddin. Neill Hockey, an Australian, came from a Brethren background, and, in the tradition of his forbears, felt that community was a viable way to live out his faith in fellowship with others. He had a particular concern for education as both a teacher and student. Before long, we invited a very disturbed young Tamilian,[162] whom I'll call "Dravid Thomas," to stay with us. Dravid came from a very broken background and needed the support of a compassionate group of people. Whereas Neil represented our energy, Dravid represented our fragility, and both defined our community from beginning to end.

In spite of our desire to establish a community that was similar to Dilaram, we were all very aware of the danger of doing just that, because we did not want to import another foreign product or to provide an indigenous

160. Samuel, *An Evaluation of the Concept of Communes and its Scope for Application in Youth Ministry in Urban India*, 56–57.

161. This narrative is taken from the dissertation I submitted in 1985 to the faculty of social work at the University of Queensland, which was entitled "Aashiana: A Study of an Intentional Religious Community Located in New Delhi, India." The narrative was reconstructed on the basis of a chronology of events kept by Neil Hockey and Susy Masih. Without them remembering, much would have been forgotten, but their recollections provoked the memory of the group. Suzi Deane then wrote her account, and Lawrie Deane wrote his account. Based on these written contributions and the verbal reflections that were forthcoming through innumerable conversations, an outline was written, circulated for comments, and then edited. This was the result.

162. Tamils are people who inhabit parts of southern India and Sri Lanka who speak a Dravidian language.

import substitute that was exactly the same as the foreign product with a different brand name. The foreigners in our group did not want to control the processes of the community, and the Indians in our group did not want the community to be controlled by foreigners. We wanted to develop a community that would be authentically Indian, but we weren't sure how to draw from the experience of the foreigners while offsetting our influence. Together, we agreed on a number of things.

First, we foreigners agreed to devote time to an intensive study of the language and culture. We studied Hindustani rather than Hindi because it was the language of the common people. Furthermore, we studied the art, religion, economics and politics of the society. We were most affected by the culture as it had been reinterpreted during the renaissance earlier in the twentieth century, particularly the poetry of Rabindranath Tagore, the compassion of Mother Teresa and the politics of Mahatma Gandhi and his disciples.

Second, we all resolved to discover the meaning of our faith in Christ within the Indian context from a traditional Indian leader. We felt this was important for all of us, since we had all been brought up in an educational system that had been largely influenced by the West (even those of us who had not been brought up in the West). Thus we all felt the need to become more in touch with our Eastern context. We stayed for three weeks in Bharuch, a small town in western India Gujarat, and learned from Subodh Sahu, who initiated us all into the Indian art of meditation, an inductive study of the Scriptures and dialogue with neighbors of other religions. Later, we invited Archarya Dayaprakash from *Sat Tal Ashram* to hold a *satsang*[163] in our house. He introduced us to the radiance of our faith in Christ in the light of other religions. Consequently, we came to understand our faith with contributions from both Western knowledge and Eastern wisdom, thereby forming a uniquely Indian synthesis.

Third, we agreed that we would, within the framework of India and infused by a faith that was Indian, make our decisions about how to develop the community through consensus. There has been some debate about whether or not consensus is an Indian practice. Indian people were described by Louis Dumont in 1972 as "*Homo Hierarchicus*"[164], suggesting that the very concept of equality is foreign in India. Yet Vinoba Bhave, a National Teacher and spiritual successor to Mahatma Gandhi, maintained

163. *Satsang* is a Sanskrit word that means "gathering together for the truth"

164. Dumont, *Homo Hierarchicus.*

that the concept of equality was no more foreign than the *vedas*,[165] and the equality of all is vouchsafed in the *vedic* notion of the Oneness. Moreover, Jayaprakash Narayan, a National Leader and socialist protégé of Mahatma Gandhi, advocated the practice of *lok niti* (direct participatory democracy, which involves all the adult members of a community) as the archetype of authentic Indian politics. To these disciples of Mahatma Gandhi, it seemed that nothing could have been more Indian than the development of community through consensus. Indeed, this was the Mahatma's dream. So in our own community, we sought to make this dream a reality, and it is a principle that we practiced with profound effect. As Nimmi says, "so much precolonial and even postcolonial missionary zeal has been borne of an unconscious spirit of patronism and it has produced a sense of inferiority and shame among Indian people." In reflecting on *Aashiana*, Nimmi contends that "a sense of very real equality exists among the members of the community" and "one of the main outcomes of *Aashiana* has been the gradual restoring of a sense of real dignity for the Indians in the group."

Fourth, we decided to reinforce this process by seeking to be as financially self-sufficient as we possibly could be. We would take funds to support projects for others, but as much as possible, we would not take money from abroad to support ourselves. In practice, the foreigners had to depend on foreign funds for their personal support, and the local members of the community generated their own income from within the country. One time, a wealthy man from abroad offered us substantial sums of money, and we discussed it and then kindly declined the offer. Another time, when Nimmi and Susie's families offered furniture and a vehicle to the community, they were accepted with much appreciation. This reinforced the sense of dignity in our identity as an Indian community.

Our emphasis on our Indian identity did not eliminate the tension between the foreign impetus of the model and the indigenous shape of the model for community—nor did it eliminate tension between those from the East and those from the West within the group. Rather, tensions continued to exist between everyone. Yet the community intentionally made decisions that would offset the influence of its non-Indian (or even anti-Indian) historical antecedents in order to facilitate the development of a fellowship that would reflect a creative fusion of the East-West tension. To begin, that fusion had a decidedly Western accent, but as time went by, it became more intermixed with Eastern rhythms. This intermixing was echoed in our name, which was Urdu (rather than an English). *Aashiana*, which literally means "nest," connotes "a place of protection, support, nurture and sustenance."

---

165. The *Vedas* are religious texts written in *Sanskrit* originating in ancient India.

In typical Indian fashion, Nimmi and Susie sought permission from their families to move in, and to our delight, their families not only agreed, but also gave all the help that they could. Nimmi's mother, Mrs. Parambi, gave Nimmi furniture for the house, and Susie's father, Captain Mathai, gave Susie their family car for our extended family to use. Through this process, we became particularly aware of our interdependence with the "traditional natural families" of our "intentional extended family." We were determined to honor the mutual expectations that comprised these relationships.

We recognized that accepting a person into the community also meant accepting a responsibility to their relatives, and so we sought to relate as a family should relate to other families, with respect and reciprocity. We made decisions that affected more than one family in consultation rather than unilaterally. This was particularly critical when we counseled people who were members of our intentional community and also members of a local clan, especially when it came to the subject of marriage. This approach made the development of the community very complex and slowed down the pace considerably. But it also made the community more relevant, relational, and true to our beliefs about the development process through our ongoing communication with, consideration for and commitment to one another. We felt that any frustrations or difficulties were worth it if they afforded us the opportunity to develop our community with care.

Finally, on 10 July 1978, our family, Neil and Dravid and Nimmi and Susie moved into a house at K13A South Extension (Part One), near the Ring Road in South Delhi. We were to make made this house the home for our extended family for the next two years.

Our times of prayer together became one of the most important aspects of our common life. We began each day with prayer, and each time we gathered for a meal, we prayed, and each time we gathered to make decisions, we prayed. In times of prayer, our hope was revived, our unity was restored, our energy was renewed and our agenda was established. We often went into prayer seeking to escape our duties and obligations, but came out of those times of prayer with a determination to do whatever needed to be done. Consequently, we were able to do what we thought we were unable to do. It took time. It took effort. It was not easy. But eventually, we began to adjust to each other and to grow together as a group. Susie says that "it took nearly six months for . . . us to get used to each other . . . [but] we tried to understand each other, change some of our ways to accommodate each other, so as to live in harmony. . . . At the end of six months we felt united and confident." Nimmi indicates that this confidence was not in vain, for "in the solidarity of the friendships that were formed . . . the painful self-revelations we experienced in living together, through the discovery of our own wounds, [we] were being healed." We were in the process of becoming a community that expressed its common life as an extended family in an extended household. Susie recalls that, at the time, the community functioned as an extended household, sharing expenses, possessions, family times and being accountable to each other. Sometimes it was difficult, but it was also a lot of fun. It was good to know "we were not alone." When Satender Bahadur came to live with us, he wrote an article for the *Traci Journal* and said that "the community . . . is more of a family . . . [in which] each person is respected as an individual. We eat, drink, and talk in togetherness. This helps enhance the family atmosphere."[166]

Susie says that "at the end of six months we felt confident to be the core of the household and open our doors for other people to become a part of the house." The people who came to house were, by and large, people we already knew. They were family members or people whom we had met at college, work or at church. A college friend of Nimmi and Susie, Meera Menezes, came to live with us, along with their friends Thomas Joseph, Dorothy and Sam Rao and Sanjiv Ailawadi. Vijay Masih moved in with us in September and was quickly incorporated into our common life. Vijay made significant contributions to the community through his knowledge of the language and culture of India, particularly with *hindi bhajans*.[167] C.B. also moved into the community in September and brought his concern for critical reflection and concrete action. Both Vijay and C.B. also brought laughter into what was otherwise a much too serious group of people. Bert Cherian and Chandrakant Shourie joined the community, and they brought along Sasi Kumar and, later, Ashok Jain, Srinivasan and Man Singh, and we realized the real fun had just begun. The revolutionary solidarity began with this phase, when we really flung open the doors of the community.

Another consequence of this phase was our realization of the possibility of developing relationships far beyond the confines of the community and, through those relationships, to influence a lot of people in society at large. In this regard, *Aashiana* was in stark contrast to Dilaram. In Dilaram, we helped disciple people, and then we sent them home to "work out their salvation" in their home country. In *Aashiana*, we helped to disciple people in their own home country and simultaneously tried to support them as they discerned what "working out their salvation" meant for them in the context of New Delhi. As the community became more affected by the experience of the general population, we also became more aware of the

166. Satender Bahadur, reprinted in *Go* (1980): 16.
167. Traditional Indian worship songs

need to take action to help the plight of people in the city, who had recently been hit by a devastating flood. As a community, we got involved in the hands-on, hard work of flood relief in Burari, a village in North Delhi. As we got involved, we began to realize the desperate need of getting other young people involved in grassroots engagement with disadvantaged groups. Neil visited student groups, encouraging them to "become a potential source of productive social change" rather than "the future office bearers of a brutal status quo." We challenged as many young people as we could to join us in the struggle, as C.B. might say, to reconstruct our personal and corporate lives according to the spirit of freedom, love and service exemplified in Jesus of Nazareth.

Towards the end of 1978, C.B. married Selina Prabhakar, which was the first of many marriages in *Aashiana*. It was celebrated with much enthusiasm, and C.B. was released from his commitments to the community so that he and Selina could decide on the future of their involvement with the community after they had established their marriage and knew what they wanted to do as a couple. Because C.B. and Selina chose to live close to the community, we continued to experience fellowship without the pressure of any special expectations. After sometime, C.B. and Selina decided to participate fully in the community again.

For some time, Ange and I knew we wanted to have another child, and we decided to adopt a child who needed a home yet did not have one. Though everyone agreed this was a good thing to do, because there were many orphans who were not being cared for around the country, we felt frustrated at every turn by insensitive bureaucrats and restrictive bylaws. We persisted with prayer, particularly Evonne, who persisted in praying for a baby sister. Finally, in 1979, we were able to adopt a newborn baby girl, Rukhmani, whose mother had died in childbirth and who was dying from diarrhea in *Bal Mandir* (the government orphanage in Kathmandu, Nepal). When Ange returned with the baby, whom we named Navdita, there was much rejoicing and then jubilation as Navdita, whom many did not expect to survive the ordeal of the first few days of her life, grew into a healthy baby and began to smile readily.

During the summer of 1979 the entire community, which typically included between ten and fifteen people and sometimes up to twenty, went camping together in the foothills of the Himalayas. It was a good time as we strolled along the winding paths through the hills, stopping for *chai* in the hillside *dhabas* and chatting with each other. It was also great to have the opportunity for quiet reflection and relaxation. Suitably enough, we studied the Sermon on the Mount, contemplating the implications of Jesus' teachings for our life together. It was a time of delight and encouragement through which we were restored for the task before us, which was much more demanding than we might have imagined. We were to fail as often as we succeeded as we tried to grapple with the responsibilities that became ours as a consequence of our commitments. But the simple, natural, spontaneous, human joys of marriage, children and our common life became a source of divine strength to us in the midst of all the struggles that were to come.

In the beginning of 1979, Lawrie Dean arrived in New Delhi. Lawrie had a real love for India. At the age of seventeen, he had left Canada for India, and on a later visit, he visited *Dilaram* and then stayed on to be a worker in the community. He was returning now—and welcomed with open arms—because he wanted to be a part of what was happening in *Aashiana*.

Later that year, Neil had to go to Australia for a while, but while he was gone, another Australian, Tony Kmita, came to stay and take on some of Neil's tasks. Tony had been working with *Dilaram,* but they had decided to close their center in Delhi for some time, and Tony wanted to stay on in India so he volunteered to work with us.

Both Lawrie and Tony came quietly, without any fanfare, and they were an expression of divine support as they worked alongside us as friends in the tasks we had to do. They were responsible, cooperative and worked hard without complaint, exceptional qualities that are essential for any community enterprise.

As a community, we wanted to practice revolutionary solidarity with both the at-risk people who came knocking at our doors as well as those who would never knock on our doors, such as the people eking out a living in the slums. Once our involvement in flood relief in Burari in North Delhi was finished, we looked for an illegal *basti* settlement in South Delhi with which we could be more involved and came across one near our home in Gautamnagar. We were very enthusiastic, as we had just done some very effective relief work and felt quite confident about the work before us. We had visited the Amul Cooperative in Anand, which is the showpiece of cooperation in India, and we were quite impressed. Amul has a vast membership of poor farmers who have gained just prices for their product through the cooperative and have organized an amazingly effective and efficient enterprise. Amul even impressed the U.N. We envisaged something on a much more modest micro scale emerging from the *basti* in Gautamnagar. We also visited the Association for Comprehensive Rural Assistance (ACRA) in Madhya Pradesh, which was started by our friends Vishal and Ruth Mangalwadi to empower the rural poor. We wondered if we could do something similar with the urban poor in our city.

But when we began visiting the *basti*, we were confronted with something very difficult, in which we didn't want to be involved. In the *basti*, there were more than two hundred little huts with thatch roofs supported by bamboo poles, and each hut housed a family of five or more. Around the huts, the dusty ground was covered with waste, trash and fecal matter. There was no trap or pump for drinking water, only a pool of stagnant water that was breeding malaria-infected mosquitoes. A few pigs scavenged around the huts. Most of the people lived by scavenging the intestines of goats and the skulls and claws of chickens from the waste bins of butchers, along with rotten fruit and putrid vegetables thrown away by vendors. The people's heads were infested with lice, and their bodies were infested with worms. They were illiterate outcastes and illegal squatters who were avoided by the public and harassed by the police. To cope with their conditions, they were always joking—often about the most terrible realities in their lives—and laughing about their fate. In spite of their dehumanizing circumstances, they lived with tremendous dignity, but behind the smiles there were always tears. The joke was always on them—and it was not so funny after all. They felt hopeless, and meeting them made us feel hopeless, too.

Nonetheless, we were determined to get to know them, relate to them and be involved with them. We began by visiting regularly, sitting and chatting together about their concerns. We tried to discover what we could do together about their predicament, but it was an agonizingly slow and sometimes exceedingly awkward process. There were many questions and very few answers. How could we really get to know these people? What did we know about anything they had to endure every day? How could we relate to them? Wasn't it paternalistic to try to help them? Wouldn't we create dependence if we attempted to do something to respond to their poverty? How could we do anything constructive with such a paucity of resources within such an oppressive cycle of relentless poverty? What were we doing there? God, what could we do?

Throughout 1979, three very different people joined our growing community. What happened in their personal lives had a profound effect in different ways on the life of our fellowship, but they all encouraged us as a community to struggle with hope against despair.

The first was a Parsi from Bombay, whom I'll call "Homyar Khubyar." Homyar was a very troubled person who beat his hands on the table, his head against the wall and constantly talked to himself. His existential anguish was, as Kierkegaard described, "a sickness unto death," and he had very nearly died of it. When Homyar came to stay with us, Tony looked after him. This care was difficult for Homyar to accept, and he would refuse to eat because he did not want to impose on our hospitality. Homyar's constant companion was despair, but he came to know hope and spent many hours in its company. This made such a difference to him—and therefore to us.

Then when Neil returned from Australia, he visited Allahabad and learned about a young man whom I'll call "Ghaazi Waqas." Ghaazi had been diagnosed as a schizophrenic and was reputed to be violent. His sisters, who had been looking after him since their parents' deaths, were at a loss about what to do. Neil brought Ghaazi back to New Delhi to stay with us, and over time, Ghaazi regained his mental and emotional equilibrium, got a job and even got married. For Ghaazi, despair had been the prospect of never getting better, never making any progress or improvement. But during his time at *Aashiana*, Ghaazi found hope for himself—the hope of getting better, making progress, improving and no longer being defined by his diagnosis.

Then one day Ange and I were called by Jim Hunter, who was working with university students, to see if we could help with a guy who was running around the university, acting crazy. His hair was unkempt and matted, and his eyes were wide and wild. Tossing his head from side to side, he talked in a constant stream of incoherent gibberish. He was the last person Ange wanted to bring home, but she finally agreed. At first, we didn't know what to call him, because he switched between three well-developed personas: "Abdul Razak," "Jerry Mendoza" and "Lemuel Simon." Initially, we suspected he was Jerry Mendoza. Then we took him to Dr. Chakraboorty, a psychiatrist, who suggested that he was Abdul Razak. Then after a chance encounter with someone who knew him, we learned that he was the man we will call "Lemuel Simon" or "Lem."

The prognosis for Lem was not good, as the psychiatrist told us that if Lem cooperated, which he doubted, it would take seven years of intensive psychotherapy before he could readjust enough to function in society. Lem had been traumatized by his father's death when he was a child, had raged against God for allowing the tragedy and then rebelled against his family and society. He had gotten into using and dealing drugs, was arrested and imprisoned many times, but always found a way to escape and get back into using and dealing, which gradually began to affect his capacity to function. His abnormal behavior made him hard to deal with. Lem used to burn Neil with his *bidi*[168] when he walked past, and he once attacked Neil with a knife. I confronted Lem about his behavior and told him that he was accountable for his actions, which were wrong. I told him that I knew that he knew what was right and that I believed with God's spirit and our support, he could get

---

168. Small hand-rolled cigarettes made of tobacco and wrapped in tendu or temburni leaf

it together. I said we were with him, but if he couldn't try to do what was right, he should leave. And he did.

Months later, Lem returned and said he was ready to change. He opened himself to God's spirit and the support of the people in the community. In a few days—not weeks, not months, not years— Lem was completely transformed. People could scarcely believe it. We don't know whether or not his transformation was a "miracle," but in spite of the psychiatrist's prognosis, Lem became less hyperactive, more quiet, controlled, coherent and contemplative. His weird behavior and violent outbursts became a thing of the past. He studied seriously, and his life reflected his growing awareness of good values. He was given a job, part-time at first with and then full-time. Lem was not so interested in telling his story as in living his story by extending to others the same compassion that had been extended to him. Lem began to take an interest in the *basti* in Gautamnagar, and as he started to visit, he developed relationships with the people and gradually realized that his calling was to work for the people in the *basti*.

We took every opportunity we could to encourage other young people to follow the way of Jesus by entering into revolutionary solidarity with those who were suffering. We chatted with the youth group at Free Church in Green Park. We contacted college students at the Birla Institute of Technology (BITS) in Palani, Jawaharlal Nehru University in Delhi (JNU) and Delhi University. Matthew Titus from JNU started visiting us regularly, along with Bert Cherian, Chandrakant Shourie, Sasi Kumar and Ashok Jain from BITS. Through our initial contact with the *basti*, Bert, Shourie and Sasi made it a regular commitment and initiated Luke Samson's in-depth involvement there. In time, Luke resigned his job and became the first full-time worker with the *Kanjars*[169] in Gautamnagar. After working with the urban poor, Bert, Shourie and Sasi went on to work with ACRA in Chhatarpur and then to work with the rural poor in Nagod.

Ivan Hutnik, who had been working with ACRA, came to work with *Aashiana*. After visiting for awhile, Nimmi and Susie's friend, Meera Menezes, also came to stay. Meera decided to give up the prospect of a secure position as an economist in the State Bank of India to work as a teacher in the *basti* in Gautamnagar. Nimmi's students, Gloria and Celia Burrett, visited regularly and stayed occasionally. Our times together were very mutually encouraging. Celia went on to join the Sisters of Charity, working with the destitute and dying in the slums of Kolkata.

We also participated in a student's camp organized by the Evangelical Union students at Rajpur Road, Old Delhi, where we made friends with

---

169. A nomadic tribe or group of people of North India, Kashmir and Pakistan.

Joy Mahadevan, Rebecca Stephen and Blessina Jesudas, three young women who were completing studies in health work. Joy was training to be a doctor, and Rebecca and Blessina were training to be nurses. The camp was a turning point in Joy's life, as she realized that following of Jesus meant using her skills to work with the poor. Joy joined Meera in the *basti* in Gautamnagar. Rebecca and Blessina joined Bert, Shourie and Sasi, along with Dorothy Rao and Sanjiv Ailawadi, in committing to create an intentional community to work alongside the rural poor, which they eventually called *Aashrai*.

As the *Aashiana* fellowship continued to grow, the house on South Extension was no longer sufficient to accommodate us, and so we had to take on other housing. Then on 26 March 1980, we moved into a huge house at E-453 Greater Kailash II, and soon after took on the rental of an adjacent accommodation at E-537. The men resided in E-453 and the women resided in E-537.

In that first year in Greater Kailash II, we studied a course called "Jesus the Liberator," which stressed the radical truths of the gospel. We hosted a seminar on "God and the Poor," which was led by Dr. Ron Sider, whose famous critique *Rich Christians in an Age of Hunger* challenged Christians to practice their faith in Christ in the context of the poor. We organized a combined conference for all our friends who were involved in various experiments with intentional community and social involvement, which included everybody in *Aashiana*, ACRA and *Aashrai*.

We also continued to be very involved in the *basti* in Gautamnagar. The local people there asked us to help them install a small hand pump so that they could have access to fresh water. We also started literacy classes for adults and children, organized a community health program and held *satsangs* every fortnight for the people who lived in the *basti*. Then someone bought illicit liquor for a wedding celebration in the *basti*, which was cheap and plentiful because it had been mixed with paint stripper. The *basti* community quaffed the adulterated booze in large quantities at the celebration, much to everyone's delight—until the paint stripper hit their stomachs and caused excruciating pain. Writhing in agony, people fell to the ground, and those who could function tried to help their friends, but many died on the spot. Some were brought to our house for help, but by the time they arrived, they were beyond help and died in terrible pain in our lounge room. Among the ninety families with whom we worked, eleven people died, leaving behind many widows, orphans and a terrible grief.

To make matters worse, the newspapers picked up the story and made it a media event in the city. The city government did not want to seem slow to respond, and so they decided to condemn the victims of the tragedy for dealing illicit liquor and evict them from their illegal squatter settlement.

Deprived of elders, fathers and mothers, brothers and sisters, breadwinners and loved ones, the survivors plunged into an even deeper grief as they had to suffer police harassment that was approved by the government. *Kya kare?* What to do?

Luke describes our response to the eviction order as follows: "Upon the suggestion of a *basti* community leader . . . we took a petition up to the Lieutenant Governor of Delhi. There was a considerable mobilization of the *basti* people, who witnessed success in their united stand for justice." In response to our petition, the government allotted the people land at Mongolpuri, but the people resisted taking this option because the opportunities for employment and the availability of services were grossly inadequate in that area. We discussed the matter with the *baradari* (the decision-making elders in the *basti*) and together we decided that the people needed to agree to move to Mongolpuri to secure a stable land base for their community. However, we also assured them that we would work with them to explore possibilities for income-generating schemes as well as medical and educational services. As Luke describes the results of these explorations, "After much thought, talk and prayer, the most viable project for assisting the basic economic needs of the people in Mongolpuri seemed to be the *Kabadiwalla* Project, recycling paper, bottles and all sorts of metal. This scheme proposed to employ income earners for (each) family." The *Kabadiwalla* Cooperative provided three employment opportunities: it offered *Kanjars* fair prices for recyclable scrap; it offered them an opportunity to own a rickshaw through a hire-purchase scheme; and it gave them a chance to operate their own income-generating venture. Alongside the *Kabadiwalla* Project, Joy Mahadevan organized a health clinic, and Meera Menezes organised a school. Luke immersed himself in the affairs of the *Kanjar* community, supporting the *baradari* as it sorted out the complicated process of resettling the people in Mongolpuri.

This period was particularly difficult for Ange. On top of all the stress associated with living in the same house with heaps of high needs people, she had been experiencing serious physical abdominal pain that doctors had been unable to treat effectively. When her sister Sophie came for a visit, we decided that Ange and Evonne and Navi should return to Australia with Sophie to take a break and seek other treatment options. After making arrangements for our absence, I followed soon after to join Ange in Brisbane. While in Australia, Ange got treated at the Royal Brisbane Hospital (RBH), and Ange and I went through counseling with Charles and Rita Ringma to review how we might better cope with our life as a family.

During the course of this counseling, my approach to our "sacrificial involvement" in the world was challenged. While Charles and Rita agreed with the need for "sacrificial involvement," they felt that my approach was "too simplistic" in dealing with "complex issues." Moreover, they suggested that Ange had suffered because I was too "impatient with the complications" that constituted the nature of our day-to-day life in a residential community among so many distressed and distressing people. While this feedback was very affirming for Ange, it was very confronting for me and led to a lot of intense conversations and soul searching. That wasn't made any easier by the fact that the staff at the RBH couldn't find anything physically wrong with Ange and suggested that it might be psychosomatic.

I was mortified to think that I had been "too focused"—"too fanatical," someone said—to the detriment of Ange's welfare, and so I entered into lengthy negotiations with Ange about how I could do better by her in the future. The question we needed to answer was whether that future was going to be in India or Australia, but we weren't sure what to do. To complicate matters further, Ange was still sick, and the best treatment available in Australia wasn't helping her—and the best treatment available in India was not likely to be any better. As we struggled with this decision, we decided to do something that we had never done before and have never done since: we asked Charles and Rita to pray for guidance and then tell us what they thought we should do.

To our surprise, their advice was that we should return to India on three conditions. First, we should move out of the main house in *Aashiana* and balance our proximity to the community with privacy from the community. Second, I should follow through on making the changes in our relationship that I had agreed to in order to ensure that Ange would feel more supported. Third, Ange should follow through on seeking medical treatment for her abdominal pain in Delhi. After some consideration, we accepted their advice and returned to India.

Most reasonable people probably would have thought that it was insane for anyone as sick as Ange to return to India. No responsible mission agency I know would have permitted such a ridiculous decision. But we went back to India, and it worked out better than we could have imagined. First, when Ange and I returned, we moved out of our shared accommodation at E453 into our own flat at D23 nearby. Second, when we set up our home, we established a much more sustainable routine for our family. Third, when Ange consulted a local gynecologist, she gave Ange a hands-on examination and found what the Royal Brisbane Hospital, with all its high-tech interventions, couldn't find. Ange had a big amoebic cyst that had fused her intestines with her womb and was causing her great pain. Once the doctor operated and removed the cyst, Ange quickly and completely recovered the best of health for the rest of our time in India.

In the meantime, *Aashiana* was slowly transitioning into a family-friendly community. Ruth Samson, Luke's sister, arrived with her fiancée, Eddie Mall. They had been so impressed by the transformation in Luke's life that they decided to come to *Aashiana* after they got into trouble. Eddie had been working as a manager in a five-star hotel in Bombay where he had good working conditions and great wage checks. But the corruption at the heart of the hotel industry had been too much for Eddie to handle, and he had a nervous breakdown. Eddie and Ruth decided they should both come to *Aashiana*. When Eddie got on the train, he had just enough money to get to Delhi, but he didn't worry because he felt that everything would turn out all right. While at *Aashiana*, Eddie recovered, and he and Ruth became much-loved members of *Aashiana* because of their stability, common sense and easy-going style.

Around this time, Pete and Kate Fitzgerald and their kids joined *Aashiana* from Dilaram. They had been asked to lead a small Dilaram House in Kathmandu in Nepal. Then they were asked to lead a large Dilaram community that had been started on a houseboat called "The Ark" near the central railway station in Amsterdam. We were delighted when Pete and Kate came to work with us at *Aashiana*, because they were very down to earth and had their feet firmly on the ground, and they helped our fellowship become more realistic and less self-conscious. Pete and Kate laughed at the "fancy language" and "fanciful ideas" for which I was famous. This concern for reality, which was practiced with tremendous compassion, provided a concrete model of a healthy family and community balance.

Bernard Devasahayam, who'd been sent from Bangalore to work for the government in Delhi, arrived and had myriad suggestions about fun things we could do. Through Bernie, we often found ourselves at the movies or on a picnic or playing a football match. Bernie was always ready with a cup of chai or coffee, which are so essential to a community.

The number of people in the community had virtually doubled every year since its inception in 1978, when there were only four of us. By the beginning of 1982, there were twenty-eight of us—and more were yet to come that year. As the community got bigger, the number of interests also expanded. But *Aashiana* had become identified with residential care and counseling and, later on, community work in slum and resettlement areas, so people began to wonder if they could still be considered part of the community if they had other principal ministry interests. This was exacerbated by the fact that as interests became more diversified, accommodations became more dispersed. We had all begun by living in the one household, with one couple and a number of single people. As each succeeding couple became married, they set up their own separate household. We all agreed that each household should be within walking distance of the main community household (E-453) so that we could maintain the viability of a close fellowship, but with all the changes, we needed to redefine the meaning of that fellowship.

We took time to consider who we really were and identified *Aashiana* primarily with the people in our community and only secondarily with the ministries in which everyone was involved. We came across the concept of a covenant that we could make to one another to articulate the nature of our responsibilities and expectations and to affirm one another in our common commitment as a community. After checking out the covenants of other communities, we adapted one from Patchwork Central in the U.S. that expressed much of what we believed and adopted it as our own.

> We will seek to be a tangible demonstration
> of the Good News of Jesus Christ.
> We will seek to stand together with all people
> regardless of race, color, caste, class or creed,
> especially with local groups of people,
> regardless of religion or denomination,
> who are also seeking to be a tangible demonstration
> of the Good News of Jesus Christ.
> We will seek to be a witness to the necessity
> for peace through a concern for justice,
> the confrontation of evil and
> the extension of forgiveness.
> We will seek to serve the needs
> of those around us,
> particularly standing with those often
> neglected, rejected or forgotten by society at large.
> We will seek to work for renewal
> within the institutions
> with which we are associated
> and we will work for the care of creation
> wherever we are situated.
> We are willing to go anywhere
> for the sake of the Gospel.

The shape of these vows expressed important elements about our commitment to Christ, each other and the world around us. The spirit of these vows was meant to be directive, but not dogmatic. The vows were meant to describe the active, moral, flexible, dynamic and relational agenda of our community. We added a final resolve to these vows, which was made famous by the *Sat Tal Ashram* in North India, because it summarized our vows in beautiful, poetic and aspirational terms:

> Here we enter a fellowship
> Sometimes we will agree to differ.
> Always we will agree to love and unite to serve.

Each Monday morning, most of us would have breakfast together, and on Tuesday and Thursday nights, we had dinner together at the main house. These meal times were really critical to our sense of being and belonging together, as they were relaxed and often rowdy occasions that promoted an easy sense of camaraderie and companionship. Over time, we decided to gather in small groups so that we could share our individual concerns more intimately. These groups were organized around the emerging families so that each family could hold their particular concerns with others. We also met as a larger group, which included the coordinators of the emerging ministries, so that we could share our collective concerns. The whole community continued to meet once a week for prayer and collective decision-making around matters of mutual concern. We had fewer formal community meetings so that people would have more time to get together informally.

The community was soon alive with many children. Stewie, Meghan, Cameron and Patrick, Evonne and Navdita, Sandeep and Kavita were joined by Joshua, Pranay, Sarah, Nadine, Malathi, Jessica and Dhiraj. Their presence turned things upside down and inside out. Meetings were disrupted by shrieks of laughter over their antics. Our gatherings were interrupted time and again by cries for attention. The chaos of our life together refused to conform to the order of the day, making us realize the importance of not taking organization too seriously—even as we were trying to organize ourselves more assiduously. The major issue we addressed as a community during this time was the degree to which people should be encouraged to continue taking risks in reaching out to care for others while caring for their own embryonic families. We decided that each family should decide that for themselves.

Around this time, David and Marion Boice got involved with *Aashiana*. They had been on the edges of the community for some time, but now wanted closer fellowship with us and to collaborate with us in our work among the poor. David came from a working-class family in England and felt a strong affinity with the working class in India. Marion was from a middle-class, down-to-earth family in Germany, and she wanted to get down to business wherever she was. Both David and Marion learned Hindi and wanted to work among the *Hindl*-speaking people of the city, so they gave themselves to the work in the *basti* in Gautamnagar.

Then Paul, Luke's older brother, arrived. He'd worked and studied hard and gone on to do postgraduate work in the United States, but the U.S. wasn't his cup of tea, so he returned to India and joined us in *Aashiana*. Not long after Paul arrived, the rest of the Samson family came to Delhi: his sisters, Ega, Anna and Maria, and his mother, Rosa. Ega eventually married Neville, and they joined *Aashlana* and gave themselves unreservedly to the work of rehabilitation. Paul ended up marrying Dawn and set about establishing a home, but in settling down, Paul did not want to opt out of the issues about which they were concerned. Paul wrote a report that surveyed the slums and resettlement areas of the city, identifying all the resources that were available to the people in these areas through government and non-government agencies. He also gave an account of various attempts that had been made to connect the people with the resources in ways that were constructive. This report was used by people in the slum and resettlement areas to access the resources they needed, and it was also used by people around the city who wanted to help them, but didn't not know where to start.

Though organization was not our primary focus, we still considered it to be essential. Lawrle and Susie organized *Sahara*, a Centre for Residential Care and Rehabilitation, as a distinct ministry from *Aashlana*. When they left for further studies, Tony and Days took over the leadership. After Tony and Daya left, Neville and Ega assumed responsibility for this ministry.

In 1981, *Sharan,* the Society for Serving the Urban Poor, was legally registered, but it was organized and then reorganized between 1982 and 1984. *Sharan* operated with a managing committee from *Aashiana, Aashrai* and ACRA, which met three times a year. Luke, the secretary, was legally accountable for *Sharan's* programs, which provided educational opportunities for both children and adults, health-related services (both curative and preventative), employment-related opportunities via the *kabadi* cooperative and economic assistance through government schemes. Luke and Meera, Eddie and Ruth and David and Marion moved to Janakpuri to be closer to the people with whom they worked in Mongolpuri.

C.B. and I organized two training programs related to the concerns of *Sahara* and *Sharan*. The first was under the auspices of *Sahara*, and the second was under the auspices of the Evangelical Fellowship of India Commission on Relief (EFICOR). *Sahara* also sponsored a special training program for people interested in residential care and counseling by Paul Swaroop and Sundar Daniel, who were sent from Union Biblical Seminary.[170] C.B. was appointed as the Associate Training Coordinator of EFICOR in North India, who sponsored many training seminars to help Christian groups and agencies become involved with the plight of the poor in India.

At the end of 1984, in an attempt to control foreign support for the Sikh *Khalistan* independence movement—which had led to the assassination of Prime Minister Indira Gandhi by her two Sikh bodyguards, and in turn had led to revenge attacks on innocent Sikhs in Delhi (in which I had tried to intervene)—the Indian government demanded that all foreigners without visas leave the country immediately. Ange and I, along with thousands of other Commonwealth expatriates, who up until then had not been required to have any special visas to stay in India, were informed that we had to leave, and so our wonderful, life-changing sojourn in Delhi came to an abrupt end.[171]

In 2018, Ange and I took our daughter, Evonne (who is now known as Ruby), and her two teenage children, Lila and Kaedin, on what we think could be our last visit to our dear friends in Delhi.[172] We hired a driver and searched for the places we had lived in Delhi. After an hour or so of negotiating the stop-start, dodgem chaos of Delhi traffic (which most drivers negotiate with consummate skill), we found 27a Friends Colony and then F9/4 . The Friends Colony House had been rebuilt and was completely unrecognizable, so there was little to remind us of our wonderful days there. The open entrance to the driveway had been replaced by a locked gate, and the warm welcome of our beloved and bouncy boxer dog, Smack, had been replaced by the cold threat of an anonymous guard dog patrolling the walled grounds. The House of the Peaceful Heart, which had once been a place of fun and laughter and hugs and tears for so many of us from around the world, had been replaced by an inaccessible set of multi-storied luxury apartments. The Vasant Vihar House was still recognizable, but had been completely repurposed into the "Vasant Visions Ultrasound Colour Doppler X-Ray Clinic." As we looked at the cold, hard façade of the clinic, there was very little to relate to or resonate with, but we still remembered

---

170. Rev. Dr. Paul Swarup is now Presbyter in charge of Green Park Free Church in New Delhi. Sunder Daniel went on to serve as the executive director of NEICORD.

171. After we all had to leave India, Pete and Kate Fitzgerald came to work with me in TEAR Australia, an International Christian aid agency. Through TEAR's partner aid agency, Serve, Pete is still working for the people of Afghanistan, where his life was transformed forty years earlier.

172. We also visited our dear friend Meera Menezes, and we would have loved to have written about her, but she asked us not to.

the joy of being able to bring our daughter, Evonne, home as a baby into the embrace of some of the most beautiful, life-affirming, life-transforming communities we have ever known.

Ange and I visited the extended family of our former cook, George Peters, and his wife, Grace. Though George and Grace had died, their children, Carol and Queenie, provided us with a wonderful meal of *biryani*,[173] followed by our all-time Dilaram favourite desert, vanilla ice cream and *gulab jarmuns*[174] Then George and Grace's grandchildren, Joshua, Elijah, Abhishek and Valbhav, who are in a band called "The Brothers Four,[175]" sang inspirational English and Hindi songs of praise, including *Yeshu Nam*.[176] Ange and I wept, knowing how proud George and Grace would have been.

We visited our friends Matthew Titus and Anuvinda (Anu) Varkey and their daughter Deepika. Titus has been involved with innovative micro-finance programs, ensuring that people who aren't wealthy can access the financial services they need to survive and thrive. Anu is involved in organizing a disparate coalition of health agencies, advocating changes to government health policies that would reflect a commitment to quality healthcare across the country. Anu's great grandfather, SK Rudra, was the first Indian Principal of the famous St. Stephens's College in Old Delhi, which Ange and I had visited when we lived there. SK Rudra was a friend of C.F. Andrews, whom Rudra had sent to South Africa to persuade Mohandas Gandhi to return to India to lead the Independence Movement. After Gandhi returned to India, he and Andrews stayed with Anu's family for four months while they plotted the next steps of their campaign. My grandkids said that Deepika treated them like family even though she'd never met them before. These people know the ancient art of how to nurture good friendships, and we are grateful they are our friends.

We visited our friends C.B. and Selina, whom we have known for more than forty years. I can remember visiting C.B. at seminary in Yeotmal before he returned to Delhi to marry Selina. Since then, all through their married life, C.B. and Selina have helped other couples in their marriages. C.B. not only went on to become the director of EFICOR, but he also became a world-renowned Bible teacher who has challenged the Christian world to rediscover the gospel option for the poor. One of my favorite memories is participating in a 2012 global conference of Micah International, a coalition

173. *biryani* (dish made with highly seasoned rice and meat, fish or vegetables)

174. *gulab jarmin* (sweet consisting of a ball of deep-fried paneer boiled in a sugar syrup)

175. One of the grandsons is an event manager, and the other three are music teachers.

176. *Yeshu Nam* (the name of Jesus)

of Christian aid agencies. The conference was organized by Sundar Daniel, and C.B. and I were both keynote speakers, and it was a gift to remember how the three of us had started out together so many years before in *Aashiana*. Our time together was formative for so many of us, and many have sought to continue to live in light of the faith, values and the lifestyle that were shaped by that wonderful little idealistic community. When we visited C.B. and Selina, their daughter Kavita was also visiting, and she is continuing to live out the family tradition by working with poor people with disabilities in remote communities in the Himalayas.

We visited our friends Sasi and Blessi Kumar, who were involved with us in *Aashiana* and *Ashrai* and whom we have known for almost forty years. Since those crazy, exciting, experimental, try-anything, try-everything, let's-do-the-impossible days, Sasi and Blessi have gone on to do really significant work, courageously providing emergency relief in Darfur during the war, meticulously writing policy papers for the Indian government on treatment of people with HIV-AIDS and relentlessly advocating with the World Health Organization (in an unpaid capacity) for people who are suffering with TB through their consultations in many countries around the world. At the same time, they have managed to raise two wonderful daughters, Bhavana and Arthi, exemplary young women who are friends with our daughters, and to whom we were able to introduce our grandchildren. It's a great joy for us to introduce the next generation to so many committed, capable comrades.

We visited our friends Sanjiv and Sushila Ailawadi, who were involved with us in *Aashiana* and *Ashrai,* and whom we have known for almost forty years. During that time, we have seen them establish a contemporary church that we visit when we're in town called "New Generation," whose vision is to "reNew Delhi," a city that has a history of horrendous sexual violence and was recently rated as "the most unsafe city in the world for women."[177] With the help of their daughter, Shruti, and son, Ashish, they run online and real-time workshops in colleges and schools, challenging traditional modes of patriarchy, advocating radical two-thirds-world womanism (rather than bourgeois first-world feminism), women's equality, equity and empowerment, while also rehabilitating trafficked women and rescuing young boys and girls who have been abandoned on the streets.

Before we left Delhi, I also went to visit our dear friend, Neville Selhore, who was dying of cancer. Neville and Ega had led *Sahara* heroically for many years. They helped establish the *Sahara* Centre for Residential Care and Rehabilitation, which has been widely regarded as one of India's oldest

---

177. https://poll2017.trust.org/

drug rehabilitation organizations, running programs that many have seen as their "last hope"—not only in Delhi, but also Shillong, Kohima, Imphai, Mumbai, Pune and Hyderabad.[178]

Practicing Transformative Reciprocity

I've tried to practice "the Spirit behind the script" in terms of *transformative reciprocity.*

In 1984, when Ange and I returned to Australia with Evonne and Navi from India, we had nothing but our cherished memories of Dilaram and Aashiana. We had used all the money we had made from selling our house in Brisbane to fund the work we did in Delhi. In our twelve years there, we had lived from hand to mouth, kindly supported by the charity of friends, and had never been paid a salary. Having no home and no money to rent a place of our own, Ange's mum and dad invited us to stay with them at their place, 31 Julia Street in Highgate Hill.

For the next six months, I cried. I hadn't chosen to leave India, and I didn't want to be in Australia. People thought I would be happy to be back, but I wasn't. I felt as if I was in exile in my own country, and I was separated from the communities that had meant the world to me. Ange gave me those six months to feel sorry for myself and then confronted me with my self-indulgence, which rendered me useless to her, the children and everyone else. Happy or not, she said I was to start where I was, use what I had, and make the most of it.

After staying with Ange's mum and dad for a year, Ange and I decided it was time for us to get a place of our own. Nick Platts, who had been with us in Delhi, generously shared his inheritance with us so we could afford to buy a quaint little old ramshackle workers cottage at 8 West Street in Highgate Hill, which is in the greater West End area.

Since we wanted to continue to work with marginalized and disadvantaged people who were struggling to resolve their problems, West End was a great place for us to be because it had its problems. When we moved into West End, up to 75 percent of the population were living below the poverty line, and over 50 percent were living in insecure rental accommodations, which were becoming increasingly unaffordable due to gentrification. At that time, we were told that West End had the highest rate of murder, attempted murder, conspiracy to murder, manslaughter and robbery, as well as the second highest rate of car theft, the third highest rate of break-and-enter home invasions, and the fourth highest rate of sexual assaults in the

178. https://bit.ly/2lZgFZq

entire state of Queensland. These stats were reflected in the fact that many of our friends only felt safe to visit us during the day, and a couple who were brave enough to come over for dinner one night had their car stolen while we were having supper. On another occasion while I was away, someone broke into our house, so Ange fled with our kids to her mum and dad's house, which was then broken into later that night. Many nights Ange and I have lain awake listening to the fights that break out in our street. If it's a fair fight, we leave them to get on with it, but if someone is being badly bashed, Ange kicks me out of bed to go sort it out, with the assurance that if I'm not back in five minutes, she'll call the cops. Only last night, after all these years, a man across the street was threatening to cut a women's throat with a knife, and we had to call the cops.

But of course West End is bigger and better than its problems. It has a strong sense of community, which is a great resource for creatively resolving our problems. There are five significant characteristics of West End, which both reflect and reinforce the ongoing sense of community in this place.

The first characteristic is geography. The greater West End area, which includes West End, Hill End, Highgate Hill and South Brisbane, is not a suburb that loses its identity as it bleeds into the surrounding amorphous sprawl. Instead, the greater West End area is a distinctly identifiable and vibrant urban village, which is bounded by a bend of the Brisbane River and bordered (for the most part) by beautiful parklands.

The second characteristic is economy. The artery that keeps the life-blood of the locality pumping is Boundary Street, which is not a privately owned mall controlled by big corporate interests that suppress community life, but rather a village high street with a little strip of small local businesses, where you can walk from place to place at a leisurely pace along the footpath and get to know all the shopkeepers and shoppers by name.

The third characteristic is hospitality. From the very beginning, the very heart of the area was a significant meeting place for Indigenous peoples, long before it was named Musgrave Park. People from all over Moreton Bay used to come to *Kurilpa,* the place of the Water Rat, to feast communally on its wild fruits. Since settlement, waves upon waves of migrants coming to Queensland from Europe, the Middle East, Indo-China and the Horn of Africa, alighted from the trains that stopped at South Brisbane Station and were invited to settle their families in *Kurilpa.* In spite of dispossession, the Indigenous tradition of hospitality defined West End.[179]

179. This view focuses on the lighter side of our history. If you would like to read an article about the darker side of our history, I would suggest Brown "The History of Musgrave Park."

The fourth characteristic is a balance between homogeneity and heterogeneity. A significant number of similar people have lived in West End for a long time and have created a culture of safety, security, stability and responsibility. But there is also significant diversity among the people who all live together in West End: Aboriginals, Greeks, Lebanese, Vietnamese and Chinese; Christians, Muslims, Hindus, Buddhists and Pagans; rich, poor and middle class; upwardly mobile, down-shifters and side-liners; old, young and middle aged; quiet achievers, rabble-rousers and cross-dressers; straight, lesbian and gay; tradies, students and artists.

The fifth characteristic is creativity, which emerges from the distinctive mix of order and chaos in West End. The Jews say that God creates both *peace* and *pandemonium*. The Hindus say that Vishnu creates *harmony* while Shiva creates *havoc*. The Chinese say that we need both *yin* and *yang*. In West End people pride themselves on the creative mix of order and chaos in the community. This mix is held within a relatively protected and culturally equipped community that has a high degree of diversity and complexity with an incredible capacity for adaption and development.

Humans are attracted to cities because they were invented as "places of exchange"[180] to facilitate the exchange of culture, knowledge, skills, goods, resources, services and so on. This exchange is more difficult if people are scattered all over the countryside without access to centralized places of exchange. Cities are a concentration of people, structures and processes that maximize the potential for mutual exchange to take place while minimizing travel. The challenge for people in an inner-city community such as West End is to realize the transformative potential of mutual exchange for all people, including the most marginalized and disadvantaged, through committed reciprocity.

This is exactly why the West End Waiters Union was established. No one is quite sure when the Waiters Union began, but it seems to have emerged in 1985, after Ange and I returned from India to Australia and expressed an interest in doing the same kind of faith-based community work in West End as we had done in New Delhi. We were joined by two other couples, Chris and Ruth Todd and Nigel and Sue Lewin, who had met us in India and moved into West End and then helped us start the network

The network was called the West End Waiters Union because we wanted to be "waiters" in West End. We didn't want to set agendas for people, but wanted to be available, like waiters, to take people's orders and do what we could to help them. We wanted to help to develop a sense of hospitality

---

180. This is from my friend, David Engwicht, *Towards an Eco-city.*

in the locality so that all people, especially those who are usually displaced, could really begin to feel at home in the community.

Dilaram was a residential community, where we all lived the same way of life in the same house. Aashiana was an intentional community, where we all lived in different houses but were committed to living the same way of life. The Waiters Union is more of a local community network, where we all live in different houses but are committed to living the same way of life with others, including the marginalized and disadvantaged people in our locality.

As our website puts it, the Waiters Union is a "network of residents in West End who are committed to developing a sense of community in the locality with our neighbours, including those who are marginalised, in the radical tradition of Jesus of Nazareth."[181] There are three distinctive characteristics in this definition. First, we are not a community in ourselves. We will only be the community we aspire to be with others in our locality. Second, we will only be the community we aspire to be with others in our locality if we include the people who have been traditionally excluded in our locality. Third, we can only include the people who have traditionally been excluded in our locality if we do not operate as an exclusive Christian community but, like Christ, include people who do not identify as Christians.[182] That being so the Waiters Union is always under negotiation, always a matter of conversation, sometimes a matter of contestation. Anyone who knows the Waiters Union knows this is a topic of endless discussions and debates. If you asked lots of different people associated with the Waiters Union to define or describe the Waiters Union, chances are you'd get lots of different answers. On our Waiters Union website, there are nine different definitions of the Waiters, which reflect our different personalities and different perspectives.

These different definitions are based on the nine perspectives of the Enneagram. The One reflects the Reformer's Perspective, which is that the Waiters are "a sincere bunch of people working honestly and authentically with marginalized and disadvantaged people without pretense or compromise." The Two reflects the Helper's Perspective, which is that the Waiters are "a great group of really nice, kind and compassionate people, helping the people in the community who need us most, as sincerely and sensitively as we can." The Three reflects the Achiever's Perspective, which is that the Waiters are "a great alternative, post-evangelical community movement in Australia with an outstanding track record of great work with the poor for over thirty years." The Four reflects the Designer's Perspective, which is that

181. www.waiters union.org

182. www.waiters union.org

the Waiters are "a niche inner-city community, creatively serving the poor in our own remarkable way, despite the sacrifice—and people's apparent inability to appreciate our innovative approach." The Five reflects the Scholar's Perspective, which is that the Waiters are "a well-educated cadre working holistically with socio-economically disadvantaged groups of people to facilitate a transformational model of developmental mission that mobilizes inclusive, participatory, people-centered responses to systemic injustice." The Six reflects the Believer's Perspective, which is that the Waiters are "a discipleship community seeking to love God wholeheartedly—and to love our neighbors as faithfully as we love ourselves, just as it says we should do in the Bible." The Seven reflects the Dreamer's Perspective, which is that the Waiters are "a happy gang of punters who love nothing better than to party enthusiastically with our neighbors as they discover the extravagant joy of being fully human and fully alive." The Eight reflects the Protester's Perspective, which is that the Waiters are "a community of activists strongly committed to marching shoulder to shoulder with the poor in the righteous fight against poverty till the last battle is won or the last drop of blood is spilt." The Nine reflects the Peacemaker's Perspective, which is that the Waiters are "a well . . . ummm . . . you know, we just like live in harmony with God, in tune with ourselves, and in solidarity with others . . . if that's . . . er . . . okay with everyone else."[183]

Given these various perspectives, its not surprising that the Waiters don't have a community covenant that everybody agrees to sign. Instead we have a liturgy, an affirmation if you like, that reflects many of our aspirations.

> The Waiters Union is a network of residents
> working towards community in our locality,
> so as to realise the love of God for all people,
> particularly those on the periphery of our society.
> Our example is Jesus of Nazareth,
> whose way of life serves as the inspiration
> for the simple, practical and compassionate path
> we want to take in relation to the planet.
>
> Our hope would be that we would not slavishly copy Jesus,
> but would voluntarily make the same choice Jesus made,
> to accept life, respect life and empower people to live life to the full.
> We want to know God, the source of life, more fully.
> We would like to cultivate the disciplines
> that would help us develop a relationship to God
> in the midst of our ordinary everyday lives.

183. We adapted these definitions from our friend Kristen Jack

We would seek to live in harmony with the heart of God,
sustaining our selves, supporting one another
and serving those around about us
in an increasingly steadfast, faithful, life-affirming manner.
We want to be aware of ourselves,
and the gift of life that each of us can bring to this community.
We recognise not only the reality of our weaknesses,
but also the reality of our strengths.
And we would seek to grow individually as people
in our capacity for self-care, self-control and self-sacrifice
for the sake of the community.
We want to be aware of one another
and the gift of life that everyone else can bring to this community.
We acknowledge not only the reality of our brokenness,
but also our potential for wholeness in relationships.
And we would seek to grow collectively as people
in our capacity to speak truthfully, listen attentively and work coopera-
    tively for the sake of the community.
We particularly want to remember people in the community
who are neglected, rejected or forgotten.
We would like to affirm our commitment
to the welfare of the whole of the human family.
And we would seek to make ourselves available
to brothers and sisters who are marginalized
in their ongoing struggle for love and justice.
We disagree about many things, but one thing we agree on:
the need for us to join together to develop a community in our locality
that is more devoted, more inclusive and more nonviolent.[184]

In the early days, people in the network talked a lot about our aspirations. We dreamed of a world in which all the resources of the earth would
be shared equally between all the people of the earth so that even the most
disadvantaged among us would be able to meet their basic needs with dignity and joy. We dreamed of a great society of small communities cooperating
interdependently to practice personal, social, economic and political compassion, love, justice and peace. We dreamed of people developing networks
of friendships so that the pain we carry deep down could be shared openly
in an atmosphere of mutual support and respect. We dreamed of people
trying to understand the difficulties we have in common, discussing our
problems and possible solutions and working together for personal growth

184. www.waitersunion.org/liturgy.htm

and social change in light of the love of Christ. We yearned to make this dream a reality in our own locality.[185]

Because the Waiters Union has no membership, no one is quite sure how many people there are in the network, but there have never been very many people at any one time. Thirty years ago we started with two or three households, and there have rarely been more than twenty households at any particular time during the network's journey. Many who are happy to be associated with the Waiters may not be regarded as a Waiters household.

We are not a high profile group, and we intentionally try to keep a low profile in the area. The activities and initiatives we are involved in do not carry our name, but instead reflect the names of the groups who organize them. Though we contribute, we do not control, and so a lot of people in our area may know us well as people, but they may not know that the Waiters Union even exists. This is fine with us, because we exist to promote the community, not our group, and we can function more effectively as a catalyst in the community if we are prepared to be more or less invisible rather than attract attention to ourselves at the expense of other groups. Yet we are not secretive, for we welcome inquiries and answer questions as freely and fully as we can. We aim to be inclusive, inviting anyone who is interested to tell us how they think we can work together in joint groups, sharing processes and projects as partners.

Jesus once said, "The kingdom of heaven is like yeast that a woman took and mixed into a large amount of flour until it worked all through the dough" (Matt 13:33). We see our network as "yeast" and the neighborhood as "dough." The yeast can only do its work when it is mixed into the flour until you cannot tell the difference between the yeast and the flour. Only then does the yeast make a difference, causing the whole milieu to rise. Based on this parable, we feel we need to let go of a distinct, visible public identity in order to merge with our neighbors and fulfill our role as a dynamic, invisible catalyst for reciprocal transformation.

All our work is intended to be self-directed and other-orientated, and we tend to work informally through existing networks. Whenever we engage the community formally as a collective, we work together as a small group rather than a big organization. Being part of this small group depends on participation. We don't join by jumping through any hoops, but through our participation in the group. Once someone is part of the group, they have the right to help manage the group, because we believe people should have the right to shape the decisions that impact their lives. We also believe

185. This section is based on Andrews and Beazley, "The Network," in *Learnings*.

that the best way for us to shape the decisions that impact our lives, both individually and collectively, is through the process of consensus, and so we work *with* the people that we work *for,* seeking to enable those who *partner* with us to realize their enormous potential as men and women who are made in the image of God.

Monday mornings, from 6:30 to 7:30 AM, we meet for worship, reflection and planning for the week ahead. Throughout the week, people meet in a range of groups to nurture their souls and sustain their faith and values. Every year different groups emerge to meet different needs, and once those needs are met, the groups disappear as quickly as they appeared. Year in and year out, on Sunday night from 6:30 to 8:00 PM, we meet for public worship with local people in the basement of St. Andrew's Anglican church.

Every two weeks, we have had a community meal, to which everyone is invited. Every six weeks, we have had a small gathering for fellowship with people in the network. Every eight weeks, we have had a large gathering with people in our region who are not in our network, but who need continuing support for their faith-based community work. Every six months, we have had a two-week, live-in community orientation program, which provides an intensive introduction or re-introduction to the spiritual disciplines that are the foundation for our faith-based community work. Every twelve months, we have had a camp so that we can get away and relax together.

The most intensive learning experiences within the network have been in households dedicated to formation. Between four and six people have lived in these community formation households at any one time. Many of the people in the network have spent time living in these more intense households at some time or another. These households have served as a resource for ongoing in-service training in compassionate community development.

Many groups help the Waiters explore spirituality, philosophy, politics, lifestyle and so on, including short-term study groups, reading groups, documentary groups, women's groups, men's groups, and various groups focused on social justice issues. Some of these groups have been around for years, and some simply come and go as the needs arise. These group meetings are managed by the people who participate in them, and while one person may act as a contact across meetings, the role of the facilitator usually alternates.

The network has been very involved in helping to promote the aspirations of the Indigenous inhabitants of our neighborhood by lobbying for them to have permission to build a cultural centre in Musgrave Park in the middle of West End. The network has also sought to support refugees by sponsoring their settlement and the settlement of their families and helping them work through the anguish that they experience as "strangers in a strange land."[186] Through a whole range of groups, people in the network have sought to relate reciprocally to those in the neighborhood with physical, intellectual and emotional disabilities as friends rather than as clients, consumers, or users.

None of these things seem particularly great, but we constantly encourage one another to remember that true greatness is not in doing big things, but in doing little things with a lot of love over the long haul. That is exactly what we are trying to do!

Sharing a range of other people's perspectives about the Waiters is important, because these perspectives provide a counterbalance to my own, which, from time to time, other people have felt has not been balanced and therefore is not truly representative of the community. The best way to give you a fair, all-round, multifaceted feel for the Waiters is by sharing a range of different views about the network.

In 2010, Helen Beazley and I edited a book for the twentieth anniversary of the Waiters Union, which featured twenty different views of the Waiters by twenty different people who have worked in, around and alongside the Waiters. In the acknowledgements of the book, we wrote the following:

> . . .every community has a dark side as well as a light side. And we'd . . . like to begin . . . with an acknowledgement of all those people who would have had difficulty in writing anything celebrating their association with the Waiters Union: people who came to the Waiters with high hopes, but left with deep disappointments; people who didn't experience the Waiters as hospitable or helpful or supportive; people who experienced the Waiters as exclusive, not inclusive, but cliquey—experienced the Waiters as elitist, self-righteous and judgmental of others. We know that community amplifies our experiences. It makes good experiences better and bad experiences worse. So any pain people may have experienced in the context of the network would have certainly been intense. And we want to acknowledge that. Having said that, we'd still like to share these bright diamonds mined from the dark coal. Stories of our successes, wrested from our failures, are the more valuable for being rare. These reflections highlight the bit of progress we have made in

---

186. Exodus 2:22.

the midst of our struggle to live with each other and work with one another.[187]

The first reflection I'd like to share is from my wife, Ange. In 2011, when Ange turned sixty, I published a selection of her reflections and shared them with her family and friends at her birthday party. The following is an excerpt she wrote about the approach we took when we returned to Australia.

In 1985 Dave and I returned to Australia. We were determined to live in Australia in the light of the lessons we had learnt in Afghanistan and India. We prayed that we could preserve our vision of hospitality and reinterpret how we could live out the value of compassion in this place. I knew I could only start where I was with what I had. Where I was—was in a neighbourhood with all these wallahs who were marginalized. And what I had were all my rels looking on to see what I was going to do.[188]

So with some forty first cousins all watching over my shoulder I began to write the next chapter of the history of our family in this area. Had I given it a title at the time, I would have called it "Inclusion." I knew that if I was going to translate my experience of hospitality in Afghanistan and India into my community in Australia, it would need to start with inclusion.

Inclusion was important for me, because I had learnt that at the heart of hospitality was compassion and that compassion with open arms always started with inclusion. So I began by including the marginalized people I met in the neighbourhood into the core of my family by treating all the wallahs I befriended as my rels.

As you can imagine many of my rels would stop me in the street and ask me: "Angie why are you doing this? You are a good girl, why are you hanging around with these bad people?"

I would tell them: "They are not bad people. They are troubled people. Because many of them have had bad things happen to them in their lives. And you'd be troubled too, if the same things had happened to you."

"Yes. Angie. That may be true. But why should you be involved with them? After all, you are a mother, with your own children and you should be caring for your own children."

"That's exactly the point," I would say. "I believe God wants us to care for our children and to teach them to care for others just like their own relatives."

I was really happy when my daughters Evonne and Navi began to bring troubled people home. I remember Evonne going out of her way to befriend lonely kids at school and bringing them home for me to meet so we could talk

---

187. Andrews and Beazley, *Learnings*, Acknowledgements.

188. Ange often uses idiosyncratic expressions. Two of her favorites are *wallahs* and *rels*. *Wallahs* is an Indian term for *persons*. *Rels* is an Aussie abbreviation for *relatives*.

with them about how we could support them. I remember Navi bringing home a fourteen-year-old girl who was pregnant. She was under a lot of pressure to abort her baby. So we talked with her about her options. And said that if she wanted to keep her baby, and needed a place to stay, she was more than welcome to stay with us.

One of the basic rules in community work is: never do on your own what you can do with others. So when I began including the marginalized people I met in the neighbourhood into the core of my family by treating all the wallahs I befriended as my rels, I invited others to join me on my journey. A group of students told me they were interested, so we decided to go on the journey together. We used to meet at my house to study a passage about the importance of inclusion from a book I had by Mother Teresa, remind ourselves of the people in our neighbourhood who were forgotten, then visit a group living with disabilities in a hostel.

One day I remember saying to these students that if we were really going to relate to these wallahs as our rels we needed to not only visit them in their hostels, but also invite them back to our own homes. The students said they were happy enough to visit people in the hostels, but were afraid to invite people back to their own homes. But I said to them, as followers of Jesus, we are called to "not be afraid,"--to "not be afraid" to relate to these "brothers and sisters" as our "family." I knew one of the students was having a house warming party that weekend. And I encouraged her to invite the hostel wallahs as well as her other rels. Eventually she decided to include them, and they had such a great time that they became good friends and have stayed good friends till today.

It was the beginning of a revolution of inclusion. As word went around about what we were doing others asked to join us. We would talk to them about the legacy of Jesus, about his vision of hospitality as a way of life, about his call to be filled to overflowing with a spirit of compassion. We would specifically talk to them about Jesus' challenge to include people in our parties who were left off other people's party lists. As a result of these discussions we decided to host an open community meal on a Friday night at someone's house every fortnight.

Right from the start we decided this would be a shared meal where everyone was encouraged to bring something to share, rather than a soup kitchen where everything was provided by someone else. So right from the start there was an expectation that not only would everyone be included but also everyone would contribute. Those who had more brought hot pots. Those who had less brought tea bags. And the tradition continues to this day.

What has changed over time is how people interact. When we started the community meal there was very little direct eye contact. People used to come in silence, with no smiles. With their heads hung down, they would collect their meal [and] eat their meal without talking to anyone and leave as quickly as they could. Now, people arrive hours early and stay on as late as they can. There is lots of hubbub as people greet each other and give one another hugs. There are still some people who choose to sit in silence, but most people laugh and cry as they talk over their meal about their week. And most people are happy to pitch in with setting up, serving and cleaning up.

Over the years it has become clear that through the spirit that is at work within us, somehow or other, none of us knows how, we have discovered the power to help one another and to heal one another. One night when I was sick Ted came to my house. He stood outside in the dark. I could not see him, but I could hear his voice, saying he felt for me and he was praying for me. It was as if an angel had come to comfort me. Another night, when my brother died, after he had thrown himself off the Storey Bridge, Dave was telling people about his death. And Dean came up to Dave, wrapped his arms around him and said, "Don't worry Dave. I'll be your brother-in-law." When my adopted daughter Navi, who was born in Nepal, was being taunted by racist skinheads, it was people from a nearby hostel who came to her aid and offered her their protection. And when my daughter Evonne decided to marry, she extended an open invitation to all the people from the hostels. Many of them attended the wedding and some of them were in the wedding party. The presence of these wallahs together with the rest of our rels was a small glimpse of heaven on earth.

I always wanted to be mindful of those who were far away, as well as those who were nearby. When we bought a house, we bought at the bottom end of the market and decided to pay the mortgage off little by little so we could set aside money to give to others overseas. When Navi turned eighteen, she wanted to track down her birth family. We flew to Nepal and tracked down her sisters and their families. Two of the three sisters were very poor, so we helped them buy small plots of land and build their own houses.

I wanted to welcome strangers, particularly refugees who came from far off lands, so I joined the Refugee Learning Centre in West End. There I was able to meet refugees, welcome them to Australia, teach them English, talk with them one by one, listen to their stories, assess their needs and then find volunteers in the community who were happy to help them. These volunteers eventually became known as the West End Refugee Support Group. Twice a year for the last twenty years I have taken a session in the Community Orientation course we run when I talk about the work of the West End Refugee Support Group.

I continually stress that the core role of our volunteers is to use the opportunity of helping refugees to be with them, befriend them and be faithful to them in their time of distress—dispossessed of country, property, family, friends and even their own identity. A no-fees, no-interest revolving loan scheme [was started] to enable refugees with visas to pay for their fares to Australia. About a hundred refugees have come through that scheme. And there have been zero defaults on loan repayments.

We started a special torture and trauma support group with them. Waves upon waves of refugees came to Australia fleeing war-torn regions: Indo-China, Central Asia, South Asia and the Horn of Africa. So we started an interfaith dialogue group for Christians, Buddhists, Hindus and Muslims to get to know one another.

And the work goes on. Recently I helped in a complex two-year refugee settlement case, assisting the reunification of an Eritrean refugee in Australia with her fiancé in a refugee camp in the Sudan. Then I organised volunteers to help her through her complicated pregnancy and subsequently arranged work for her and her husband.

But often there is no work or the work that is there is not suitable for single parents who have lost their partners in wars and need to work at home so they can supervise their children. So Judy Collins-Haynes and I have negotiated contracts for bulk orders of conference bags then organized volunteers to train refugee women to sew at a professional level and to supervise the production of the conference bags by the refugee women sewing in clusters at home.

Most of the work I have done has been unfunded or has been underfunded. So we have had to have to put on lots and lots of fundraising events to raise money for our work with refugees. And I've never been happier than working alongside my daughters, putting on dinners for hundreds of people to raise money to support refugees.

One of my most significant memories was when Evonne and her husband Marty were living in the Bristol Street Household with our younger daughter Navi, their childhood friend Olivia and a couple of others. The Bristol Street Household, located on the main street of West End, was a place devoted to developing an everyday spirituality that gladly put itself at the disposal of the people who came to the door of their house looking for help. And they invited Dave and me to move in with them.

The next eighteen months proved to be one of the best times of our lives. We got on well. We prayed together, laughed and cried together, cooked and cleaned together and grew together. And I was able to see how my children had grown into adults and were now including their rels into their lives, along with all the other wallahs.

It is my prayer that all of us who have been involved in the network we now know as the Waiters Union will all find our own way of living out our vision of hospitality in our community.[189]

The second reflection I'd like to share is by Steve Collins-Haynes, who lived in West End for twenty years. This reflection offers a brief glimpse of the experience of a local person who encountered the Waiters Union.

I got to know a couple of members of the network through a protest about rising rents around the time of the 1988 World Expo. Since then I've become friends with quite a few people in the Waiters Union and participated in many activities of the network.

Another big thing the Waiters Union has done for me has been to bring my wife, Judy, and I together. We met at a community meal one Friday night many years ago. We got to know each other as friends when we lived in the Bristol Street household. This household was committed to personal growth and justice. Living in the Bristol Street household provided a great context to work on my own life and to establish a lasting relationship. After being friends for many months, Judy and I decided to get married.

In my time of involvement with the Waiters Union I've had at least three major breakdowns. These breakdowns have been long painful experiences for me and my family. People from the Waiters Union have helped in many ways. Some have visited me regularly in and out of hospital. Some have supported my wife Judy through these times. A past member counselled Judy and I through one of my breakdowns.

A couple of people started a local Grow group, which helped significantly with my mental health. I'm part of a men's group, which meets once a fortnight at my place. The group provides a safe space to express our trials and successes, to learn from one another and to offer and receive support. It was through the support of a couple of people in the Waiters Union that I've been able to create and sustain my self-employment. I run a small carpentry business from home. Many of my customers are from the network.

The Waiters Union has been a great network to be involved in over the years I have lived in West End. I feel I've experienced a level of support that many people wish for. I feel privileged to be a part of it.

The third reflection I'd like to share is by Maddie Anlezark, who lives west of London, where she works as a social worker with older people in hospital. This reflection offers a longer, more in-depth account of the

189. Andrews and Beazley, *Learnings*, 22–32.

transformative experience of a person who encountered the Waiters in a time of crisis.

In 1986 I was at university studying for a degree in social work. My journey to this point in my life had been a tough one. I was abused physically, emotionally and sexually. As a young adult I ran from my family to Australia. I then married an alcoholic who was abusive and sometimes violent. [In 1986], I had just left him.

Dave Andrews was one of my social work tutors. He introduced himself as a follower of Jesus, who had recently been living in India with his wife and children, [where he lived] with drug addicts and people with psychiatric conditions. He encouraged us to look at our dreams of how we would like the world to be and consider how we could help to make this happen. As he talked I became excited and glimpsed a God who really cared about people and was on the side of those who struggled.

One Saturday I felt desperate and could not work out how I could carry on. . . . I went to the telephone box and dialed Dave's number and when he answered I cried and told him I needed to speak to someone. He drove over and got me, took me to his home, introduced me to his wife and children, made a cup of tea, and they sat with me around their kitchen table. I began to weep bitterly, reached out and clutched them and asked them to hold on to me.

After I had cried for some time Dave asked me if I would mind if he prayed for me. He told God that my heart was broken into tiny pieces and that I did not see that it could ever be put back together. He asked God to show me that God could mend my broken heart and would do so, not necessarily by changing the circumstances of my life, but from within my heart. It was as if I was physically jolted and had found the God I had been looking for all my life. I could not believe that these people had tried to understand my pain and that they thought there was life ahead for me despite the death of so many of my hopes.

I began to get involved with some of the things they were doing with marginalised people in our neighbourhood. My progress was slow and stumbling, the pain was sometimes excruciating, but I was starting to find a God who loved me, called me to follow him and could cope with the mess that my life had been so far. I struggled with doubts and I was scared of trusting God and of trusting the new people in my life because all my past experience screamed at me that I would only get hurt again. It was like a fight went on inside me. I can remember saying on several occasions that knowing God certainly did not make life painless, but it did make it possible to go on and believe for a better future.

After a while, I moved into the Bristol Street household where people learned to live out their Christian values with those on the margins of our local

community. Here I learned a great deal more about God and learned gradually to trust the people with whom I lived. It was still a real struggle for me to
trust and living with others at very close and crowded quarters brought home
to me how broken I was. It must have been very difficult for them to live with
me when I was so easily hurt, did not really trust them or believe that they
wanted me to be with them, and spent a great deal of the time crying bitterly
as I got in touch with my pain and brokenness.

However these amazing people loved me and nurtured me and truly accepted me. I learned with these people how to begin to live out the dream of
creating with God the kind of world that we wanted to live in, and I got in
touch with dreams I had had long ago but been unable to carry through. A
highlight was when I was no longer living at Bristol Street, I was asked by the
residents of the house to be their external supervisor. This entailed attending a
weekly household meeting and spending regular time with the female residents
each week. My role was to help them both communally and individually to be
clear about their dreams and to seek ways of demonstrating God's love for each
other and those in our local community. It was a watershed in my understanding of the Christian life, and an encouragement to us all, to realise that this
"wounded healer," me, could be used by God to pastor others, even those who
had been her pastors in the past. Later, I worked as a colleague with Dave on a
project with women who had been sexually abused as children within church-
run orphanages. This, too, we experienced as an amazing testimony of God's
healing power and the true possibilities for freedom within the Christian life.

I have now been back in England for seven and a half years and all that
I learned with the Waiters has led me on in my journey with Christ. I am
part of a team that runs a course called "Workshop," encouraging people to
look at what it means to follow Christ and make our world the kind of place
God intends it to be. With Street Pastors I go out on the streets of Kingston
on Friday or Saturday night and walk around talking to those out, chatting,
building relationship, helping out if needed. With some friends I help to orga-
nise a group at our local homeless hostel to befriend and support each other,
share our dreams and struggles, talk about Christ, develop relationship with
God and pray together.

Through my experience with Waiters Union God transformed me and
showed me how to work with him to transform his world and to enable others
to know his transforming, redemptive compassion.[190]

The fourth reflection I'd like to share is by Mark Delaney, who lived
with his wife, Cath, and children, Tom and Oscar, in slums in India for over

190. Andrews and Beazley, *Learnings*, 211–216.

twenty years. This reflection offers a perspective about how those who encounter the Waiters are encouraged to engage both local and global issues in radical ways.

In the early 1990s, Cath and I were thinking about heading to India. Cath and I had been to India as singles in the late 80s on short-terms during our university holidays. At that point, Dave and Ange Andrews had not long returned from their twelve years in India, so they had shared their wisdom in India with Cathy to help her prepare. While on those short-term visits, [which] Cath and I had taken separately, we were struck to the core by the incredible disparity between life for the poor folk we met and our own experience of middle-class life in Australia. I remember meeting a man outside his "house"—a plastic tent—and hearing that his wife had just given birth to their baby days before, right there in their tent! This was December in North India—winter—when the temperatures get close to freezing. I shook hands to say goodbye. His hand felt like a block of ice! It was a simple interaction. With my limited Hindi it took perhaps only five minutes, but it was the turning point in my life. I returned to Australia with a deep sense that the world is not right and an idealistic resolve to do something about it.

A couple of years later, after completing my studies and working in Brisbane, I met and fell in love with Cath. We realised quickly that we were very similar in our desire to go to the developing world, so we married in 1993, intending to get back there within a couple of years. Before subjecting ourselves to the rigors of the majority world, however, we figured we'd better learn how to care for each other in the relative ease of Australia. We rented a little place in Highgate Hill for a year, during which we also started getting involved in the Waiters. After our first year, we moved into a share house with other Waiters folk in Highgate Hill, the idea in our minds being that we should learn to be in community with others in Australia before heading overseas.

As in any community, that household was a good, yet painful, year. I remember various wandering folk dropping in at any time of the day for a chat, as well as the lengthy discussions on cooking schedules, how often to eat together and so on. All simple, hair-tearing stuff. Yet, as expected, great learning too. The skills we learned there and in other communities we'd lived in—how to listen, be honest and, where necessary, to confront—were to prove invaluable later in India.

Meanwhile we were also meeting with Dave Andrews once a week to discuss readings he gave us in preparation for overseas. He suggested that we still go to India for a couple of years while we were young and relatively unencumbered. We could make the decision about the longer-term future from there, on the basis of that experience, rather than from the relative comfort of justice work in Australia. Only in retrospect have I come to appreciate that more

about the Waiters. The spirit of freeing others up to do what God is asking of them, rather than them asking folk to stay in Brisbane with the Waiters itself.

So we went to Delhi in March 1995 to experience, think and decide. We joined a group called Servants to Asia's Urban Poor (now just Servants), whose workers attempt to live with and work with the poor in the slums of Asia's mega cities. We moved into a poor neighbourhood in south Delhi and began to learn Hindi and to understand a little of how poverty ticks in India. We tracked down a number of Indian Christian leaders, many of whom had been involved in Dave and Ange's communities in Delhi. We asked them whether they felt there was still a place for foreigners in mission in India. Their consensus was, yes, there was a place, if we were willing to work in partnership with them, the Indians, rather than come in as the expert boss. That seemed entirely reasonable, as we certainly didn't feel like any form of development expert!

After our first couple of years we figured that we could be useful in India, so we stayed and have been here ever since! We've deliberately attempted not to set up our own projects, but rather work to encourage and equip the many committed Indian Christians working for the poor. In our own neighbourhood, we help to link our poor friends with government services like education and healthcare that should be available to them, but which often remain out of reach due to corruption or laziness on the government's part or simple lack of awareness or confidence on our poor friends' part.

Our two boys, Tom and Oscar, were both born here and are doing really well. As ridiculous as it might seem, we've come to the view that a north Indian slum is actually a rich environment for raising our boys. Here they are exposed to real issues for the majority world—crowded school rooms, the rising price of flour and the ever-present rats, all in a context in which we can talk together about the best response. On top of that, we also have a lot of laughs together, not least at how crazy it is that we, the introverted Australians, should be here in an incredibly crowded Muslim slum in Delhi!

When we return to Australia for a break every couple of years, we generally stay with our friends Greg and Katie in the Gabba[191]. It's the closest thing we've got left to a home in Australia. We also find a warm welcome at the various Waiters activities: Project Hope, Men's Group [and] Sunday evening service at St Andrews. In these groups we find a place of acceptance from many who've had similar experiences overseas. Unlike many Australians who look to us for results, numbers and stories of God's miraculous interventions, we find in the Waiters folk a quiet understanding—a knowing that helping to bring

191. "The Gabba" is short for Woolloongabba, which is the site of a famous cricket ground

the Kingdom in the forsaken places is usually more hard work and tears than striking results.

On the other side, when we're in India, we try to provide a place for the many folk who want to experience something of the majority world. In fact, as I write, we're looking forward to our good Waiters friends coming to spend a couple of weeks with us over Christmas. We hope and pray that a couple of weeks in an Indian slum may be as formative for them as those early community days in the Gloucester Street community house were for us. Let's see![192]

The final reflection I'd like to share is by Peter Westoby, who at the time of writing was Associate Professor at the Queensland University of Technology. This reflection offers a comprehensive systematic analysis of the Waiters approach to community development from a person who was part of it. (If theory is your thing, this is for you; if not, you can skip it.)

I had been a part of the Waiters for several years when one afternoon I sat down with Dave Andrews and said something like, "We're doing a lot of stuff, getting involved with lots of people—it all feels a bit chaotic and mad." In a nutshell his response was, "there is a method in the madness." My mention of "madness" and Dave's response about "method" in some way frames how I would like to consider the Waiters Union as a model of community development and . . . community development as a method of social change.

The Waiters is "a model" of community development—[as] there are many ways of understanding "community" and "development.". . . To say that the Waiters is "a" [model] and not "the model" does not imply that the Waiters model does not reflect some orthodoxies around what normative community development is generally understood to be. The community development of the Waiters is reflective of some key orthodoxies that are typical of community development, such as a set of social practices through which people assist, enable and facilitate groups of people to build relationships, develop analyses and work bottom-up to address issues that are impacting on their lives.

The Waiters is then one model of how people have embodied this set of normative practices. People who are part of the Waiters network purposefully engage in such social practices—assisting others, enabling them and bringing people together in groups. If nothing else, normative community development is a collective process of social change; it is "stuff" people do together to move their private concerns into public processes of deliberation and action.

When I was involved with the Waiters I either observed others or participated myself in social practices that embodied bringing together people who had mental health problems, women experiencing domestic violence [and]

---

192. Andrews and Beazley, *Learnings*, 177–183.

people wanting to be in solidarity with both refugees and with local Indig-
enous people. In the coming together of people who shared similar concerns, or
similar pain, people were able to support one another in making sense of their
world and then choose tactics, strategies or actions that could address some of
those pains or concerns.

Ironically, it should also be noted that one important part of the Wait-
ers community development work is when people come together to develop
a "community analysis." Sometimes the agreed analysis is to . . . foster ac-
tivities and projects that facilitate the opposite of bringing people together in
groups. Sometimes the [agreed] analysis directs the work towards actually
helping people who have often been grouped together by the service-delivery
industry (e.g. [helping] people living in hostels with mental health issues to see
their individual worth through other kinds of friendships within the broader
community).

Orthodox community development argues that social change usually
does not occur through individual action alone—it requires people creating
"community" as groups who together want to bring change. And while the
Waiters would agree with that, they would not agree with collapsing the indi-
vidual into the collective—the individual is considered to be hugely important.
The Waiters is an orthodox model of community development that enables
collective action that still validates the significance of the individual at the
same time.

Having established that the Waiters are doing orthodox community de-
velopment, we need to ask, is there anything unorthodox—or unique—about
the Waiters model? The Waiters model is unorthodox in that it is an inten-
tional community development model that is not essentially dependent on any
kind of funding or donor. People are a part of the community they work in as
people who dream of social change in a very practical sense. The key unortho-
dox element of the Waiters model is that those who are purposefully engaged
in such social change work in the community are not so much working for, or
even with, those who are marginalised, but as people who are actually living
amongst those people.

The Waiters model is "in situ," whereby people come and participate in
the network as citizens who want to learn about doing community develop-
ment through doing it. There is no sense that people must first become "ex-
perts" in community development or accumulate experience elsewhere prior
to joining in.

The Waiters model is "relational" [in that it is] centred on some key
ideals, such as simplicity, solidarity and service. Such concepts reflect a deep
commitment within the model to relational rather than institutional language,
such as "quality standards," "best practices," and "codes of conduct." Without

wanting to disparage the latter, it is important to say that the Waiters model . . . is focused on relationally oriented ideas rather than institutional ideas.

The Waiters model is "reciprocal" [in that it is] based on mutual aid rather than service delivery. People are welcomed in to receive the support that the Waiters "provide" on the condition they will also reach out and support others. There is no notion that some are the "professionals" and some are "clients." All are considered to be people with both "resources" and "needs." The Waiters model attempts, as a relational network, to link need [with] resource as closely as possible.

The Waiters model is "spiritual" [in that it is] oriented towards a spiritually defined centre, mostly within the Christian tradition, although strongly aligned to a Gandhian interpretation of that tradition. The spiritually defined centre orients the network to put love and justice at the centre of its defining mission.

The Waiters model is "political" in that there is a genuine effort to construct and maintain an open, anarchist decision-making process. There are no official leaders, no elected bodies. There are open regular meetings on Monday mornings at 6:30 am, gatherings, and annual planning days that people can come to who want to participate in decisions that affect the network.

And the Waiters model is "communitarian" in that it invites people within the network to live up to their own ideals within community. Morality is "constructed" in the context of relationships—one cannot be a moral person as an isolated individual, a case of "just-me." Morality is worked out as justice (as opposed to "just-me") which can only be measured in the context of community.

The Waiters model is not only unique as a model of community development, [for], in my experience, it . . . is also unique as a method of social change.

Firstly, the Waiters practise what I call elsewhere "supportive co-responsibility." There is a key recognition that most people change their lives for the better when accompanied by someone else. People who are downtrodden, those who cannot pull themselves up by their bootstraps, so to speak—these are the kind of people whom the Waiters try to invite into their lives, or to be invited into. [These people] need help, but not necessarily a patronising help. It is a help forged by relational practice, whereby people come alongside one another and hold one another to account in bringing about desired change. Such supportive relational practice has endured for literally decades within the Waiters. People have been supporting one another and holding one another to account in pursuing their desired changes for many years. And because the whole model is non-dependent on funding and "professional" workers, that is, it is an intentional model, then such long-lasting relational work is possible.

Secondly, in order to practise "supportive co-responsibility," the Waiters practise "networking"—weaving people into a web of relationships that enables people to be both supported and also to provide support, to be accountable and [to] hold others to account [and] to link people with need to resources as "effectively" as possible.

Thirdly, in order to practise "supportive co-responsibility" in their "networking," the Waiters practise building relationships that are "purposeful." Relationships are forged, groups are nurtured, networks are constructed, with a directional hope that people will gain more capabilities and therefore more freedom. There is certainly a lot of sitting around sipping tea, loving coffee, and sharing meals. Such "ordinary" activity is part and parcel of community, but for many within the Waiters, there is often purposefulness to this—a conscious commitment to building community, with full awareness that within modern society, such "ordinary" activity is often undermined by fragmentation, business, mobility and so forth.

Fourthly, the Waiters method is "hospitality-focused" and imbued with a radical hospitality, welcoming the stranger, the "other," the marginal. Within the Waiters model the praxis of such hospitality starts within each person's household, then engages with neighbours, and then with other marginalised people within the neighbourhood.

Fifthly, the Waiters method is "solidarity-oriented" and infused with a spirit of mutuality and standing alongside—not of providing a service within the logic of a patron-client relationship. This practice means people within the network are conscious of the damaging impacts of many professionally defined relationships that are infused with anything but mutuality.

Finally, the Waiters method involves social practices of building "community-oriented structures and processes" that support people's involvement and engagement within the neighbourhood and beyond. Such structures, which are in themselves unique, have been specifically "designed" to support action, rather than take energy away from action. Such processes are minimalist, ensuring that people do not waste scarce time participating in an endless spiral of meetings. The Community Initiatives Resource Association, for example, frees people to participate in community and community-oriented activities instead of squashing initiatives or sucking time and energy and creativity out of those initiatives.

It is not . . . any one of these elements that makes the Waiters unique; it is in the holding of all these elements together that makes the Waiters Union a unique model of community development and method of social change. The Waiters model and method, infused by the practice of love and the hope of justice, are an important contribution to the life of many people in West End, mine included. It is also a model that enables many people in other locations to re-imagine community development in all its breadth and depth and multiplicity.[193]

The Waiters Union has always been a non-formal community network, but over time, we came to recognize the need for a formal community organization as an auspice for some of our community activities. Usually groups solve this problem by turning their non-formal community network into a formal community organization, but in the movement towards institutionalization, they tend to lose the very charisma of the community. The free and flexible, strong but gentle spirit of the community at the beginning ends up being bound, hand and foot, by rules and regulations and thereby becomes a slave to the system that it sought to overthrow.

As an act of prophetic resistance, we decided not to institutionalize our community under any circumstances. Instead we set up a formal organization as a parallel structure alongside the non-formal network so that if anyone in the community needed an officially recognised, legally registered auspice for certain activities, they could use the Community Initiatives Resource Association.[194]

In line with this vision, the Resource Association Management Committee works in a spirit of servanthood, empowering the Waiters Union and other groups who seek its support, rather than having its own agenda and co-opting groups and their activities to drive that agenda. In this spirit, it has helped establish many community programs by providing healthy guidance, services and accountability without unhealthy control.

Since its inception, the Resource Association has managed the finances for community property, provided compulsory public liability insurance, become the employer for people whose grants have required that arrangement and supplied workers and volunteers with the umbrella that is necessary to carry community-based projects.

The Resource Association has also helped establish many community groups, some on their way to becoming their own incorporated association—including some which are now very prominent in the local community and or community sector—and some who have remained informal and had a finite life. These groups include Micah Projects, the Creative Stress Solutions Project, the Inner City Citizens Advocacy Group, West End Community Association, Spiral Community Hub, Local Power and the Praxis Community Cooperative.

193. Andrews and Beazley, *Learnings*, 189–195.

194. The Waiters Union mobilizes many volunteers to participate in many local community groups, which may or may not identify with the Waiters Union. See Waiters Union Activities

The Community Praxis Co-op is a not-for-profit workers' cooperative that was established in 1998 by a group of community development colleagues who were part of the Waiters Union. There are currently nine members of the Co-op and a network of more than fifty colleagues from a range of community backgrounds, who work together on a range of projects. Community Praxis Co-op exists to empower people and to resource and strengthen the capacities of groups and organizations by developing peaceful, just and sustainable communities. It operates as an education, training and consultancy agency for individuals, neighborhoods, non-government organizations and government authorities.

The Community Praxis Co-op was originally under the auspice of the Resource Association, and while it still includes people who are also part of the Waiters Union, it is a completely autonomous agency, without any formal association with the Waiters Union. Much of the training philosophy and the training materials, resources and programs that the Community Praxis Co-op uses were developed in the Waiters Union. However, though the training delivered in the Waiters Union is specifically aligned to the Christian tradition and explicitly articulated as Christ-centered, the training delivered by the Co-op is more generic community work training. The Co-op seeks to practice traditional cooperative principles, which are explicitly articulated as soul-centered (and implicitly Christlike, if not Christ-centered), encouraging the development of acceptance and respect, spirituality and compassion, solidarity and participation, responsibility and competence in individuals, neighborhoods and organizations.

As well as practicing transformative reciprocity through the auspices of the Waiters Union, the Resource Association and the Community Praxis Co-op, I have served as an educator with TEAR Australia and an elder with Servants To Asia's Urban Poor, and I now serve as a facilitator for a group of multi-faith leaders, a group of local ecumenical ministers, two groups of post-evangelical community chaplains, pastors and coaches, and two groups of secular, spiritually committed and politically active community workers. I find what might be called "eldering"—that is, encouraging, equipping and empowering the next generation to develop their spirited practice of transformative reciprocity—really very meaningful.

The Prophetic Inspirator

Richard Rohr says, true prophets have some sort of "amazing, positive experience of theophany - God appearing to humans - that fills hearts . . . with ecstasy that has to be shared." He says "They experience a special calling that comes directly from God, and their message comes from their experience of God. . ."[195]

The role of prophetic inspirators incorporates "energizing" people to get "back on track," not just "on script," but "in touch" with the amazing, positive "Spirit behind the script" by cogently "verbalizing" their inspired passion and compassion through their writing, singing, preaching and teaching. Prophetic inspirators "believe God is with us. Their confidence in [the Spirit's] presence and power, and their ability to arrange an encounter with this present and powerful [Spirit] infuses people with inspiration. It lifts people out of their self-referential cycles and points them to the possibilities of a new reality."[196]

Spiritual Inspiration

I've always believed in the importance of the Spirit in spiritual inspiration.

The Spirit is God *incognito, the self-effacing face of God,* who has no face.

The words used in the Bible for "spirit" are *ruach* in Hebrew and *pneuma* in Greek. Both words refer to *moving air,* such as wind or breath, which you can't actually see, but the effects of which are obvious for all to see. Thus conveying the idea of the Spirit is vital, but it is essentially anonymous, and so it is easily overlooked, just as we often don't think about the significance of the next breath we take.

Through the Spirit, God energizes us. In fact, our English word "enthusiasm" comes from the Greek *en-theos,* which literally means "in-god." This suggests that if we want to maintain our enthusiasm, we need to be *filled with the Spirit.* The Spirit enhances our vitality, sensitivity and responsibility, so that we have the power to struggle for real personal, social and political change.

I love the way John Taylor describes the role of the Spirit in our lives in his beautiful book *The Go-Between God.* He reminds us that Jesus says, "when . . . the Spirit of truth comes, he will guide you into all truth" (John 16:13). The Spirit is "the one who presents all reality to us," so when "it comes to us," it "strikes us," "commands our attention" and we are "face to

---

195.. Rohr "Understanding the Prophet," adapted from Rohr, *Prophets Then, Prophets Now.*

196. Catchim, *The Prophetic Ministry,* Part 2.

face with *the truth of it*—not merely *the truth about it*. . . . To be in-the-Spirit is to be vividly aware of everything (and everyone) that the moment contains."[197]

John Taylor goes on to say that the Spirit helps us interact with one another face to face attentively and authentically in a way that creates true community. Thus Paul prays for "the fellowship of the Holy Spirit [to] be with you all" (2 Cor. 13:14), where the "fellowship of the Holy Spirit" refers to "the communion," the in-between-ness of the Holy Spirit. As John Taylor observes, "It is often translated 'fellowship', but 'fellowship' is the result which we can feel and see. What causes the 'fellowship' is the gift of awareness which opens our eyes to one another."[198]

God is not merely the "ground of our being" but the "ground of our meeting." "The Holy Spirit [is] the elemental energy of communion itself, within which all separate existences may be present and personal to each other." [199] The Spirit, as Martin Buber would say, turns all our "Its into I's;" our "Thou's into Ourselves," "You to me" and "me to You;" our "I's and Thou's" into "I-and-Thou's," and thus our "We's into One Another's."[200]

When the Spirit came at Pentecost, it helped people create true community. My friend Paul Tyson says, "Pentecost is the redemptive inverse of Babel." Babel was an attempt to build a central global political economy based on technology rather than morality, using a single, universal common language. Pentecost is an attempt to develop a global community of local communities, which are decentralized rather than centralized, and empowered by the Spirit to relate to "different people" in "different languages" with the "same kind of sensitivity." [201]What are the indicators of the presence of the Holy Spirit? In Galatians 5:22–23, Paul says that the "fruit" yielded by the Spirit is "love, joy, peace, patience, kindness, goodness, faithfulness, gentleness and self-control. Against such things there is no law." Any community that has the gift of the Spirit will yield the fruit of the Spirit. At a *personal* level, there will be love (passion, compassion, and joy), awareness, appreciation and peace (trust and tranquility). At a *relational* level, there will be patience (persistence and kindness) and sweetness (not bitterness). At a *social* level, there will be goodness (generosity) and faithfulness (fidelity). At a *political* level, there will be tolerance, non-violence, self-control, and self-management. Paul stresses that "against such things there is no law."

---

197. Taylor, *The Go-Between God,* 6, 8–11, 12, 15–16, 18, 20.

198. Taylor, *The Go-Between God,* 18, 21–22

199. Taylor, *The Go-Between God,* 18, 21–22, 29, 126–7

200. Quoted in Taylor, *The Go-Between God,* 126–7

201.. Tyson, *A Divine Society,* 88

So in "spirited" organizations, there should be no laws that discourage the development of these qualities. On the contrary, all the structures, processes and protocols should be specifically designed to facilitate the development of these characteristics.

The Spirit is always at work. The Spirit will make things happen. We need to be present and open to the ebb and flow of what happens. We need to go with the flow and help others go with the flow. We need to create processes that allow us to go with the flow and structures that allow us to go with the flow. When the flow is over, we need to recognize that it is over. We need to grieve the end of the old and wait patiently for the new movement of the Spirit.

We can create space for a new movement of the Spirit by cultivating what Harrison Owen calls "Open Space," where the Spirit is free to operate.[202] We do this in our community by encouraging people to consider something they really care about, something they really want to do something about, and we encourage them to identify it, name it and own it for themselves. Then we encourage them to extend an invitation to meet with others who care about the same thing. Those who respond to the invitation come into a circle that they hold open, as a host, for mutual conversations. We encourage the host not to control these conversations, but to let people come and go as they please, trusting the Spirit to bring order out of chaos, clarity out of confusion, conviction out of concern. We encourage those who are hosting multiple conversations to welcome any expression of passion, compassion and responsibility as signs of the Spirit's prompting in a particular direction. Then we encourage people to organize processes and structures that will support the activation of this critical mass of spirited interest.[203]

Jesus said there is always a mystery about the way the Spirit breathes vitality into our lives. Sometimes it comes screaming into our lives like a gale in a storm, rattling through the valley of dry bones at the bottom of our souls. But most times it comes with a whisper on a zephyr that blows so gently that we scarcely notice it speaking a still, small word into our subconscious minds. Jesus said that no one really knows how or when or where this wind will come. He said, "the wind blows wherever it pleases. You hear its sound, but you cannot tell where it comes from or where it is going."[204] However, Jesus also said that we need to be open to it so that when it does come, we can make the most of the opportunity to be "born again of the Spirit" (John 3:8).

202.. Owen, *Wave Rider.*

203. Owen, *Wave Rider* 3.

204. John 3:8.

The last thing Jesus told his disciples before he left was that they should not go anywhere until they were "filled" with the Spirit. He said that the day would come when they would all be "immersed" in the Spirit, and if they were open and receptive, and if they created a hospitable space in their hearts, then they would be "filled" with the "Spirit as well (Acts 1:4). We can't define or predict the movement of the Spirit, but we will know what it is when we encounter it. We can recognize when team spirit, or *the esprit de corps,* is present, or not. No matter how weak we may feel, "when the Spirit of a people is strong and vibrant," as Harrison Owen says, "wonderful things can happen."[205]

Inspiring through Writing

When I started writing, I had to make a choice about how I would write. I was studying at university, and the more impersonal, abstract, formal academic university style would have been a safer style of writing for me to adopt. But at the time, I was living in community in India, and I felt challenged to adopt a more humble, vulnerable, accessible, personal-political writing style in the spirit of the early twentieth-century activist authors that I admired, who lived missional lifestyles in Asia. Thus I sought to copy the inspirational writing style of Stanley Jones' *Christ Of The Indian Road,* C.F. Andrews' *Christ In The Silence,* Mahatma Gandhi's *Experiments With Truth* and Toyohiko Kagawa's *Love – The Law Of Life.*

I wrote *Not Religion But Love,* my best-known and most widely translated book, with the help of my friend and fellow community activist, David Engwicht. We wanted to point "people to the possibilities of a new reality" by "practicing a radical spirituality of compassion." It was first published as *Can You Hear the Heartbeat? A Challenge to Care the Way Jesus Cared,* but after *Christi-Anarchy* caused such a stir, *Can You Hear the Heartbeat?* was released as *Not Religion But Love* as a kind of *Christi-Anarchy* "in action," as it were.

In *Christi-Anarchy,* I critiqued a closed-set perspective of Christianity and then introduced the centered-set perspective of a radical, Christ-centered spirituality of compassion.[206] Even now, I often find myself sitting across from somebody I'm having coffee with in a coffee shop, drawing diagrams on a serviette, and talking about the significance of the centered-set perspective, which is "defined by a centre and movement towards the

---

205. Owen, *The Power of The Spirit,* 1.

206. These perspectives draw from Hiebert, *Anthropological Reflections on Missiological Issues.*

centre." In a centered-set perspective, a "set of people who have a connection to Christ show they are part of the set not by choosing to subscribe to a certain set of beliefs and behaviors within certain set boundaries, but by choosing to overcome any boundary of belief or behavior that might prevent them from moving towards the free, beautiful, compassionate spirit of Christ, which they have made the centre of their lives." [207]

For me, the essence of relating to Christ from a centered-set perspective is all about becoming Christlike and encouraging everyone to become Christlike, whether or not they become Christians. In *Christi-Anarchy* I explain that "conversion means turning towards Christ, whether we know him by that name, or not, beginning to judge our own lives for ourselves, in the light of his love, and beginning to trust his love to sustain us on the journey of personal growth and social change that he is calling us to make." [208]

While there are some disadvantages associated with a centered-set perspective, because it can seem a bit fuzzy and confusing, there are many advantages. The first advantage is that it is centered. Once you "get the centre right . . . the circumference takes care of itself." The second advantage is that it is centered on Christ. Christ is "the Best to which all Good points," but "Christianity has become eccentric, off centre, away from Christ. The world has too much Christianity and too little Christ." The third advantage is that "as we move towards the centre, Christ, we can move beyond the Scriptures, creeds, rites, rituals, ceremonies, and even religions that divide us towards the One who can unite us as human beings made in the image of God." [209]

When I share the centered perspective, most people say that it makes sense of the way that they want to relate to Christ, but haven't had the words to say it. Moreover, it gives them a way to share their faith in Christ with people of other faiths and those who have no faith that is more inclusive, more appreciative and more respectful.

Inspiring through Singing

Lech Welensa was asked, "What did the church contribute to solidarity?" He said, "Music."

I'm a church-based community worker, and I've worked in solidarity with disadvantaged groups for over forty years. During that time I have written, sung and recorded fifty songs we can sing along the way to sustain us in our struggle for genuine spiritual, personal and social change.

207. *Christi-Anarchy*, 63

208. *Christi-Anarchy*, 64

209. Andrews, *Christi-Anarchy*, 68–71

The songs I've written are not "Hill Songs," but what I call "Valley Songs," easy-to-play, easy-to-sing songs about the joys and sorrows of ordinary people working quietly for love and justice "in the valley of the shadow of death." I'm not a musician. I'm a community worker. The songs I've written over the years were not meant for performance, but participation. They are for people who are traveling through "the valley of the shadow of death" to sit with, stand with, walk with and sing along with.[210]

I started out with a very basic three- or four-chord, do-it-yourself, song-writing-for-dummies approach to writing songs, so they are all easy to play and easy to sing. In actually writing the songs, I worked through a simple three-step process.

First, I picked a theme by being present in my community, observing the issues people are struggling with, keeping my eyes, ears and heart open and then picking a Christlike theme that is both important to my community and matches their mood—not just the highs of hope, but also the lows of despair.

I can remember a time when there was a lot of painful conflict in our community, and we desperately sensed a need for forgiveness, so I began to write a song that expressed our deep need for mercy in the form of a prayer.

Second, I selected a melody by choosing a style that is popular in my community. I used to consider some melodies by popular artists, but not ones that were so well-known that everyone knew them. I would select a tune with a good hook that would catch people's attention. If the music was too complicated, I'd simplify it to ensure that it would be easy enough for people in my community to play and sing.

I remember searching for a melody for the prayer for mercy song when I came across Van Morrison's "Lover's Prayer." It was a typically lively Van Morrison melody, but few people in our community knew it, and so it was a perfect fit.[211]

Third, I wrote and rewrote the lyrics. I started with a draft, usually a pretty bad draft at first, knowing I could fix it up later. Then each time I did a re-draft, I tried to make it a bit better, over and over again, until I got it more or less right. I know I've got it more or less right when the lyrics match

210. Happily, in recording these songs, I was helped by some of the most talented musicians I know: Peter Branjerdporn, Andrew Kennedy, Dave Fittell, Rob Haysom, Paul Young, Luke Page, Martin Richards, Evonne Richards, Hudson Read, Eleanor Owles, Rachael Brady, Andrew Wilcox, Katei Chang, Benjamin Hooper and Marty Kendall. In writing down this music, I was helped by Greg and Katie Manning, who notated the music, which can be downloaded with the lyrics, chords and mp3s at www.daveandrews.com.au/media/songs.

211. You can hear the original at http://www.youtube.com/watch?v=r8opWKSSeb8.

the melody—when they are memorable and meaningful, and they say what I want to say and what I think my community wants to say.

I remember writing and rewriting the lyrics and melody for "Need Your Mercy," which emerged gradually and eventually became a much-beloved prayer song in our church.

> *Lord, Lord, Lord, Lord, Lord. Won't you listen, Lord*
> *Lord, Lord, Lord, Lord, Lord. Need your mercy, mmm.*
> We don't wanna hang about, fightin' anymore.
> Don't wanna leave nobody hurt, lyin' at the door.
> Resentment causes vengeance, vengeance causes pain.
> Pain breaks like a cloudburst, tears pour down like rain.
> We don't know quite what to do, we're under so much strain.
> Don't know who's there to talk to, the line's on hold again.
> Often feel like givin' up, layin' down and dyin'.
> But you told us we could call on you, I guess we'll keep on tryin'.
> *A desperate prayer . . . oh yeah!*
> *We need you there. Need you to care.*
> We need to hear you, gently speaking to our soul.
> Whisperin' forgiveness, grace that makes us whole.
> You leave us with the feelin', you're givin' us a chance
> To get ourselves together, to join in with the dance.[212]

As time has gone by, I've gained confidence in writing my own melodies. I believe that people learn much of their theology through songs, so we need to write good songs to teach good theology. I think that it's even possible to communicate quite complex theology through simple songs. For example, I have translated a radical theology of the cross into a song cycle.

1. Confession: At The Foot of the Cross

My song cycle on the cross begins with a confession at the foot of the cross.

When we read the story of the cross, we are confronted with the most profound and terrifying critique of humanity in history, for we realize, to our horror, that it is not God who killed Christ, but *the powers that be—and people like you and me—*who killed Christ and have therefore "killed" God.

Jesus acknowledged that people often "did not know what they were doing" when they collaborated with the powers. Even when the crowds, who were stirred on by the priests, were baying for his blood, he prayed,

---

212. You can hear an mp3 of our recorded version at http://www.daveandrews.com.au/media/songs/03_need_your_mercy.mp3.

"Father forgive them, for they know not what they do."[213] As Studdert Kennedy, the keen observer and author of *Indifference,* writes, "All through the ages [people] have crucified God, not knowing what they did. Crucified Him through their ignorance, stupidity, dullness of imagination, feebleness of mind, and a host of other factors—as well as their deliberate choice of wrong against right."[214]

But at the foot of the cross, people are forced to face *the truth* about themselves at last—clearly, unmistakably and unavoidably. Here, at the foot of the cross, people are forced to confront the truth of *who they are* in the light of *what they have done.* They look at the body in front of them, then look at the blood they have on their hands, and hear that still, small voice whispering in their hearts, saying, "*You* put him to death, you know."

There's no time to run. There's no place to hide. We are totally exposed, stripped of all excuses. We may have been ignorant, but we know that ignorance is no justification. We may have been stupid, but we know that stupidity is no defense against culpability. We may have been dull, but we know that lack of imagination is hardly an acceptable defense for the execution of innocents. As feeble and fickle as we may have been, we know we must own the truth: out of some misplaced sense of obligation, habit of obedience, desire for approval, fear of punishment, hope of reward, bout of laziness or fit of spite, we have crucified the Messiah, and we have nobody to blame but ourselves.[215]

"Christ that Bleeds"

Standing here at the foot of the cross. I see life as it is . . .
The flesh flayed raw. The crowd cry more. The wounds that weep.

Some of us would kill for hire; some of us kill for desire;
Some of us would kill for fear; some of us kill for power.

We crucify with sophistry. We crucify with style.
We crucify with bigotry. We crucify with bias.
We crucify with pleasantries. We crucify with smiles.
We crucify with treacheries. We crucify with lies.

At the crux of this tragedy, it's painfully clear to see. . .
If we crucify even the least, it's Christ that bleeds.[216]

213. Luke 23:34.

214. Studdert-Kennedy, *The Best Of G.A Studdert-Kennedy,* 84.

215. Andrews, *Crux.*

216. From *Songs of Grace and Struggle*: http://www.daveandrews.com.au/media/songs/08_christ_that_bleeds.mp3.

2. COMMEMORATION: THE FACE OF COMPASSION

The next song in my cycle on the cross continues with a commemoration of the face of compassion.

Through the ages God has always been prepared to suffer greatly and to forgive greatly, but because God is invisible, no one can see the tears that God cries.

Only the prophets, who lived in sympathy with the heart of God, had any appreciation for the greatness of his *grace*. Until, at the right time, God stepped onto the stage of human history, visibly, as a human being, and, in Jesus, showed us the boundless depth and breadth of his *grace*.

God's grace is vast enough to embrace our pain, absorb our rage, forgive our sin and encourage us all towards completely revolutionary personal growth and social change.

In Jesus on the cross, we can see that God embraces our pain. Frederick Beuchner tells a story that he describes as "a peculiarly twentieth century story." You only have to hear the story once to know it's just the kind of story that Jesus himself might have told.

> It's a kind of parable of the lives of all of us. It's about a boy of twelve or thirteen who, in a fit of crazy anger, got hold of a gun and fired it at his father, who did not die straight away but soon afterward. When [he] was asked why he had done it, he said that he could not stand his father, because his father demanded too much of him. And then later on, after he had been placed in a house of detention, a guard was walking down the corridor late one night when he heard sounds from the boy's room, and he stopped to listen. The words that he heard the boy sobbing out in the dark were, "I want my father, I want my father."[217]

"Our father," Beuchner says, "we have killed him, and we will kill him again."[218] But Jesus, on the cross, cries out as one of us, saying, "Father. Forgive them. For [I know] they know not what they do."[219]

In Jesus on the cross, we see that God not only embraces our pain, but he also absorbs our rage. As Gale Webbe, in *The Night and Nothing*, says, "There are many ways to deal with evil. All of them are facets of the truth that the only ultimate way to conquer evil is to let it be smothered within a willing, living, human being. When it is absorbed there, like a spear into

217. Beuchner, *The Magnificent Defeat*, 65
218. Beuchner, *The Magnificent Defeat*, 65
219.   Luke 23:34

one's heart, it loses its power and goes no further."[220] As Scott Peck says in *The People Of The Lie*, "The healing of evil can only be accomplished by love. A willing sacrifice is required. The healer must sacrificially absorb the evil."[221] Jesus on the cross absorbed our evil. He took evil into his heart as assuredly as the spear that was thrust into his side. But it went no further. There was no reaction, no demand for restitution, no demand for retaliation. The cycle of violence stopped right there and then with Jesus, forever.

In Jesus on the cross, we see that God not only absorbs our rage, but he also forgives our sin. "One thing I know," William Barclay says that

> . . .because of Jesus Christ and what he did [on the cross] my relationship to God is changed. Prior to Jesus Christ [we] did not fully know what God was like. The holiness of God [we] did know; but the marvel of the love of God [we] had never dreamed of. When Jesus healed the sick, comforted the sad, fed the hungry and forgave his enemies, he was saying, "God loves you like that. Nothing that [you] can ever do will stop God loving [you]." Because of Jesus Christ I know God is my friend. He is no longer my enemy. He is no longer even my judge. There is no longer any unbridgeable gulf between him and me. Daily, and hourly, I experience the fact that I can enter into his presence with confidence. [And as a result] I am more at home with God than I am with any other human being in the human world.[222]

In Jesus on the cross, we see that God not only forgives our sin, but he also encourages us all towards completely revolutionary personal growth and social change. When I gaze at Jesus on the cross, my heart is strangely moved. Someone dying for a cause doesn't make it right, but a manifesto of love written in blood cannot be easily dismissed. A movement, which has proved to be worth dying for, may be worth living for. The martyrdom of Jesus lights a beacon for compassion, an inextinguishable fire that scorches the apathy and hypocrisy hidden in the dark corners of my soul. His agony breaks my heart and, in the process, breaks down some of the barriers that I have erected in my heart against my own humanity. His anguish brings the sound of others who are crying to my ears, which otherwise I would not hear, and brings the sight of others who are suffering to my eyes, which otherwise I would not see. The death of Jesus is not the end, but the beginning of a whole new way of life committed to the way of Jesus.[223]

220. Webbe, *The Night and Nothing*, 109.

221. Peck, *The People Of The Lie*, 269.

222. W. Barclay, quoted in Peck, *People of the Lie,* 134, 130, 129.

223.. Andrews, *Crux,* 59

"What Love Is This?"

> Strung out, naked on the cross, assaulted by our age.
> We see the cuts. We hear the cries. You suffer our disgrace.
>
> Around your brows form lines of kindness.
> In your eyes there's care.
> Down your cheeks flow tears of sadness.
> On your lips a prayer.
>
> What love is this, as strong as death,
> that lives life as it should?
> What love is this, with its last breath,
> sets bad aside for good?
>
> Love never looked so sorrowful. Love never looked so sore.
> Love never looked so beautiful. Love never looked so pure.
> Love never looked so remarkable. Love never looked so great.
> Love never looked so lovable. As it looks upon your face.[224]

3. CONSECRATION: IN THE FOOTSTEPS OF CHRIST

My song cycle on the cross concludes with a consecration in the footsteps of Christ.

The *new covenant* was different from the *old covenant* in two important respects. First, it was recognized as a relationship that was based on love rather than the law. Second, it was a relationship that was restored, not by any sacrifice we might make to God, but by the sacrifice that God, in Christ, made for us. And, of course, the hope is that the *new covenant*, which is written on our hearts in "the blood of Christ," would "cleanse our consciences from acts that lead to death to serve the living God!"[225]

For Paul, the *new covenant* was the good news, and he encouraged us to celebrate the good news of the new covenant regularly at the Lord's Supper. "Do this," the Lord says, "whenever you eat of this bread, and drink of this cup," in "remembrance of me."[226]

---

224. From *Songs Of Grace And Struggle:* www.daveandrews.com.au/media/songs/09_what_love_is_this.mp3.

225. Hebrews 9:14.

226. 1 Corinthians 11:23–27.

One of the crucial questions that we must face is, what does this mean for us? What does it mean for us to "do this" in "remembrance of" Jesus today?

Carlos Christos, a Catholic from a middle-class family in Brazil, who got involved as a lay brother working with the poor and was put into prison for four years for his efforts, wrestled with this question. In a letter from prison to his parents, he wrote:

> Last year I meditated a great deal on the mystery of the Eucharist. Jesus instituted it in his last meal with his apostles, when he told them of the sufferings he would have to endure for their redemption. He took into his hands those most ordinary of foods, bread and wine, and he consecrated them. "This is my body which will be broken for you. This is my blood which will be shed for you. Do this in memory of me." What is the meaning of these words we repeat every mass? Do we simply mean that the consecration of the Mass is performed in memory of Jesus' sacrifice? No, they do not mean simply that. It is true that the Mass makes his sacrifice present here and now. But it also summons us to repeat Jesus' redemptive acts so we might be truly imitators of him. When the priest repeats the words in the Mass, "Do this in memory of me," I interpret it as Jesus saying to us: "I have loved you completely, so much that I willingly died for you. I've given all that I am to free you. Having nothing left but my life, I didn't grudge you that either. I gave it up to show you that the limits of love are to love without limits. I have given you my body and my blood. I have made this gesture a sacrament so that at any time or place in human history you may receive it and re-enact it in your own life. When I said, "Do this in memory of me," I did not mean you should merely commemorate what I had done. I meant you should do likewise, that you should offer your body and blood for the redemption of humanity. Just as at the Mass you receive my body and blood, so in your lives you should offer up your own, so that my acts may always be present in the world through you." Unfortunately, many Christians do not realize that Mass is something to be lived rather than attended, and that it is to be lived to the extent that we are willing to sacrifice ourselves for the liberation of human beings, and so become *God's sacrament in the world.*[227]

I believe that this view that Carlos Christos advocates so eloquently in his letter—that we are called not only "to receive" the sacrifice of Christ, but

227. Christos, *Letters From A Prisoner Of Conscience*, 15–16.

also "to re-enact" the sacrifice of Christ by "repeating Jesus' redemptive acts in our own life"—represents the call of Christ for all who are seeking to follow in his footsteps.

"The Way of Christ

> This is my body broken for you. This is my blood that I shed.
> Do it to . . . the least of these . . . In memory of me."
> There's no faith where there is no grace.
> No grace where no sacrifice.
>   No way but the way of Christ—
> A love that lays down it's life. (x2)

>   No other way but redemption. No other way but prayer.
>   No other way but compassion. No other way but care.
>   No other way but devotion. No other way but love.
>   No other way but dedication. No other way but the cross.

> There's no faith where there is no grace.
> No grace where no sacrifice.
>   No way but the way of Christ—
> A love that lays down it's life. (x2)[228]

This is the revolution of Christ. We need to sing this revolution into reality.

Inspiring through Preaching

I am the son of a Baptist preacher, who taught the art of preaching at the Queensland Baptist seminary. My father used to teach me to preach by having me prepare a sermon for Sunday and then preach that sermon over and over again on a Saturday to rows of empty pews until it was good enough to preach to the congregation. I can remember my dad sitting at the back of the vacant auditorium, taking notes, giving feedback and encouraging me to speak loudly, clearly and cogently. He taught me that while teaching and preaching both require a reverential interpretation of the Word, teaching focuses on transferring reliable *information*, whereas preaching focuses on transmitting stimulating *inspiration*.

My father was a pastor in charge of multiple churches, some big and some small. While there were plenty of volunteers to speak at the bigger churches, there weren't as many willing to speak at the smaller churches. So that's where I got my chance to start preaching when I was seventeen years

228. From *Songs Of Grace And Struggle*: www.daveandrews.com.au/media/songs/10_the_way_of_christ.mp3.

old, during my last year of school (where I coincidently won the school debating competition).

I remember one occasion, when my father was preaching in the big church, he lost his voice and asked me to preach the rest of his sermon. Though I used my father's notes, my presentation was different. He was very formal, very careful, very cautious, and I was not. I have always been a bit more fervent, flamboyant and demonstrative.

As I write this, I am in my seventieth year. I have been preaching now for over fifty years, and I've preached in more than thirty countries around the world.[229] Some of the more memorable places that I have had the chance to speak are: under a canopy in a poor caravan park in Sunnybank, Queensland; at a public meeting in the city library in Bendigo, Victoria; at the All-Indigenous Annual Convention in Katherine, Northern Territory; in a home group in a village in Chhatarpur, Madhya Pradesh; in a small hut in a slum in Kolkata, West Bengal; to a large gathering in the city of Faislabad, Punjab; in a camp site in the Swat Valley, North West Frontier Province; on top of a bus at an EU-sponsored cultural animators event near Wroclaw, Poland; under an oak tree at the Slot Art Festival in Lubiaz, Poland; in a pub in TaCesta, Prague; on the stage of an old theatre in Aldershot, Hampshire; on a platform facing the grandstands at the Cheltenham Racecourse in Prestbury Park, Gloucestershire; on a hippie houseboat called "The Ark" across from the central station in Amsterdam; on the steep slopes of a mountainside in the Swiss Alps; in training school at Schloss Hurlach, Landsberg am Lech, Germany; in a prayer conference at the Powis Castle in Powys, Wales; at a hard-rock festival called "Freakstock" in Gotha, Germany; in a hard-core, alternative anarchist commune in Meziprostor; at the Greenbelt Art, Faith and Music Festival near Kettering, Northamptonshire; at The Wild Goose Festival, a story-driven, faith-inspired gathering in Hot Springs, North Carolina; at the Surrender Conference at Belgrave Heights, Victoria, encouraging people to be committed to radical, incarnational mission; in the ancient San Pablo del Campo Monastery in Barcelona; in a contemporary monastery at Ngatiawa, New Zealand; in a new monastic conference in Kloosterboeredrij, the Netherlands; in the new monastic community The Simple Way in Philadelphia, Pennsylvania; in an underground seminary in Yangon, Myanmar; in the basement service

229.. Australia, New Zealand, Canada, the United States, England, Scotland, Wales, Holland, Germany, Switzerland, Poland, Spain, Austria, Armenia, the Czech Republic, Uganda, Kenya, South Africa, Afghanistan, Pakistan, India, Nepal, Sri Lanka, Myanmar, Cambodia, Thailand, Malaysia, Singapore, Hong Kong, the Philippines and Papua New Guinea.

at St. Andrew's Anglican Church, South Brisbane; in a wee Baptist Fellowship in Perth, Scotland; in a small Baptistengemeinde in Steyr, Austria; in the charismatic Westside Vineyard Church in Santa Monica, California; in the colorful Kuki Congregation in New Delhi; in the home-grown Srijanna Church in Kathmandu; in the venerable Münster Cathedral in Basel; in the Blackburn Cathedral in Lancashire, the Bradford Cathedral in West Yorkshire and the Coventry Cathedral in West Midlands; outside on the steps of St. John's Anglican Cathedral in Brisbane; in a Muslim Youth Camp on Mount Tamborine, Queensland; in the Muslim Training College in Cambridge; in the Masjid Al Farooq in Kuraby, Logan; in the Apex Mosque in Raleigh, North Carolina; in the Islamic Center of Boston, Massachusetts; in the Omar Moschee in Wiesbaden, Germany; and in the grand London Central Mosque in Regent's Park, London.

No matter how many different places I have preached, I have always preached the same message. When I first realized this, I felt embarrassed. Other people preach about many things, but I only preach one thing. I have only one word to say, and that is "Jesus." Yet over time I realized that I shouldn't feel embarrassed, because Jesus himself was only "one word—the "One Word" that counted most in God's conversation with the world. My task is not to preach many words, but to preach this "One Word" with enough fervor and power "to awaken the dead."

The Christmas of 2018, I remember preaching the "one word" Jesus at the Srijanna Church in Kathmandu. My adopted Nepali daughter, Navi, has a birth sister named Uma, who with her husband, Hemraj, and their son, Uhem, lead a Nepali congregation, which sits sedately on the floor, hour after hour (the service is four hours!), and then gets up to sing and dance with gusto from time to time.

It was great to see Hemraj, who is the senior pastor, choose to play a humble role behind the scenes, welcoming people at the door, making sure people had a place to sit, and seeing that everyone else was feeling comfortable, rather than being up front where everyone could see him. Hemraj only receives petrol money from the church to do visitation, and so he supplements his income by delivering the *Rising Nepal* newspaper early each morning from 4 to 8 AM as a radical worker-pastor.

Because it was Christmas, I spoke to this first generation of Christians, who were all from Muslim, Hindu and Buddhist backgrounds, about our celebration of Jesus, the Christ.

I began by asking them what was so enchanting about Jesus that he became the most well-known, well-loved human being who has ever lived.

I told them that the Hindus I know have great regard for Jesus and how Mahatma Gandhi said, "The gentle figure of [Jesus] Christ—so patient, so kind, so loving, so full of forgiveness he taught his followers not to retaliate when struck, but to turn the other cheek—was a beautiful example of the perfect person."[230] I quoted the Dalai Lama, who said, "Don't compare me with Jesus. He is a great master."[231] He also said, "As a Buddhist, my attitude toward Jesus Christ is he was a fully enlightened being—a [true] *bodhisattva* [who aids others to enlightenment]."[232]

I said that the Muslims I know also have great regard for Jesus and quoted Ahmad Shawqi, who said, "Kindness, chivalry and humility were born the day Jesus [Christ] was born. His coming brightened the world, his light illuminated it, like the light of the dawn flowing through the universe, so did the sign of Jesus flow. He filled the world with light, making the earth shine with its brightness. No threat, no tyranny, no revenge, no sword, no raids, no bloodshed did he use to call to the new faith."[233] I also quoted Khalid Muhammad Khalid, who said, "Jesus was his message. He was the supreme example he left. He was the love which knows no hatred, the peace which knows no restlessness, the salvation which knows no perishing."[234]

I told them that I honor Jesus because he wanted to make the love of God manifest on earth as it is in heaven.

I said that I honor Jesus because he envisaged the world as a "kingdom of heaven on earth," where the meek would "inherit the earth" (Matt. 5:5), those who gave mercy would "receive mercy" (Matt. 5:7), the hungry would be "filled" (Luke 6:21), those who hungered and thirsted for justice would be "fulfilled" (Matt. 5:6), those who mourned would be "comforted" (Matt. 5:4), those who had wept bitterly would "laugh" happily (Luke 6:21), the peacemakers would walk proudly as "sons and daughters of God" (Matt. 5:9) and all who were pure in heart, regardless of their religion, "would see God" (Matt. 5:8).

I honor Jesus because he advocated heaven as a way of life that people could experience here and now, on earth, in this life as well as the next, saying "yours *is* the kingdom of heaven," so take it and make it your own, teaching us to pray, "May your kingdom come, may your will be done on earth as it is heaven," every day (Matt. 6:10).

230.. Gandhi, *The Message of Jesus,* Foreword.

231. http://bit.ly/2ivTxMua.

232. http://bit.ly/2yybdSv, 83.

233. Shawqi, *Al-Shawqiyyat,* Vol. 2, 12.

234. Khalid, *Ma'an 'ala-l-Tariq: Muhammad wa-i-Masih,* 188–189.

I honor Jesus because he embodied heaven on earth for people whose lives were hell on earth. The Pharisees said with scorn, "This man welcomes sinners," but Jesus said to those who were weary, bearing the terrible weight of public disapproval, "Come to me, all you who are weary and burdened, and I will give you rest" (Luke 15:2; Matt. 12:28). Jesus brought real healing to the sick, disabled and distressed, restoring their broken bodies and their battered souls. One evening, "after sunset the people brought to Jesus all the sick and Jesus healed [them]" (Mark 1:32–34).

I honor Jesus because he especially loved the people no one else really loved. He demonstrated a compassion for people that was more powerful than his concern for himself, his own comfort or his own safety. When confronted by a man with a sickening case of leprosy, Mark says that Jesus was "moved with compassion . . . stretched out his hand," and literally touched the untouchable (Mark 1:41). He touched a man that everyone else in his society was too scared to touch, and so followers of Jesus, all around the world, still seek to touch in his name the men, women and children in our society that others are too scared to touch.

I don't just preach the gospel *about* Jesus, I preach the gospel *of* Jesus.

I remember being invited to speak to a convention of Aussie evangelists who had been preaching "the gospel" in city malls and on street corners round Australia for twenty, thirty, forty years or more. I asked the organizers whether they really thought I was the right person for the gig. After all many people would not consider me an evangelical, let alone an evangelist. They assured me that they thought I was the right person for the job, and so I accepted the invitation.

I began my presentation by asking the evangelists to tell me, given their years of preaching "the gospel," how they would define "the gospel" they preached.

They were all ready with ready-made answers. "The gospel is accepting Jesus as our Savior." "The gospel is repenting of our sins." "The gospel is being justified by faith." "The gospel is being washed in the blood of the Lamb." "The gospel is being born again." On and on they went, one after another, articulating their classic biblical evangelical answers to the question.

When they finished, I said, "Two things are clear. One is, you know your Bible, and all your answers to the question I asked are unquestionably biblical. Two, not one of you has answered the question the way that Jesus would have."

I went on to say that, as far as I was concerned, Jesus would have said, "The gospel is the kingdom of God."

From day one of his ministry, Jesus announced the alternative future that he imagined as the "gospel of the kingdom of God" or the "gospel of the kingdom of heaven." While Matthew primarily uses the term the "kingdom of heaven" and other Gospel writers use the term the "Kingdom of God, the meaning is the same.

The main message of Jesus was not being "born again," which is mentioned only twice in one Gospel, but the kingdom of God / kingdom of heaven, which is mentioned more than seventy times in the four Gospels. Jesus came saying, "The time is fulfilled, the kingdom of God is at hand, repent and believe the gospel"(Mark 1:14–15).

Jesus never tries to define the "kingdom of God," but he describes it in many ways so that we can experience it, whether or not we understand it completely.

Jesus explains the divine society he imagines as the "kingdom" through his *parables*. Many of us know what it is like to feel lost, but Jesus says that the kingdom is wherever a good shepherd finds the sheep that are lost, and whenever lost children find themselves in the arms of a loving parent who gladly welcomes them and happily restores their broken and battered souls (Luke 15).

Jesus explicates the divine society he imagined as the kingdom through his *relationships*. Jesus advocates a kingdom of friends for all who are friendless. The Pharisees said with scorn, "This man welcomes sinners," but Jesus says to those who are weary, bearing the weight of disapproval, "Come to me, all you who are weary and burdened, and I will give you rest" (Luke 15:2; Matt. 12:28).

Jesus elucidates the divine society he imagined as the kingdom through his *responses*. Jesus advocates a kingdom of dreams that come true, where there is real healing for the sick, disturbed and distressed. One evening after sunset the people brought to Jesus all the sick and Jesus healed [them]" (Mark 1:32–34).

Jesus exemplifies the divine society he imagined as the kingdom over against the empire through his active, radical, alternative *practice*.

Following John the Baptist, *Jesus denounces the exploitation of the poor by the rich*. John told the armed forces, "Don't extort money and don't accuse people falsely—be content with your pay." He told the tax collectors, "Don't collect any more than you are required to." He told his followers, "The man with two tunics should share with him who has none, and the one who has food should do the same" (Luke 3:11–14). Similarly, Jesus confronts Zacchaeus, an infamous tax collector, personally about his extortion. As a result of this encounter, Zacchaeus promises to give "half of my possessions to the poor" and "if I have cheated anybody out of anything, I will pay back four times the amount." Then Jesus says, "salvation has come to this house" (Luke 19:8).

Jesus advocates for the liberation of disempowered groups of people through the empowerment of the Spirit. Jesus attacks the key religious leaders of the day as "lovers of money" who maintain a façade of sanctity by saying long prayers in public, but "devour widows' houses" (Luke 16:14–15). When Jesus sees a widow "put everything, all she had to live on," into the collection box, he condemns the temple for extorting the last coin from the kind of person it was set up to protect (Mark 12:38–44). Jesus breaks up the monopoly on forgiveness that the temple developed through the sacrificial system that it controlled. He baptizes people in the Spirit and gives them the authority to forgive sins, saying, "Receive the Holy Spirit," and "if you forgive anyone his sins, they are forgiven" (John 20:22–23).

Jesus promotes countercultural communities that will be led by people who will serve the people rather than oppress them. Jesus encourages people to liberate themselves from captivity to the political economy by developing compassion for people that will transcend society's sick, obsessive and compulsive preoccupation with power, position and property. "God is compassionate," Jesus says. "Be as compassionate as God" (Luke 6:35–36). He denounces all oppressive forms of politics and affirms charismatic leadership that is based on experience and exercised within a decision-making framework that functions according to group consensus. Rather than having the bosses call the shots and the heavies throw their weight around, Jesus says, "That is not the way we are going to operate. Whoever wants to be the leader of a group should be the servant of the group" (Matt. 20:25–26). He renounces all exploitative forms of economics. He expects generosity and teaches that wealth should be freely shared by the rich with the poor in an earnest quest for genuine equality. He teaches his followers to "Be on your guard against all kinds of greed" (Luke 12:15) and to "give to everyone who begs from you, and do not refuse anyone who wants to borrow from you" (Matt. 5:42) and to "lend, expecting nothing in return" (Luke 6:35).

Jesus creates communities that are committed to doing justice to the marginalized and disadvantaged. The dominant value of much of Jewish society at the time was purity, but the dominant value of Jesus is inclusivity. While the Jews despised Gentiles, Jesus declares, "my house shall be called a house . . . for all nations" (Mark 11:17). While the Pharisees ostracized sinners, Jesus invites outcasts to his parties (Mark 2:16). In his countercultural communities, Jesus encourages people to consider other people to be of enormous importance—not just as producers or consumers, but as people in their own right. The people that were usually considered the least important and so were consequently pushed to the side in Jesus' day were treated as the most important and given a place of respect in these countercultural communities. Jesus says, "When you give a luncheon or dinner, do not invite your friends, your brothers, [sisters, relatives, or rich neighbors]; if you do, they may invite you back and you will be repaid. But when you give a banquet, invite the poor, the crippled, the lame, the blind, and you will be blessed. Although they cannot repay you, you will be repaid at the resurrection of the righteous (Luke 14:12–14).

The counter-cultural communities that Jesus developed never smashed the political economy to which their society was captive, and they never completely reconstructed the political economy, though they prayed for its total liberation. Yet they did break some of the mechanisms of control, and they did manage to reconstruct a liberated—and liberating—alternative political and economic reality, to the degree that their experience has served as an example of true love and true justice ever since. According to eyewitnesses, they all met together, breaking bread in their homes and eating together with glad and jubilant hearts. They had everything in common, selling their possessions and giving support to anyone who asked for help. There wasn't a single person with an unmet need among them, and all the people spoke well of them (see Acts 2:44–47; 4:32–35).

Jesus demonstrates active, radical, sacrificial nonviolence that will free people from cycles of violence and counter violence. He says,

> I am the good shepherd. The good shepherd lays down his life for the sheep. The hired hand is not the shepherd who owns the sheep. So when he sees the wolf coming, he abandons the sheep and runs away. Then the wolf attacks the flock and scatters it. The man runs away because he is a hired hand and cares nothing for the sheep. I am the good shepherd . . . and I lay down my life for the sheep. All who ever came before me were thieves and robbers. I am the gate; whoever enters through me will be saved. He will come in and go out, and find pasture. The thief comes only to steal and destroy; I have come that they may have life, and have it to the full. (John 10:8–18)Jesus turns to his friends and says, "Greater love has no one than this, that he lay down his life for his friends" (John 15:13).

Under his guidance, the Jesus movement became an active, radical, sacrificial peace movement.[235] For three centuries, Christianity remained more or less a pacifist movement. The Apostles taught Christians the pacifist principle: "Love does no harm to its neighbor" (Rom. 13:10). Paul taught Christ followers to "Bless those who persecute you; bless and do not curse.

235. Stassen and Gushee, *Kingdom Ethics*, 152.

Do not repay anyone evil for evil. Be careful to do what is right in the eyes of everybody. If it is possible, as far as it depends on you, live at peace with everyone. Do not take revenge" (Rom. 12:14–19). On the contrary, "If your enem[ies] are hungry, feed [them]; if [they] are thirsty, give [them] something to drink. . . . Do not be overcome by evil, but overcome evil with good" (Rom. 12:20–21).

Every time I preach about the love of God revealed in Jesus, the voice of an old friend reminds me that I can't preach about the love of God revealed in Jesus authentically without practicing the love of God revealed in Jesus myself.

Inspiring through Teaching

Because of my passion for the gospel of Jesus and for seeking to incarnate the kingdom of heaven on earth, albeit imperfectly and partially and ephemerally, I have always had an interest in radical spirituality, liberation theology, incarnational missiology and faith-based and inter-faith community development.[236]

The most well-known formal course that I have taught is called "Compassionate Community Work." The inner dimension of this course is a church-based, Christ-centered, community-orientated spirituality. The outer dimension of this course is the Australian National Training

---

236. I have studied at the University of Queensland, completing a Bachelor of Arts in 1971 (in literature, history and psychology), a postgraduate Diploma of Education in 1972 (including educational psychology), a postgraduate Diploma of Social Planning in 1981 (including social analysis, social change, social planning, sociology of development, and community development), and a Master of Social Welfare, Administration and Planning in 1985 (with a thesis on our intentional community in New Delhi, India, which explored the possibilities of personal growth and social change in the context of a state of despair). I simultaneously studied externally for a Master of Arts at Fuller Seminary, focusing on the study of anthropology, missiology and theology.

The most useful formal community development training I have received was at the Department of Social Work and Social Policy at the University of Queensland, where I was privileged to get what I consider to be the best formal community development education available in Australia under the guidance of Dr. Allan Halladay, who was Head of the Department, and Mr. Tony Kelly, who was the Senior Lecturer in Community Development.

I have taught in many formal educational institutions, both secular and religious, including Griffith University, University of Queensland, Queensland University of Technology, Bremer and Southbank Colleges of Tertiary and Further Education, Christian Heritage College, Brisbane College of Theology, Queensland Baptist Theological College, Bible College of Queensland, and Australian College of Ministries and Praxis in New Zealand.

Authority's community development knowledge, skills, principles, practices and competencies.[237]

In 2006, I published *Compassionate Community Work* as a religious training manual, but then in 2007, I published a generic version of the same course called *Living Community*.[238] Though *Living Community* uses the same framework as *Compassionate Community Work*, I rewrote it for a general audience and describe soul-centered community work rather than Christ-centered community work. *Living Community* advocates for a spiritual approach to community work that is truly open to God and establishes the practice of prayer at the heart of the community work process, but it is intentionally inclusive for people from all religions. Instead of referring to the parables of Jesus, as I do in *Compassionate Community Work*, I refer to the stories of Paulo Coelho, which are contemporary tales with nonsectarian, universal appeal.

Alongside this formal training, I have developed informal training options in situ for small groups in local communities, using community education processes and incorporating flexible content that is prepared by practitioners to create co-learning communities that will test their learning through action and reflection in the context of ordinary, everyday life.

Some time ago, as part of a reform process in Queensland after the famous "Fitzgerald Inquiry" into police corruption, I was asked to teach a course for law enforcement officers. In order to respond to the culture of corruption in the police service, which had been brought to light by the inquiry, *transformation* rather than *information* was supposed to be at the heart of this course. Through the course, the participants were encouraged not only to discuss and debate issues of personal integrity and social justice, but also to develop a commitment to personal integrity and social justice themselves.

237. I've also taught courses on Perspectives on Community, Community Practice, Community Work, Community Welfare, Community Service, Christian Community Work, Interfaith Community Work, International Community Work, Mission, Mission Aid And Development, Community Development Practice, Community Development Practitioners and Compassionate Community Work. I have taught this course for Christian Heritage College, Brisbane College Of Theology, Queensland Baptist Theological College, Bible College Of Queensland, Australian College Of Ministries and Praxis (New Zealand). And in 2006 the content of the Compassionate Community Course was published by Piquant Editions in Carlisle, England as well as EFICOR in New Delhi, India, who printed a cut-price Asian edition, which was distributed around the world through the Micah Network, a global community of over 750 Christian aid agencies, non-governmental organizations, mission associations, educational institutions, local congregations, denominational secretariats, networks, and alliances committed to integral mission, who used the course to teach their workers.

238. Published by Tafina Press and distributed by the Community Praxis Coop.

Though it is easy to *teach* about personal integrity and social justice in the classroom, it is difficult—if not impossible—to *learn* personal integrity and social justice anywhere but the ebb and flow of ordinary, everyday life in the community.

So we invited students from the colleges where we were teaching to come and live in our community for two or three weeks to learn experientially about personal integrity and social justice.

We introduced them to Aunty Jean, an Aboriginal elder, who not only told them the story of her people and their painful dispossession, but also took them with her to meet her people—some in a maximum security prison, languishing in their cells, and others in a human rights organization, fighting for their release.

We also introduced them to Father Kefle, an Eritrean priest, who showed them the scars of thirty years of civil war. They visited refugees who had been torn away from their families, tortured by the very people who were supposed to protect them, forced to flee for their lives and were struggling to rebuild a life for themselves as strangers in a strange land.

Some of the students had never met an Aboriginal or refugee face to face before, let alone heard their stories or seen their struggles for themselves. These encounters confronted the students with questions that we all have to answer one way or another, such as:

How do we, as members of a "white" society, deal with our "black" history? How do we, as members of the human family, respond to the desperate plea from our brothers and sisters, not just to address the superficial symptoms, but the underlying causes, of their ongoing pain? What are you—and I—going to do about it?

These are questions *to us*, which call for answers *from us*—not merely *theoretical* answers, but *practical* answers. Answering these questions is a *moral imperative* that we can either accept or reject, but which we cannot ignore.

One of the students who accepted the moral imperative to answer these questions as honestly as he could was a cop I'll call Brad, who had been on the beat for many years.

Like a lot of police, Brad had only ever related to people either as sources of information about "criminals" or as potential or actual "criminals" themselves. He had become quite cynical about the public. But when he took the opportunity to get out of uniform and to meet the people he'd stereotyped face to face, as fellow human beings, he began to *change*.

The first stage of change was *perspective*. What we *see* depends on *where* we stand. Standing with the very people that Brad and his fellow officers had often been expected to take a stand against helped him to see a different side to the struggle on the streets than he'd seen before.

The second stage of change was *responsibility*. What we *hear* depends on to *whom* we listen. Listening to the very people to whom Brad and his fellow officers normally didn't listen helped him not only to hear a different side of the history of our society than the story he'd heard before, but also helped him to accept his part as a police officer in perpetuating that history.

The third stage of change was *pain*. How we *feel* depends on what we *do*. Recognizing that what Brad and his fellow officers were doing was often part of the problem rather than part of the solution helped Brad feel the impact of the issues much more acutely than he'd ever felt them before.

The fourth stage of change was *responsiveness*. We have two options for managing the *pain* that comes from recognizing the gap between who we are and who we are meant to be. One option is *rationalization,* where we try to *change the ideal* so that it is closer to who we are. The other option is *transformation,* where we try to *change the reality* so that we draw closer to who we are meant to be.

The chance for Brad to choose *transformation* rather than *rationalization* came along one day quite unceremoniously when a local *murri* asked him for a smoke. Instead of moving on as he usually did, Brad chose to stop and have a smoke and a bit of a chat, just as he would have done with any of his other mates. This *small* change was a *big* deal for Brad.

Brad was in this fourth stage of change when he completed the course. I spoke to him about how encouraged I was about the changes he had gone through so far, but I cautioned him, saying that it would all be in vain unless he continued to take the change a stage further.

The fifth stage of change is *practice*. We are what we do *repeatedly.* Transformation, then, is not one act, but the *habitual practice of personal integrity and social justice.*

My friend Andy Pratt, who was a policeman for 28 years in the UK and the former Chief Superintendent National Community Tension Team, suggests we need to make four *changes in structure* of the police service to encourage such an ongoing *change in practice.*

Firstly, communities need to recruit police based on a demonstrable history of honesty and empathy. Secondly, community members need to constitute the majority of members on recruiting panels for the police service, so the recruits are clear that as police they are working *for* the community. Thirdly, police need to get out of their cars and walk and/or cycle around the community in which they are located in order to develop relationships with people in the community and learn to do policing that is not just *for* the people but *with* the people in the community. And fourthly, people in the community need to intentionally develop respectful reciprocal relationships with the police, so the police feel supported *by* the community and feel responsible *to* the community. Such changes can transform policing.

Inspiring Mobilization

People tend to get involved in movements when they get excited. We can get people excited either through *manipulation* or *motivation*. *Manipulation* involves imposing our vision upon others and pulling their strings to get them to do what we'd like them to do. *Motivation* involves exploring a vision we share with people and tapping into their passion for what they'd like to do to in order to make their dream come true.

We need to develop training approaches that are *motivational* rather than *manipulative*. There are a range of *motivational processes* that we can use to help people explore their vision of community and help them tap into their passion to make their dream come true.

Articulate Vision

The first process is helping people to *articulate their vision*.

Articulating our vision is a vulnerable process in which we reveal the desperate hopes we hold dearly in the deepest parts of our hearts.

I remember how scary it was for me to own my vision. It seemed too romantic, too idealistic, too unrealistic—and more like Martin Luther King Jr.'s than my own. But for better or worse, it was what it was, and I needed to own it, both privately and publicly.

> *I dream of a world*
> *in which all the resources of the earth*
> *will be shared equally between all the people of the earth,*
> *so that even the most disadvantaged among us*
> *can live with dignity and joy.*

> *I dream of a great society*
> *of small communities cooperating*
> *to practice personal, social, economic,*
> *cultural and political integrity and harmony.*

> *I dream of vibrant neighborhoods,*
> *where people relate to one another*
> *genuinely as good neighbors.*

*I dream of people developing networks of friendship
in which the private pain they carry deep down
is allowed to surface and be shared in
an atmosphere of mutual acceptance and respect.*

*I dream of people understanding the difficulties they have,
discerning the problems, discovering the solutions,
and working together for personal growth
and social change according to an agenda of
sustainable justice and peace.*

Every time I share this vision with other people I feel very self-conscious, but I have found that if I am prepared to disclose *my* dream, others will normally be willing to share *theirs*.

In an atmosphere of acceptance and respect, it's easy to get people talking about their vision for the ideal kind of community that they would really like to live in themselves.

COMMUNICATE VISION THROUGH STORIES

The second process is helping people to *communicate their vision through stories.*

Stories are the best way for people to share their vision. Stories are inclusive. Different people can apprehend them at different levels, both intellectually and emotionally. Stories are also inspirational. They put soul into the body and flesh onto the bones of our airy-fairy dreams.

One of the stories that I love to tell people is about Ronnie and Leon.

Some time back, a loud fight broke out next door, but before I could move, my neighbor Ronnie sprang into action. Ronnie called out to the angry, young man next door, whom we'll call Leon, "Leon, Leon! What's going on in there? Tell me what's going on in there!"

But there was no reply, only the pathetic sound of crashing and screaming, as if bodies were being knocked about the place. Ronnie suspected Leon might be beating up his elderly parents, so he rushed through his house, out the front, and around to the neighbor's house, where he started banging on the front door and demanding a response. "Leon!" Ronnie cried. "Come here! I want to speak with you!"

Again, there was no reply, but the sounds inside the house began to subside, and somebody opened the door. As soon as the door opened, Ronnie walked straight in. While Leon hurled his fists about to prevent Ronnie from interfering in the fight, Ronnie calmly strode up to Leon, put his arm around his shoulders, and carefully ushered him out of the house.

After Ronnie had taken Leon around the block a few times, Ronnie brought him over to join Ange and I on the verandah. While I spoke with Leon, Ange went over to speak with Leon's mum and dad about what could be done about his abusive behavior in the future.

As I sat there sipping my cup of tea, sharing a plate of biscuits with Leon, I reflected on the events of the evening. It hadn't turned out as I expected and was far more traumatic than I had imagined, but it was also far more momentous than I had imagined.

People like Ronnie make community a reality in our locality. They assume responsibility for the welfare of their neighbors because they don't project the responsibility to help onto anyone else. They understand that in a crisis, responsibility requires action. They don't prevaricate, but act promptly and appropriately. As a result of their action, they minimize the damage that we do to one another.

Whenever I tell a story like this, other people soon pitch in with their stories of people they know who make the dream of community a reality in their locality. Every story people tell encourages others to believe that the dream is *not* an impossible dream. Every story people hear encourages them to believe that they, *too,* might be able to make the dream come true!

Demonstrate Vision in our Lives

The third process is helping people to *demonstrate the vision in their own lives.*

It's pretty easy to get people talking and swapping stories about their vision for community. The hard part is helping them to clarify their values, check that they are consistent with the principle of generalized reciprocity and commit themselves to incorporating those values into their lives.

It may be hard, but deep down, we all know that we need to *demonstrate* the values we advocate in our own lives. It is only as we demonstrate those values in our own lives that we can prove that it is possible to live them out in our own locality.

One night, I was walking down the street and came across a man being attacked by a couple of hoods, who were stabbing him with the jagged shards of a broken bottle. His face was covered in blood, and his hands, which he was using to protect his face, were also badly cut and bleeding.

At first, I thought, if someone doesn't do something soon, this bloke could be cut to pieces. I looked up and down the street, but no one else was around. I knew I it was up to me to do something myself, but, I must confess, I was tempted to just to walk on by, to pretend that I hadn't seen anything that needed my intervention.

I was afraid, terribly afraid, and my fear was well founded. There were two men across the road trying to kill someone, and if I tried to help, chances were that I could be killed, too. After all, there were two attackers and only one of me. They looked like street fighters, and I looked like the wimp that I was. I had no weapon, and I wouldn't know how to use one even if I had one, and they had shards of sharp glass, which they were wielding as menacingly as the grim reaper might have swung his scythe.

But I knew it was time for me to act, so I wrapped the tattered rags of my makeshift courage around me, and, with trembling hands, wobbly knees and a heart ringing like an alarm bell, I crossed the road to intervene. I didn't rush over and try to crash-tackle the assailants. That only ever works in the movies—and even then, it doesn't work all the time. I simply approached slowly until I was about ten meters away from the melee and said, from a safe distance, the most inoffensive thing I could think of, which was, "g'day."

The antagonists immediately turned my direction. Now that I had their attention, I tried to distract them from further hurting their victim, but the trick was to do it without them harming me. So I asked, in as friendly a tone as I could muster, "Can I help you?"

The aggressors looked at one another, then at me, and laughed as if it was a big, bloody joke. "Does it look like we need any help?" they asked. "No," I said very carefully. "It doesn't look like *you* need any help, but it looks like *he* might need some help. What d'you reckon?"

By now, they had stopped stabbing their prey and just shrugged their shoulders. "Well *you* help *him* then!" they said, and with that, they walked off and left me to care for the mutilated man on the side of the road. He was seriously injured, but he was still alive—and so was I.

Talk is cheap. Actions speak louder than words. There comes a time when all of us have to stop *telling* stories and start *living* the stories in our own lives.

CULTIVATE VISION IN LIVES OF OTHERS

The fourth process is helping people to *cultivate the vision in the lives of others.*

We can *cultivate* the vision in the lives of others by *articulating*, *communicating* and *demonstrating* the vision of community we have in our own lives and then *inviting* others to participate in the community we are developing.

One of the people I decided to invite to get involved with us was a kid named Dean, who lived in a local hostel and had thick glasses, spiky hair and empty gums. Dean had started his life behind the eight ball—a little kid who had cycled through an endless round of foster homes and special schools, been knocked about a lot by big, merciless blokes and constantly felt completely snookered.

At the age of eighteen, Dean was placed in a Linden Court, where I remember meeting him, because the only way Dean knew to express his emotions at that time was to thump people, and he was apparently so glad to make my acquaintance that he almost killed me.

Since that time, Dean and I have become quite good mates. We share a passion for Rugby League Football and are very passionate supporters of the Brisbane Broncos, whom Dean and I reckon are probably the best Rugby League team in the world. We regularly go out together with a bunch of friends to have a barbecue in a park down by the Brisbane River, and Dean has been known to drag me into a game of touch footy now and again, which is really too fast for an old fella like me.

Not long ago, my brother-in-law sadly lapsed into an episode of psychotic despair and jumped off the Story Bridge, which spans the Brisbane River, tragically killing himself. Needless to say, I was devastated. When I told everybody at church how devastated I was, I noticed Dean, standing in the back of the room, listening intently to me. Suddenly he made his way to the front, where I was standing, and stood beside me, put his arm around me, quietly waited until I had finished what I was saying, then gave me a huge hug and said, "Don't worry, Dave. I'll be your brother-in-law."

I'll never forget his unpretentious gesture of care, which was a sign to me that my dream of our locality becoming a community of people who really cared for one another was coming true.

CELEBRATE THE REALIZATION OF THE VISION

The fifth process is helping people to *celebrate the realization of their vision.*

Everyone who feels inadequate needs help to realize their capacity to act. Everyone who feels afraid needs help to realize their courage to act. Everyone who feels impotent needs help to recognize the potential of their actions. Everyone who feels insignificant needs help to recognize the consequences of their actions.

We can do this by commemorating every act of truth as a victory over lies and every act of love as a victory over hatred, by consecrating every act of justice as a victory over brutality and every act of peace as a victory over bloodshed, by celebrating every risk a person takes to make a stand—no matter how small—as a victory in the battle for light against the darkness.

As I have already said, each Sunday night at half-past-six, Ange and I have met with a large bunch of people from all over our neighborhood in the basement of St. Andrew's Church.

Many of the people who gather on Sunday nights are physically, intellectually or psychiatrically challenged and live in extraordinarily difficult, life-controlling social, economic and political circumstances—but we all come together to celebrate life and faith.

One of the locals you would have met if you came to St. Andrew's one night would be Kay Irwin. Kay used to go out of her way to greet everyone who came through the door at St. Andrew's with the words, "Hi. My name is Kay. I do dialysis." Kay had a life-threatening kidney complaint and had been waiting for a kidney transplant, in vain, for years, and so three times a week, she had to go to the local hospital to "do dialysis" as a matter of life and death.

But even though Kay's life revolved around dialysis, she used to "do dialysis" in style. She was upfront about her struggle and wore the scars on her arms as badges of honor. She challenged people to join her in hospital while she was doing dialysis by saying, "if you've got the guts." Until the moment she died, Kay somehow managed to transform her struggle into a sacrament for others, selling raffle tickets to raise money for kidney research and drawing funny cartoons to give her fellow sufferers a bit of a belly laugh.

If we are to keep going, we all need to celebrate every single breath we take and every single step we make—just as Kay Irwin did—and we need to encourage those around us to do the same.

Inspiring Conciliation And Collaboration

After 9/11 I went to visit the local mosque. I had never been to the mosque before and was quite nervous. I said to the Imam, "I'm not a Muslim, I'm a Christian, but we both belong to the same Abrahamic family of faith, and in the face of the upcoming propaganda storm that threatens to tear us apart, I would like to show my solidarity with you publicly by praying with you this Friday." And so that Friday, I went to the local mosque to pray.

I looked for what Jesus called "a person of peace," a counterpart with whom I could work to rebuild the bridges of communication between our communities, which the extremists on both sides were blowing up. It didn't happen quickly, but Jesus says, "seek—and keep on seeking—and you will find." Eventually, after six years, I found Nora Amath, who had been an Australian Muslim woman of the year, and she invited me to join AMARAH, the Australian Muslim Advocates for the Rights of All Humanity, which she and her friends had started.

From that point on, I began to partner with Nora. In terms of our Christian-Muslim engagement, we decided that we would do everything that we could together, and we would never do anything on our own that we could do together with others. One of the first interfaith events we organized was a mixed gathering of Christians and Muslims to come together over an evening meal during Ramadan to learn from one another how our respective traditions understood the role of prayer and fasting as a spiritual practice. This required a radical reversal of the usual way many people engaged in interfaith dialogue, because we were expected to listen and learn from one another rather than lecture and correct each other.

Together, Nora and I have tried to arrange as many authentic, empathic and appreciative interfaith engagements as we could. Sometimes our meetings have been a debacle, such as the time we went to an Anglican church to talk about "How Christians and Muslims Can Live in Peace" and were met by an angry mob with clenched fists wrapped in Aussie flags, demanding through gritted teeth for Aussies to "Resist Islam." On that occasion, all we could do was pray for grace to absorb their hostility and animosity. Other times, our meetings have been a miracle, such as the time we went to a Pentecostal church to talk about "How Christians and Muslims Can Live in Peace" and were greeted with a barrage of searching questions, and at the end of the session, the senior pastor walked down the aisle to the front of the church, knelt at Nora's feet and asked her to forgive him for his prejudice. On that occasion, all we could do was rejoice in a miraculous triumph of grace over bigotry.

Since then, we've trained Christian and Muslim young people in nonviolent conflict resolution and organized Christian and Muslim leaders to come together to stand against the scapegoating of Muslim women in Queensland. On one occasion, we were talking with some of our Muslim friends, and while they were talking about how one member of the community wearing a *hijab* (or scarf) had been attacked in the street, and another member of the community wearing a *niqab* (or veil) had been stalked and then assaulted in her own home, and another member had been abused by a complete stranger who threatened to run her over in his car, the phone rang with another report of an unprovoked attack on a vulnerable Muslim woman in Logan. So Nora and I organized Christian leaders from various denominations who were concerned about the recent attacks to come to the Kuraby Mosque and publicly stand in solidarity with the Muslim community. A group of twenty Christian leaders from many denominations (Anglican, Catholic, Orthodox, Lutheran, Quakers, Waiters, Churches of Christ, Salvation Army, Uniting Church and Wesleyan Methodist) came from around Logan City and South East Queensland, where the attacks had occurred. The Muslim community breathed a sigh of relief, and I even saw a few friends weep, to hear Christian leaders say, "We are all people of faith. An attack on any of us because of our religion is an attack on all of us. All of us have the right to feel safe on our streets and in our homes. All of us have the right to practice our faith freely without fear. We appeal to every member of our community to stop this harassment, stop these attacks, stop this climate of suspicion." There was widespread media coverage, which sent the message of solidarity loudly and clearly.

Nora and I have both been involved in faith-based aid agencies. Nora is involved in Islamic Relief, Australia, and I was involved in TEAR Australia, a Christian international aid agency. Some time ago we started a conversation between these faith-based aid agencies about how we could help each other use our respective sacred texts as a resource to educate our constituencies to move beyond alms as charity in order to work systemically for justice and peace.

Since then I have been able to also connect with Adis Duderija, a brilliant progressive Muslim scholar, in the Brisbane chapter of Spiritual Progressives in Australia. Under his guidance, I have prepared training materials for Muslims in South Asia about how to respond constructively to troubling incidents in their communities and how to develop mutually respectful relationships with non-Muslim leaders and mutually beneficial partnerships with non-Muslim organizations.

I have written four books that are helpful materials for meaningful interfaith engagement between Christians and Muslims: *Bismillah, Isa, Ramadan* and, most recently, my most controversial book, *The Jihad of Jesus: The Sacred Nonviolent Struggle For Justice.*

The Jihad of Jesus is a handbook for reconciliation and action, a do-it-yourself guide for all Christians and Muslims who want to move beyond the "clash of civilizations," join the *jihad* of Jesus and struggle for justice and peace nonviolently, side by side. The key messages of the book are:

- We are caught up in a cycle of so-called "holy wars."

- Though this inter-communal conflict is endemic, it is not inevitable.

- Depending on our understanding, our religions can either be a source of escalating conflict or a resource for overcoming conflict.

- In order to be a resource for overcoming conflict, we need to understand that the heart of all true religion is open-hearted, compassionate spirituality.

- In the light of an open-hearted, compassionate spirituality, we can reclaim *jihad* from extremists, who have (mis)appropriated it as "holy war," and reframe it in *Qur'anic* terms as a "sacred nonviolent struggle for justice." We can also reconsider Jesus as he is in the Gospels—not as a poster boy for Christians to fight crusades against Muslims, but as a strong-but-gentle Messianic figure, who can bring both Christians and Muslims together.

- Indeed, many Christians and Muslims have found Jesus and the *Bismillah* he embodies as common ground upon which they can stand together and work for the common good.

I have been advocating for our strong-but-gentle *jihad* all around the world.[239] Some time ago Bob Shedinger and I took part in a conference of the IONA (Islamic Organization of North America) as special Christian guests among roughly a thousand Muslims. Bob and I had never read one another's writings, but we had both published books on the same topic at the same time with the same publisher, and we were invited to launch our books together at the conference. Bob's book is *Jesus and Jesus: Reclaiming the Prophetic Heart of Christianity and Islam*. Bob and I both presented copies of our books to Imam Abdul Malik Mujahid, one of the most influential Muslim leaders in the world, who currently serves as the chair of the Parliament of World Religions. Imam Siraj Wahhaj, a black American Muslim, who is Imam of Masjid al-Taqwa in Brooklyn, called on conference participants to remember the example of Dr. Martin Luther King Jr and to engage in *jihad* "without violence, without violence, without violence." And IONA has published a helpful booklet by Ahmad Afzal called *Jihad Without Violence*.

While Ange and I were in Europe in 2017 we had some special encounters with Muslim leaders in Holland and Poland. *The Jihad of Jesus* was translated into Dutch by Arjaan Hijmansvandenbergh, and Ange and I were pleased to be at the launch of *De Jihad van Jezus* at a gathering of Christian and Muslim leaders that was organized by the publisher in the

239. Including Australia, New Zealand, the United States, England, Scotland, Wales, Holland, Germany, Switzerland, Poland, Spain, Austria, the Czech Republic, Uganda, Kenya, South Africa, Afghanistan, Pakistan, India, Nepal, Sri Lanka, Myanmar, Cambodia, Thailand, Malaysia, Singapore, Hong Kong, the Philippines and Papua New Guinea.

Doopsgezind Seminarie in Amsterdam. I presented the core message of a call to a sacred, nonviolent struggle for justice in the Anabaptist seminary in a room adorned by a small statuette of Menno Simons—the great Anabaptist advocate of nonviolence and one of my heroes—sitting across from me on the mantelpiece, witnessing my attempt to continue the tradition.

I presented a copy of *De Jihad van Jezus* to Mostafa Hilali, a Muslim leader of Moroccan origin, who is the founder of #nietmijnislam or #Not-MyIslam I told Mostafa that I, too, believed we are called to hear the cry of the oppressed and to be willing to intervene to protect the vulnerable against violence. I said that I thought direct nonviolent intervention was the most loving way to do that, because it is least likely to incite further cycles of violence and counter-violence. However, I also said that nonviolence should never be used as an excuse for nonintervention, and if the only intervention people can envisage to protect the vulnerable in a particular set of circumstances is violent, it is better to use violence to intervene than to use nonviolence as an excuse not to intervene. We talked about that for a while.

As you can imagine, our different approaches to *jihad* made for a very interesting, exciting and entertaining interaction. You might assume that these differences led Mostafa to reject the approach I advocate in *The Jihad of Jesus* completely, but they didn't. Rather, Mostafa kindly, warmly and enthusiastically thanked me for my positive construction of *jihad* and for bringing the concept of *jihad* and the example of Jesus back together for Christians and Muslims to consider.

While we were visiting the Islamic Centre of Wroclaw, Poland, which is the largest Islamic center in Lower Silesia,[240] we met Polish Muslims and a bunch of Indian, Pakistani and Bangladeshi expat Muslims, whom we bantered with in broken Urdu. Ange and I, along with two Polish friends, Piotr Lorek and Krzysztof Slabon, were special guests of Imam Ali Abi Issa and his wife, Iwona, and we got to have a great conversation with them about Christianity, Islam, interfaith dialogue and *jihad*. It so happened that Imam Ali's doctoral thesis was a critique of the concept of "offensive *jihad*," so over a wonderful *Eid* dinner we got to talk about "defensive *jihad*" and the nonviolent "*jihad* of Jesus." It was a beautiful meeting of head, hearts and hands. Before we left, I was able to present the Imam with a poster of *Our Nonviolent Struggle*,[241] which he said he would be more than happy to frame and hang on the wall of the Islamic Centre. We parted, with much hugging, like long-lost friends who'd met again, for the first time, after many years.

---

240. There has been a continuous presence of Muslims in Poland since the fourteenth century, when many Tatars settled in the Polish-Lithuanian Commonwealth.

241. See the poster on the website http://www.jihadofjesus.com/#welcome

While Ange and I were in Europe in 2018, we had some special en-counters with [242] Muslim leaders in Germany and Switzerland. *The Jihad of Jesus* was translated into German by Florian Hoenish, and Ange and I were pleased to be able to be at the launch of *Der Jesus Dschihad*, which was or-ganized by the publisher, Kai Scheunemann, on two consecutive nights. The first was in an evangelical church in Eschborn-Niederhöchstadt, and the second was in the Omar Mosque in Wiesbaden. Sixty to seventy people at-tended each night and engaged in great conversations about how Christians and Muslims can come together and work for justice and peace.

In Switzerland, I addressed a large, mixed gathering of reformed and evangelical Christians and Muslims from all around Basel at the historical hall of the Cathedral of Münster, which is one of the most significant sites in the city. The event, which was organized by Christian Schneider, was a full house, with more than two hundred citizens of Basel turning up to listen to and enthusiastically discuss "A Nonviolent Way Out Of Conflict Between Christians and Muslims," which I presented with the help of Birgit Krom-bach, who did a brilliant job of translating. Kerem Adigüzel, a well-known, Swiss-Turkish progressive Muslim theologian, was kind enough to conclude the evening by sharing his reflections on *The Jihad of Jesus*.

The next morning, Ange and I and our hosts, Stephan and Monika Thiel, had breakfast with Kerem, with whom we have become close friends, and then we all went to a special showing of the film *The Imam and the Pas-tor* for a great mixed group of Muslims and Christians in an old industrial hall, which the International Christian Fellowship has turned into a large but welcoming warehouse church. A well-known local Imam, Mohammed Tas, kindly made some introductory remarks before the film and then an-swered questions after the film. As anyone who has seen the documentary will surmise, the story inspired the hitherto cautious crowd to risk sharing their journeys of faith deeply and personally with one another. At the film, we met a wonderful family (whom I cannot name for safety reasons) who had been forced to flee Turkey because of their opposition to the increas-ingly Islamist politics of President Recip Tayyip Erdoğan. This family had come from Izmir, which is the same city that Ange's grandmother, Sophie, came from (though at that time it was known as Smyrna). Meeting this fam-ily was like having a reunion with close relatives we hadn't seen in a long time—such a lovely, joyful, extended family get-together.

242. *Eid al-Fitr*, also called the "Festival of Breaking the Fast," is a religious holiday celebrated by Muslims worldwide that marks the end of the month-long dawn-to-sunset fasting of Ramadan.

We conducted our *Jihad of Jesus* tour of England in 2018 as a kind of rolling series of interfaith conversations around the country, inviting a British Muslim conversational partner to join us in order to embody the spirit of dialogue we were advocating. We couldn't have hoped for a better conversation partner than Julie Siddiqi, who was honest, authentic and assertive, yet sensitive. Right from the start, Ange and I, along with the other members of the organizing team (Catriona Robertson and Andy Turner), felt an immediate rapport with Julie, who is a mentor, consultant and activist with a focus on social action, gender issues and Jewish-Muslim relations. She has a background in community grass roots work that spans twenty years, and she founded a local charity for Muslim women's needs that she led for ten years, gaining an acute knowledge of the personal challenges faced by women. Julie was listed in the *Times'* 100 Most Influential Muslim Women in the UK in 2009, and she was previously a member of the government's National Muslim Women's Advisory Group. Julie was also the executive director of the Islamic Society of Britain from 2010–2014. She is chair of her local standing advisory council for religious education and sits on the national "Anti-Muslim Hatred" working group as an independent member. She has spoken on many major news programs, including BBC Radio 4 and "Newsnight," the Christian festival, Greenbelt and the Jewish festival, Limmud.

We started our *Jihad of Jesus* tour of England at the famous London Central Mosque in Regents Park, London. The Board of Trustees of the centre is comprised of the Muslim ambassadors and the high commissioners to the Court of St. James, which reflects the cohesion and positive spirit that is present in their community. The role that the trustees play is of paramount importance in helping to foster an environment that is open to all cultures and backgrounds. The Islamic Cultural Centre has many objectives and roles as it is involved in the religious, cultural and social life of London and the UK. Chief among them is to promulgate an understanding of Islam as a religion of peace, tolerance and coexistence

The public meeting we held at the London Central Mosque was organised by Catriona Robertson from the Christian-Muslim Forum and hosted by the director-general, Dr. Al Dubayan, and Peter Bennetts, the Mosque's interfaith manager. My conversation partner, Julie Siddiqi, was brilliant in dealing some very discourteous comments from a Christian in the audience, who had come on a mission to the London Central Mosque to discredit Islam. We were grateful that the overwhelming majority of the other people in attendance were more interested in developing a deeper understanding of one another through meaningful dialogue.

In the middle of our *Jihad of Jesus* tour around England, we were invited to a private meeting with the staff and students of Cambridge Muslim College, which is dedicated to training Islamic scholars, leaders and imams for the UK. The meeting was hosted by a world-renowned Islamic scholar, Shaykh Abdal Hakim Murad (Dr. Timothy Winter) and Shaykh Ibrahim Mogra. Speaking with a college full of brilliant, educated, articulate Islamic scholars, leaders and imams in training provided us with a fantastic opportunity to have animated exchanges of faith-based ideas, but the college also provided us with a wonderful opportunity to have more intimate, vulnerable, and heartfelt conversation about our faiths. A young female scholar wearing a *niqab* told us about how she had been abused on the street that very morning by a woman wearing a crucifix, and how our evening together was lovely experience of healing for her personally.

On our *Jihad of Jesus* tour of England, we also held three wonderful interfaith meetings in three cathedrals: Blackburn Cathedral, Bradford Cathedral and Coventry Cathedral. The *Jihad of Jesus* Christian–Muslim encounter at Bradford Cathedral was organized by the Ali Amla and Catriona Robertson from the Christian Muslim Forum amidst serious threats of disruption from Robert Spencer, a key figure of the "counter-jihad" movement in the United States, and Tommy Robinson, infamous for his involvement with the English Defence League in the United Kingdom. However, it was a great evening, with one hundred and fifty Christians and Muslims participating in a wonderful atmosphere of reflective, interfaith engagement that began with Waseelah Smedley, a local Muslim vocalist-pianist, singing her inspiring songs. This was a perfect setting for Julie Siddiqi and I to share the message of *The Jihad of Jesus* and to hear an in-depth, critical-yet-appreciative response by Imam Saleem Seedat, who advocated for the nonviolent approach to *jihad* developed by his fellow Gujarati, Mahatma Gandhi, another of my heroes. In the *Jihad of Jesus* Christian–Muslim encounter that we held at Coventry Cathedral, one Christian man told Julie that she had changed his view of Muslims, and one Muslim woman thanked her for encouraging her to learn more about Jesus. Julie said, "Well, that's a job done, isn't it?" I nodded.

PART 3

THE PARADOXICAL

Ever since I can remember, I have been desperate to be righteous, but have been painfully aware of my unrighteousness. One day, in my late teens or early twenties (I don't remember exactly when), I decided to lock myself in an empty house, fast and pray for a month, vowing not to come out of the house until all my thoughts, feelings and actions were in total alignment with God's will for my life.

I fasted and prayed and fasted and prayed some more—for thirty days and thirty nights. When I emerged from my suburban hermitage, I noticed that I had definitely become more intense, intent, focused and committed than ever before, but unfortunately, I had also become more self-conscious about my hard-won, superior virtuousness. When I met my friend, Mike, he saw it straightaway and called it for what it was. My very best efforts to become a truly, totally, completely "righteous" man had only resulted in my becoming what he now correctly labeled "a self-righteous bastard!"

THE DELIGHTS OF RIGHTEOUSNESS

As I said, I have always aspired to be righteous. I was brought up by my pastor-father to believe that God was *dikaios*. (My father used to like quoting the Greek and then translating it into English. I guess it showed respect for the text. It also earned him respect from the congregation, who couldn't access the original text for themselves.) Anyway, according to my dad, saying God is *dikaios* is saying that God is "righteous," which means that God is essentially good, fair, reasonable and just—always committed to doing the right thing by everybody. And, my dad would say, because we are "made in the image of God," we are all expected to be good, fair, reasonable and just—always committed to doing the right thing by everybody ourselves.

My dad preached that it was possible for us to be righteous because God's endlessly, relentless, prevenient and proactive grace was more than enough to empower us to be good, fair, reasonable and just, regardless of how many mistake we may make. We were created good (Gen.1:31) to be good (Matt. 5:48) and to do good (Matt. 6:33). God's guidelines for our behavior are "not burdensome" (1 Jn. 5:3), for his "yoke is easy" and his "burden is light" (Matt. 11:29). God is very clear about this. He says, "what I am commanding you is not too difficult for you or beyond your reach. No, the word is very near you; it is in your mouth and in your heart, so you may obey it" (Deut. 30:11–14).

My dad would say that God gives his people choices that have life and death consequences. If we practice righteousness, it will result in prosperity and salvation. If we practice unrighteousness, it will result in tragedy and destruction. God says, "I have set before you life and death. . . . Now choose life, so you and your children may live!" (Deut. 30:15-19).

There are many great figures of righteousness in the Old Testament, but the one who inspired my growing imagination was Joseph, the kid with "his coat of many colors," who was sold into slavery by his family, but who rose to become vice regent in Egypt, "doing the right thing by everybody," even by those who had betrayed him along the way. Holocaust survivor Elie Wiesel says that as far as the Jews are concerned, "Abraham was obedient; Isaac was brave; Jacob was faithful; but only Joseph was just." He says that Joseph—and Joseph alone—"among all our ancestors is called a *Tzaddik*, a "Just Person," an "Example of Righteousness." "He assumed his destiny and tried to give it meaning from within. He lived his eternal life in the here and now, demonstrating that it is possible for a slave to be a prince, for the dreamer to link the past to the future, and for the victor to open himself to the supreme passion that is love." Thus he "transformed exile into a kingdom, misery into splendour, and humiliation into mercy."[1]

As for those who identify more with the New Testament than the Old Testament, claiming "not to live under the law, but under grace," Paul asks, "Shall we sin because we are not under law, but under grace?" (Rom. 6:15). His resolute answer to this question comes down to us through the centuries as he cries, "Never! . . . Your body should be an instrument of righteousness" (Rom. 6:15, 13). Peter fully affirms this by saying, Christ "bore our sins in his body upon the cross, so that, free from sin, we might live for righteousness" (1 Pet. 2:24). And the author of the letter to the church at Ephesus writes, "For we are what he has made us, created in Christ Jesus for good works, which God prepared beforehand to be our way of life" (Eph. 2:10).

In spite of the difficulties I've faced along the way, it has been a delight for me to seek to live a life-affirming, life-fulfilling, life-giving righteousness. Unfortunately, it has not always been as delightful for many of the people around me.

THE DANGERS OF SELF-RIGHTEOUSNESS

Jesus encourages people to be "righteous" (Matt. 5:6). In fact, he consistently challenges ordinary people to be "more righteous" than the Pharisees—the "most righteous" people of his time (Matt. 5:20). He says that the problem with the Pharisees is that they "*clean* the *outside* of the cup but *inside* [they] are full of wickedness" (Luke 11:39). Jesus wants people to be "pure"—or *clean*—"in heart" (Matt. 5:8).

1. Wiesel, *Messengers of God*, 155, 156, 182.

The word Jesus uses for "pure"—or *clean*—"in heart" is recorded as *katharos,* which is also used to describe "winnowed" wheat and "unadulterated" wine. This word suggests that one's motives should not be mixed. Jesus says that it is essential for anyone who really wants to be righteous "*to clean the inside of the cup*" thoroughly (Matt. 23:26). "Be *perfect,*" he says, "as your heavenly Father is *perfect*" (Matt. 5:48).

For better or worse, I am a strong, resourceful, assertive person. My ancestors are Scots on both sides of my family, and I'm told that our Scottish family motto is *mak sikkar!* or "make sure!" So when I hear the challenge of Jesus to be "perfect"—to be "more righteous" than the "most righteous" person I know—I am inclined to martial my determination (in all its never-say-die bloody-mindedness) to *mak sikkar,* or "make sure," that I "winnow"—separate—what is "wheat" from the "tares" in my world.

At my best, this means that I can decide to lock myself in an empty house, fast and pray for a month, vowing not to come out until have sorted through all my thoughts and feelings to make sure that my actions will be in alignment with God's will for my life. At my worst, this also means that I can emerge from my suburban hermitage as a more intense, more intent, more focused, more committed "self-righteous bastard," ready to rip into any unsuspecting people I encounter about their inexcusable "unrighteousness."

In trying to understand how my quest for healthy, holy righteousness has often morphed into unhealthy, unholy self-righteousness, I have found the Enneagram very helpful as a tool for critical reflection. This ancient tool has its origins in Judaism, Christianity and Islam and explores different personality types based on their orientation towards certain predispositions. Seven of the nine personality types are based on what the Desert Fathers might have called our dispositions towards the "seven deadly sins." I have found the Enneagram particularly helpful in the way it guides me not only to identify the deep, hidden, secret motivations associated with my personality, but also to identify a way forward that can help me monitor, manage and ameliorate the destructive aspects of the unconscious motivations inside me.[2]

2. Now, before we proceed any further in unpacking the Enneagram and its implications for me, let's be clear about what the Enneagram is and what it isn't. First, the Enneagram "is not just a personality typing system. Yes, there are tests that help you identify your primary Enneagram type, but that is often just the first step. This tool is meant to help us over a life-long journey." Second, the Enneagram "is not a strict law or code. Its categories are not meant to bind us to a certain way of being." Certainly, some people who only know a little bit about the Enneagram "think its about putting people into boxes," but it "actually works to free people from their self-created boxes." Third, the Enneagram is not a static system. It is "a dynamic system that recognizes that humans are far too complex to fit easily into simple categories; it supports the

According to the tests I took to identify my personality type, I am an eight in the nine-part personality typology, variously called "a leader," "challenger" or "confronter." This is no surprise for anyone who knows me. And, of course, it perfectly fits the archetypal persona of a "prophet." "Confronters" like me have a need to be strong, robust and resilient. We value having a sense of control, and we use our capacity to confront those who try to control others, engaging in a never-ending quest for justice in which vulnerable people are respected, protected and supported. We tend to be powerful and capable of influencing society, independent (open to being inter-dependent, but opposed to being co-dependent), decisive (quick to act or react, for better or worse), assertive (saying what we mean and meaning what we say) and protective (we defend the rights of those in our care).[3]

In a group, "confronters" like me tend to think about where the power resides. We "want to know the truth" and are "only comfortable if the truth comes to light in a conflict situation" so that we know how to confront the situation. The more information or "intelligence" we "have about progress, updates and what is going on, the more [we can] focus on the bigger picture." In fact, people like me "don't like getting involved in the detail," as our "preference lies in working on the big picture." We tend to be more concerned about vision, mission and accomplishment than others. We don't like being charmed, cajoled or compelled to do something we don't want to do. People like me are essentially "intense," which is likely to come across through "the way [we] speak, [our] choice of words, and body language." When we feel exasperated with power plays in a group, we "tend to be quick to anger and then channel this anger into action." We also "tend to believe almost any action is better than doing nothing at all." We are equally quick to justify our actions. After all, we express our respect for people through our commitment to protect and support them. Thus "when people under [our] care are being treated unjustly," we "will pursue justice and will actively work to correct wrongs."[4]

However, because "confronters" like me tend to be "decisive" and quick to act or react, "other people [who] may need a lot more time to get

---

evolving, maturing human journey." Fourth, the Enneagram is a "tool for self-reflection and spiritual transformation. But it shouldn't be our only tool. The Enneagram is most helpful when used in conjunction with other practices like study, meditation, spiritual direction, and life in community with others." Fifth, "while self-discovery is important, it is not the Enneagram's final objective. The Enneagram's purpose is to help us uncover the traps that keep us from living fully and freely as our True Self so that we will use our unique, authentic gifts for the good of others and the world." This is why I have chosen to use the Enneagram myself.

3. https://bit.ly/2m7cJFK

4. https://bit.ly/2m7cJFK

the big picture and decide what to do about it" may feel hurried, rushed, and pushed aside. "When people are unable to assert themselves," we tend to "take charge of situations." We may not like to be controlled, but our "tendency to take control assumes others will comply," which may leave other people feeling manipulated, oppressed and exploited. Moreover, because we are essentially intense, our "energy is often stronger than [we] realise." We are often not "aware of how intimidating [we] may seem to other people." People "may feel threatened," even when we are trying to "hold back" so as not to threaten anyone.[5]

I can remember that on my first trip to the USA I was enjoying participating in a missions conference, when apparently to my surprise some people felt so "threatened" by me they told my hosts they would kill me if I didn't leave immediately. So my hosts had to smuggle me out of the hotel through the rear entrance of the car park in the trunk of their car. Like most Aussies, when I got back home I was tempted to shrug it off by saying "Only in America would someone threaten to shoot you at a missions conference!" But the sad fact is that people who have felt "threatened" by me have said they would kill me in Australia too.

Most "confronters" like me function at various times at different levels along a continuum, from healthy (with Mother Teresa and Martin Luther King Jr.) to unhealthy (with Joseph Stalin and Idi Amin).[6]

When I reflect on my life in light of this framework,[7] I can see distinct characteristics of my conduct at all different levels, from healthy to

---

5. https://bit.ly/2m7cJFK

6. https://www.thechangeworks.com/images/Famous.pdf

7. Healthy Levels: Level 1 (At Their Best): Become self-restrained, mastering self through their self-surrender to a higher authority and becoming more magnanimous and merciful towards others. Courageous, willing to put self in serious jeopardy to achieve their vision and have a lasting influence. May achieve true heroism.

Level 2: Be decisive, authoritative and commanding: the natural leader others look up to. An honourable champion, carrying others with their own strength.

Level 3: Be self-assertive, self-confident and strong: learning to stand up for what they need. A resourceful "can do" attitude with a passionate inner drive.

Average Levels

Level 4: Be self-sufficient, an enterprising, pragmatic, "rugged individualist." Risk-taking, hard-working, making sacrifices to accomplish their goals.

Level 5: Be dominant, wanting to feel that others are behind them, supporting their efforts. A forceful, boastful, egocentric "boss" whose word is law.

Level 6: Be belligerent, combative and intimidating in order to get their way. Using threats to keep others off balance and to get obedience from them.

Unhealthy Levels

Level 7: Be completely ruthless, dictatorial, "might makes right." An immoral, potentially violent criminal, defying any attempt by anyone to control them.

Level 8: Be totally deluded about their importance and power. An arrogant

unhealthy. On the one hand, I can see how I have been "courageous, willing to put myself in serious jeopardy to achieve my vision," "decisive, authoritative and commanding, . . . [a] natural leader," "an honorable champion, carrying others with my own strength" of conviction, a "self-assertive, self-confident and strong resourceful man" with "a 'can do' attitude and a passionate inner drive, standing up for what is needed" as well as a "risk-taking, hard-working person, making sacrifices to accomplish my goals." On the other hand, I can also see how I have been "deluded about my importance," "dominant, wanting to feel that others were behind me, supporting my efforts," "defiant of attempts by anyone to control me," and "belligerent, combative and intimidating."

THE DELUSIONS OF SELF-IMPORTANCE

I was brought up to be "a *great* man of God." When I was a boy I would often go forward to the alter call in an evangelistic service on a Sunday night in our Baptist Church. And each time I went forward the elders would pray that I would grow up to be "a *great* man of God." When I became a young man I dreamed of becoming a missionary and made the motto of William Carey, our most famous Baptist missionary, my own. It reminded me to: "Expect *great* things from God; attempt *great* things for God." Hence I dreamed of *greatness*.

One day I imagined my moment for *greatness* had come at last. I'd got a phone call from the International Red Cross asking me if I was interested in playing what was probably a minor part in a project they were involved with supporting peace negotiations between Israel and Palestine. Because of my delusions of grandeur I immediately interpreted this minor part they were asking me to play as a potentially major part in the Middle East peace process. In my mind I could already see a picture of my face on the cover of *Time* magazine under the headline: "Dave Brings Peace To The Middle East!"

I was so excited had I held my hand over the mouthpiece of the phone and called out to Ange in the kitchen: "Ange, the Red Cross want us to go to help bring peace in the Middle East! Shall we go?" And she said a straight out "No."

I thought she must have not grasped what a *great* opportunity this was for *me, my ministry, my destiny*. So I called out to her: "Hey this a *great*

---

megalomaniac, feeling invincible and recklessly over-extending themselves.

Level 9: (At their worst) Become vengeful, brutally destroying everyone who refuses to conform to their will. Antisocial Personality Disorder.

opportunity to make a *great* contribution to history." And she said a straight out "No" again.

So I said to the Red Cross person waiting patiently on the phone for my reply: "Thanks for the invitation. It's a *great* idea. I'll talk to my wife about it and get back to you."

I put down the phone, walked into the kitchen and asked Ange: "How could you possibly pass up on such a *great* opportunity." After all, I said, "It's what we were made for. It's what people have prayed for." Then she said something to me I will never forget. She said, "Dave, they will always find plenty of people who want to do *big* jobs like that. But who will do the *little* things that need to be done in our community if we don't?"

I was gob smacked. I retired to our bedroom to seek some solace in the scripture, secretly hoping to find some proof text I could find to reprove her. But for better or worse I came across these verses in *Philippians* chapter 2 verses 6 to 8:

> Each of you should not look to your own interests, but also to the interests of others. You should all have exactly the same attitude as Christ Jesus had: For he who had always been God by nature, did not cling to his prerogatives as God's equal, but he stripped himself of all privilege, emptied himself, and made himself nothing, in order to be born by nature as a mortal. And, having become a human being, he humbled himself, living the life of a slave, a life of utter obedience, even unto death. And the death he died, on the cross, was the death of a common criminal.

Paul says the path Jesus took was not *great*. To the contrary, it essentially involved consciously setting aside any aspirations to *greatness* along the way. Paul points out, that as the story goes, Jesus moved in alongside people, as one of them. He did not try to be different. He lived the same life that other people lived, experiencing the same hassles and the same hardships as everybody else. Jesus wasn't full of himself. Rather, emptying himself, he immersed himself in the lives of others, allowing their concerns to fill his consciousness. In the midst of their common struggle, Jesus made himself available to the people as their servant, seeking in all he said and did to set them free to live their lives to the full. And when it came to the crunch, Jesus did not cut and run. He was prepared to pay the price for his commitment to the people in his community - in blood, sweat, and tears.

It seemed to me Paul was saying that people like me, who say we want to follow in the footsteps of Jesus, need to empty ourselves of our ambition *to do big things, as "great men and women of God"* - so we can make time and space to *do the little things that need to be done with a lot of love over the long haul,* "*as little brothers and sisters of Jesus.*"

I remember plaintively asking God: "Don't you have any big plans for me at all?" And in a voice that sounded a lot like Ange, I heard Him say straight out "No. None at all." So that was that. I knew I needed to empty my mind of my delusions of grandeur about being a *great man of God* in order to be able to embrace my call to be a *little brother of Jesus.*

THE NEED TO SEE MY OWN BLIND SPOTS

In reflecting on all of this, what has concerned me most are my blind spots: those aspects of my behavior that I have become blind to because of my own self-importance and self-righteousness. All too often, I haven't been able to see how being "decisive," so quick to act or react, has left "other people," who "may need a lot more time to get the big picture and decide what to do about it," feeling hurried, rushed and pushed aside. All too often I haven't seen how "when people were unable to assert themselves," I tended to "take charge of situations," "taking control in a way that left people feeling manipulated, oppressed and exploited." All too often I haven't seen how the intensity of my "energy was stronger than I realised" and how "intimidating I may have seemed to other people," who "felt threatened" by me, even when I was, consciously and conscientiously, trying to "hold back" so as not to threaten anyone. Thus it has been crucial for me to spend quite a bit of time critically reflecting on a series of incidents that have revealed the serious blind spots in my way of engaging the world.

One of my blind spots was the way that I used to "witness" to other kids in school.

At my fiftieth year school reunion, I happily remember Tony Salecich telling everyone that I had given him his first Bible when he was at school with me, how it had changed the course of his life, and he had subsequently gone on to become the chaplain of Brisbane State High School.

But I also sadly remember when I was "witnessing" in King George Square at the heart of Brisbane years ago, and I noticed a young man who seemed interested in what I'd been saying. I made by way over to him and introduced myself.

He said, "You don't recognize me, do you?"

Embarrassed, I responded, "You look familiar. Where do I know you from?"

He said, "You should know me. I was in your class at school."

"Yes," I said as his face and name gradually reconfigured in my brain. "I remember now. You're Michael"

"Yes," he said. "You're Dave. And you're the reason I don't believe any of this bullshit!"

I was staggered and took a step back. But I wanted to stay in engaged. "Why?" I asked.

And then he said something that still fills me with shame to this day. "Because you always tried to convert me, but you never really cared for me."

Another of my blind spots was the way I used to confront people in the church.

While I was studying at university, I used to live at the Baptist Theological College, and as I've said before, I used to preach at Baptist churches around town with a bunch of up-and-coming zealous preachers from the Baptist college. Any dispassionate observer would probably have given us 100 percent for sincerity, but 0 percent for sensitivity.

I remember a time a friend and I were booked to preach at a church. As was our custom, we both prayed during the week leading up to the church service, with the expectation that whoever received a "word from the Lord" would be the designated preacher. But neither of us got a "word" during the week. We didn't even get a "word" on the day itself, either driving in the car on the way to church or during the service, leading up to the sermon. So when it came time to preach, we got up, filled with self-righteous indignation, and told the stunned congregation that we had waited "on the Lord" for a "word" and there wasn't one. This was not because we had been negligent in our preparation, but most probably because they hadn't listened to a previous "word" that the Lord had given them. We told them that when they obeyed the word they had already been given, the Lord would no doubt give them another word, but until then it would be a waste of breath. Having said that, we sat down. As you can imagine, all hell broke loose at the end of the service.

Another of my blind spots was the way I used to resolve conflicts with others.

When I first looked back on the part I had played in the clash with YWAM that left me excommunicated, I couldn't recollect anything I'd done wrong. I could only remember the things I'd done right. I'd stood by my commitment to *Dilaram* and, consequently, taken a strong stand against a corporate takeover that threatened to destroy the community. I'd listened to a lot of "little" people, who were being hurt in the process, and I'd spoken up on their behalf to the "big" people, who were trampling their feelings underfoot. I'd resisted the inducements that were secretly offered to me in a bid to buy me off, and I'd fought a gallant fight in a losing battle for the sake of the liberty and the equality in which I believed.

However, in hindsight, some of my 'heroic' actions were rather less than that. No doubt my words and my deeds were well intentioned, but I think that in the heat of the debate, when my blood was up, many of the things I said and did must have been very insensitive and unnecessarily hurtful. Over time, I have come to understand that the insensitivity I displayed in the situation with YWAM was no accident, but the inevitable outcome of my tendency to be preoccupied with ideology (just holding the line) rather than love, which can extend kindness (while holding a line) to both friend and foe alike.[8]

Another blind spot was the way I used to approach incarnational mission.

When Ange and I got married we resolved to make decisions by consensus, and for most of our marriage, we did. At least, for most of our marriage, I *thought* we did. Thus it came as a significant shock to me when, after some years, Ange said to me that she had never agreed to many of the decisions we had made together. When I talked with her and tried to figure out why she felt this way, it became clear that, even though Ange and I always made decisions together, I tended to dictate the speed of the decision-making process, which left Ange, who needed to make decisions more slowly, feeling hurried, rushed and pushed into decisions prematurely.

One anecdote that illustrates how my "fanatical" approach to "sacrificial involvement" left Ange feeling that she had "suffered unnecessarily" is the story of the motorbike and the fridge. When Ange and I lived in *Aashiana* with Indian friends, we tried to have a standard of living that was similar to the standard of living for our Indian friends. Since most of our friends didn't have a fridge, we decided not to have a fridge. But over the years, as each successive summer brought the searing heat that left our fridge-less fresh food rotten, Ange suggested we revisit our decision about the fridge. Each year, I vetoed the decision in the name of "sacrificial involvement," which I said meant "sacrificial identification" with our friends who had no fridge. Then one year, when I vetoed the decision to get a fridge in the name of "sacrifice," it was too much for Ange. She asked me why I could have a motorbike, but she couldn't have a fridge. I answered that I needed the motorbike for my "ministry." She countered by saying that she needed a fridge

8. Andrews, *Christi-Anarchy*, 7–8.

for her "ministry." Then she said something I will never forget. She said that if I was radically committed to sacrificial involvement and identification, I shouldn't sacrifice something that was important to her, but should sacrifice something that was important to myself. She said that for me to take something that was important to her and sacrifice it was not radical, but hypocritical. As you can imagine, I sold the motorbike and bought the fridge. This was the obvious solution to the problem, but for years, I had been so blinded by my own "fanatical" self-righteousness that I shamefully couldn't see the obvious.

Another blind spot was the way I used to approach evangelical proclamation.

Before Ange and I went to India, I studied apologetics. I believed that Christianity was the "true truth," as Francis Schaeffer—a prominant evangelical apologist of the time—once famously claimed. Thus my task as a missionary was to witness to the "true truth" claims of Christianity over against the "false truth" claims (i.e., lies) of other religions, including Hinduism, Buddhism and Islam. The presuppositional apologetic approach that I was taught to take in relating to other religions was to expose the unreasonable presuppositions upon which other religions were based (e.g. the non-dualism of Advaita Vedanta Hinduism), unpack the unrealistic implications of those unreasonable presuppositions (e.g. without duality, there could be no morality, no right as opposed to a wrong) and then present Christianity (or at least Schaeffer's version of a dualistic neo-Calvinism) as the only reasonable, realistic way to righteousness.

You can imagine how dangerous this technique was in the hands of someone as self-righteous as me. I wielded this tool like a sword, thinking of it as "the sword of the spirit," which was "sharper than any two-edged sword, piercing until it divides soul from spirit, joints from marrow; able to judge the thoughts and intentions of the heart" (Heb. 4:12). For someone as combative, dominating and intimidating as me, the conflict between competing truth claims was a credal, zero-sum game, a win-lose clash of civilizations. I won a lot of arguments, but also did a lot of damage, often needlessly, heedlessly and publicly shaming many beautiful and sensitive souls who were nurtured in the bosom of honor-shame cultures.

DEVELOPING UNSELFCONSCIOUS RIGHTEOUSNESS

In my quest for righteousness, I have discovered four stages: stage one is "unconscious unrighteousness," stage two is "conscious unrighteousness," stage three is "self-conscious righteousness" and stage four is "unselfconscious righteousness."

My "unconscious unrighteousness" stage involved a "blissful ignorance" or a witless naiveté in terms of my moral contradictions. My "conscious unrighteousness" stage involved a "painful realization" or critical encounter with my moral contradictions. In reaction to my "conscious unrighteousness," I developed a "self-conscious righteousness," which morphed into what could only be referred to as "pure arrogance" about my self-assured moral resolution. The move from the "pure arrogance" of my "self-consciousness righteousness" stage to the "modest congruence" of "unselfconscious righteousness" has been very difficult for me. My hope has been that I could become more oblivious to my individual contributions to a collective moral resolution to "act justly, love mercy and walk humbly with God," but this journey has required what some might describe as a "supernatural intervention" in answer to the heartfelt prayers of all the victims of my arrogant self-righteousness.

In reflecting on my life, I have often heard a quiet voice within me say, "What does it 'prophet' a man if he gains the whole world and loses his own soul?" (Matt. 16:26). "You're hurting people you say you want to help. You need to stop confronting others with their contradictions and start to confront yourself with your own." Hey, "why do you see the speck in your neighbor's eye, but do not notice the plank in your own eye? Or how can you say to your neighbor, 'Let me take the speck out of your eye,' while the plank is in your own eye? You hypocrite, first take the plank out of your own eye, and then you will see clearly to take the speck out of your neighbor's eye" (Matt. 7:3–5).

In my quest for righteousness, I have to constantly confront my own self-righteousness. These days, instead of focusing on righteousness in myself, I focus on righteousness in others, for others and with others. I focus "on what is true and pure and right" in others and act on "what is good, holy, healthy, and helpful" for others and with others (Phil. 4:8). I seek to validate, celebrate and collaborate with the righteousness of the Spirit that is manifest in "love, joy, peace, patience, kindness, goodness, faithfulness, tolerance and self-control" and can be found in inspirational people of all religions—and also in those with no religion (Gal. 5:22).

TRANSITIONING FROM A CONFRONTER TO A CARER

Interestingly, the transition from confrontation to caring is exactly the movement that the Enneagram suggests for an eight: moving towards a two, or going from a "leader, challenger, confronter" towards a "helper, supporter, carer." Paradoxically, it seems I didn't need to change anything, but, simultaneously, it seems I needed to change everything.

At one level, moving from being a "confronter" to a "carer" does not require much change, because they have more in common than meets the eye. Both can be extremely compassionate and exceptionally proactive. Both can bring intensity, vitality, magnanimity, generosity and personal interpersonal skills to a situation. Moreover, "both can play the roles of provider, protector, caretaker, and nurturer while denying their own needs," because both "tend to be the strong one in relationships" and "overwork themselves." In one sense, I could make the transition and still be essentially the same kind of person.

However, at another level, moving from being a "confronter" to a "carer" requires much change, indeed. The biggest change for me has been in the way that I relate to people. A "confronter" is *for* people, but *detached* from them, while the "carer" is not only *for* people, but also *attached* to people. A "confronter" tends to *defend* people in his or her care, while a "carer" tends to *befriend* people in his or her care. A "confronter" also tends to be more strong, assertive and direct in dealing with the issues that she or he has with people, while the "carer" tends to be more gentle, attentive and indirect. So making the transition from a "confronter" to a "carer" means that I need to be totally transformed and become a significantly different person than before.[9]

I need to change the way I relate to people, so that I can be really, truly committed to people—not only to defend them, but also to befriend them. I also need to try to be less strong, assertive and direct and seek to be more gentle, attentive and indirect in dealing with the issues that I have with people. Fortunately, I have had a great guide close at hand to help me make this transition. My wife, Ange, is a classic "carer."

THE TRANSFORMATION OF A PROPHET

I have had a growing realization that I can no longer play the role of a "prophet" in the same way. In becoming a "caring" prophet rather than a "confronting" "prophet," I am committed to playing roles that are more those of a practitioner and inspirator—energizing, encouraging, empowering and equipping—and less those of an interrogator and protester—criticizing, censuring, convicting and condemning.

9. https://www.enneagraminstitute.com/relationship-type-2-with-type-8

A Transformed Way of Engaging Individuals

These days, whenever I am in a confronting situation, I remind myself of the dangers that are inherent in confrontation, and I try to remember that it is crucial for me to show care when I am least likely to do so. In the nanoseconds between action and reaction, I process my response through my version of the Jesus Prayer, which is, "Jesus. Savior. May I know your love. And make it known." Versions of the Jesus Prayer have been prayed by the Greek and Russian Orthodox for centuries, and over the past century, it has been rediscovered by contemplative Catholics and Protestants.

In the stress of my interactions, I often inaudibly ask the Spirit to put me in touch with the Spirit of Jesus. I breathe in and say, "Jesus," and I imagine taking the love of Jesus to heart. Then I breathe out and say, "Savior," and try to let go of all that is contrary to the love of Jesus in my heart. I breathe in again, saying, "May I know your love," sensing the love of Jesus for me. Then I breathe out again, saying, "May I make it known," sensing the love of Jesus for the people in front of me. I do this over and over again, as long as I need to, until I feel the love and let that love transform my response.

Recently, I found myself in a very confronting situation when I reached out to an old friend whom I hadn't met with for years and suggested that we catch up over a cup of coffee. I knew that the meeting would not be without its challenges. My friend, whom we'll call Gordon, is a very strong—some would say strident—conservative pastor, who prides himself on maintaining a strict code of evangelical orthodoxy in his church and vigorously encouraging those who might disagree to go to another church.

After greeting each other, taking our seats and ordering our drinks, Gordon started our conversation by abruptly announcing that he had met with me so he could check up on me and see if I was still a Christian. He then proceeded to go through his checklist for evangelical orthodoxy, asking me whether I believed that all people were sinners, whether I believed they needed to be saved and whether I believed they could only be saved by Christ and the blood he shed on the cross. What I thought would be a conversation had quickly turned into an interrogation. I knew that my answers to those questions wouldn't be exactly the same as his answers to those questions, and I also knew that if I didn't give him the answers that he wanted, he would disavow me, and I would miss any chance I might have to reconnect with him.

What was I to do? I was tempted to confront him about the disgraceful way he was treating me—which, ironically, was not unlike the disgraceful way that I had treated my classmate Michael all those years ago—but I reminded myself of the dangers inherent in confrontation, of the way I might end up mirroring his behavior by being similarly strong, insistent and insensitive. I remembered that if there was going to be any hope of reconciliation, it was imperative for me to show real care for Gordon—even though I felt he was not showing any real care for me—by treating him the way I wanted him to treat me (rather than reacting by treating him the way that he was treating me).

In that holy, liminal space—that precious time between his action and my reaction, in which I needed to be converted again to true care—I listened to Gordon and silently prayed, "*Jesus. Savior. May I know your love. And make it known. Jesus. Savior. May I know your love. And make it known. Jesus. Savior. May I know your love. And make it known.*"

And so it came to pass that I did not react. I did not counter-attack this man who was confronting me—in spite of my propensity to do so and my being sorely temped to do so. I simply answered his questions as carefully as I could, and then I slowly guided the conversation to his wife and family, the lessons he had learned in life, his hopes and plans for the future. And believe it or not, when he began to open up about a difficulty he was facing in his church, he asked me to help him.

I wish I'd been more of a "carer" than a "confronter" when I was younger.

A Transformed Way of Engaging Community

I am so thankful that Ange and I had the chance to have another go at doing residential community together in the Bristol Street Household, where I was able to be more of a "carer." As a result, Ange has described those eighteen months we lived together as "one of the best times of our lives."

What made this experience of community so different from *Dilaram* and *Aashiana* was the part that Ange and I were asked to play in this experiment. One day, our daughters came and asked us to move into their residential community household on Bristol Street on the main street of West End, which they were sharing with Evonne's husband, Marty, their childhood friend, Olivia, and a couple of others. We were rather taken aback that our children were asking us to move in with them. When we consulted other parents, not a single person encouraged us to take up the offer. The typical Aussie opinion seemed to be, "the sooner your children are out of your house the better. You'd be mad to move in with your children by choice." However, Ange and I were overjoyed that our adult children actually wanted us to live with them. When we prayed about it, Ange and I felt a divine nudge to do it.

So we had a talk with Evonne and Navi about moving in with them. They told us we were more than welcome to join them, but we needed to be mindful that we would need to accept three conditions. The first condition was that Ange and I needed to abide by the rules of their household. Fair enough, we said. When they lived with us, we had expected them to live by the rules of our household. The second condition was that Ange and I could change those rules if we persuaded them that they needed to be changed, but on no account were we to use coercion rather than persuasion to try to get them to change the rules. Fair enough, we said. We understood. No one likes coercion. I didn't like it. They didn't like it either. The third condition was that, in order to ensure that Ange and I would not use our position as their parents to coerce them as our children, we would need to commit to a genuine decision-making process by consensus through weekly household meetings that would be monitored by an external supervisor of their choosing. Fair enough, we said. They had every right to set up checks and balances to offset my tendency to take charge of situations and to act quickly and decisively with an "intensity" that people have told me is "intimidating" even when it is being restrained.

As it turned out, this structure not only protected them, but it also protected Ange from being hurried, rushed and pushed by me into decisions she did not want to make. Without the specter of my shadow-side dominating our life together, our time in the Bristol Street Household was delightful. As Ange said, "We got on well. We prayed together, laughed and cried together, cooked and cleaned together, and grew together," devoting ourselves "to developing an everyday spirituality that gladly put itself at the disposal of the people who came to the door of their house looking for help."[10]

A Transformed Way of Engaging a Congregation

These days, as I engage the church, I seek to balance confrontation with care by combining rigorous analysis with a gracious attitude. Most of the clergy I know are aware that I am a Christian anarchist, am opposed to ordination because it is elitist and exclusive of the laity, but am supportive of them as people. A few years ago, my friend Justin Duckworth was appointed as the Anglican bishop of Wellington, New Zealand. I sent him a text that said, "You know I can't imagine Jesus ever wearing purple, but if anyone can bring the spirit of Jesus to this role, you can." He used to say publicly that I was the only one, of all the hundreds of people who contacted him,

10. Andrews and Beazley, *Learnings*, 22–32.

that did not congratulate him. But one of the first things he did as bishop was to invite me to talk to his clergy about how they could minister in their churches with unaffected and heartfelt vulnerability. Justin knew, in spite of my reservations about ordination, that he could trust me to treat his clergy unreservedly well. A few weeks ago, Rev. Dr. Peter Catt, the Dean of St. John's Anglican Cathedral in Brisbane, did the same, asking me to speak to all the deans of all the Anglican cathedrals in Australia about how they could practice the Be-Attitudes in the Beatitudes.

Over the last thirty years, it has been a great joy for me to learn how to engage for change sensitively with my local Anglican church, St. Andrew's in South Brisbane. I wanted to work with a local church, and so as a Baptist, I looked for a Baptist church, but I couldn't find one that was interested in what I wanted to do. So I tried the church nearest my house, which was an Anglican church and had the auspicious name of "St. Andrew's." When I met the rector, John Arnold, I knew I had found a sponsor, for he'd been living in Pakistan when we'd been living in India, and we both spoke Urdu. Like Ange and I, John wanted to develop the inclusive kind of church that the subcontinent teaches people is so important, and so we joined St. Andrew's.

The change I was hoping and praying for at St. Andrew's was that we would become a transformed community—safe, accepting and respectful, where everyone would be treated as special, no matter how dysfunctional their behavior was, and everyone could participate in decisions about matters that were important to them. Our long-term strategy was to transform the hierarchy of the church through mutuality, reframing the inequality in terms of equality one relationship at a time, slowly but surely nurturing a culture of reciprocity.

We began by visiting isolated people in our area. We listened to them tell us about their modest aspirations, such as getting out of the hostel every now and again and having a nice meal with some friends. As a result of these discussions, we decided to start a community meal. Right from the start, the community meal was a shared meal. In fact, some people call it the "share meal" because it is not a welfare event, where others provide for us, but a friendship event, where we provide for one another. Those who have a lot are encouraged to bring a lot. Those who have a little are encouraged to bring a little. But everybody is encouraged to bring something to contribute to the meal, which has become a party for everyone in the area who has been left off everyone else's party list—including some of the most wonderfully fragile and freaked-out characters in the inner city.

When an ABC television crew were doing a documentary on St. Andrew's—based on the undeniable beauty of its building—the church suggested a special segment on the community meal. When the documentary on St. Andrew's featured the community meal as part of the church program, it represented the moment that our informal experiment was formally adopted by St. Andrew's. A little while later, we asked if we could move the community meal onto the church premises, and our request was granted. Some would say that since that day, St. Andrew's has never been the same again.

Ange and I attended St. Andrew's for quite a few years before we saw any significant change. Then one day, about twenty years ago, our minister came to see me. He was scheduled to go away on sabbatical, but had no priest to replace him, so he enquired whether a friend and I would take over the evening service in his absence. Seeing this as an opportunity to bring some of the changes we had been involved with on the periphery into the center of the church, we indicated our willingness to take on the job—as long as we could turn the service into a church event where the people who were already coming to the community meal would feel comfortable. Our minister was more than happy with that, because he wanted the church not only to provide a space for people to have a meal, but also to be a place where people could be at home.

With his approval, we began to transform the service from a fairly rigid form to which very few people in the community could relate into a much more relaxed format where people could feel at home. We particularly tried to change the service so that it would be more meaningful to some of our friends with physical, intellectual and psychiatric disabilities. The service became more personal and relational, inviting participation and tolerating interruptions. We made it more simple and practical, raising issues and sharing responses. We also tried to make it more inspiring and empowering by praying and partying together at church.

When our minister returned from his sabbatical, I'm sure he couldn't believe his eyes, because instead of six people, there were up to sixty people at the service—30 percent of them had a serious disability, but all of them were 100 percent involved, singing and dancing along with the everybody else. If our minister had not supported the change, it would have been difficult, if not impossible, for it to be sustained. But in spite of his misgivings over certain matters—which he spoke to us about, and which we did our best to take into account—he gave the change his blessing, and he let the revolution roll on.

Every Sunday night, our community gathers in the basement of the church. People amble in, in dribs and drabs. Gradually, a motley crowd from around the neighborhood forms into a multilayered circle of humanity. The people that come don't leave their problems at the door. We know our problems are as welcome as we are, so we come with our distress, depression, neuroses, psychoses and schizophrenia in the hope that, together, we can reaffirm our significance as people over and above our problems. We begin by lighting a candle to remind us of the radiance of hope that we have, which shines in the midst of our despair. This sounds very wonderful, but it is often the occasion for a furor, as different people often fight for the right to light the candle. Having settled that dispute, some have so much difficulty lighting the candle without burning themselves that they burst into a sustained bout of profanity as the service begins.

Like other churches, we enjoy singing together, but when we sing, it's like no other church I know. Some of the people that come just love to sing their favorite songs and demand that we sing them every time we meet. Once "Brad" gets started, no one can stop him. He's a human jukebox, with no "off" switch and an endless supply of songs. Some of the people that come can neither hear nor speak, but they pick up on the vibes when we sing, and running to and fro, they make whatever noises they can in order to join in. Once "Ron" got into clapping so much that he didn't quit for the rest of the night. He just kept on clapping right through the songs, sermon, passing of the peace and the closing prayers.

Everyone is encouraged to participate in the service on the assumption that everyone, regardless of our disabilities, has a contribution to make through the service to one another's lives. The first time that "Sally" led the service, she sat in a back seat and spoke so quietly that no one knew what was going on. The second time she led the service, she actually sat in the front, where everyone could see her, but no one could hear her. The third time, she not only sat in the front, where everyone could see her, but she also spoke loud enough for everyone to hear her.

I can never forget the time "Kate" and "Jane" led the service. They are both solo mothers who have suffered the indignity of having their children taken away from them by government authorities, and as a consequence, they have felt quite suicidal at times. Yet never has the gospel been more faithfully proclaimed than it was the night when they spoke about the good news, which is that "though we may be treated like shit, and be tempted to feel like shit, we're not shit. For the love of God can make us feel as if we're as good as gold—as good as gold!"

Through the change at St. Andrew's, the locality is coming to church, and the church is becoming a community. People are finding the confidence to be themselves and to realize their amazing potential as men and women who are made in the image of God. To me, it's a touch of heaven on earth.[11]

11. *Divine Society* 126–139.

A Transformed Way of Engaging an Organization

In my work with TEAR Australia over the course of thirty years, I had a chance to confront an organization more carefully. TEAR Australia works in partnership with other Christian groups, including churches, relief and development agencies and community-based organizations, to mobilize Australian Christians to respond to the needs of the poor communities around the world.

As TEAR began to grow a few years ago, it went through a process of organizational restructuring, which convinced me that TEAR was becoming more bureaucratized, stratified, departmentalized and specialized. During the restructuring process, I learned that some TEAR staff were also concerned that more structure would make less space for spirit. So I suggested to Matthew Maury, the director, and John McKinnon, the manager of the Australian programs team, that we host a conversation at the upcoming TEAR Australia staff conference, where people could talk about their concerns.

I wanted to host an open conversation about how we could move forward from where we were. I did not want to focus on the past, but the future, as we tried to figure out how to maintain spirit through the restructuring process. I suggested a classic "open space" conversation, where we would meet with anyone in TEAR who wanted to be part of the discussion, without any organizational experts or external facilitators, in order to wrestle with a question about which we all felt passionately. I suggested that different people could host different parts of the discussion based on their particular concerns, and then we would provide feedback and ideas to the management and board.

In an open space conversation, the framing of the question is crucial. If the question is not framed sensitively, it will not elicit the kind of conversation that people want to have. The question has to be urgent, relevant, substantive and—above all—a question people feel strongly about and can't wait to discuss.

Matthew and John gave me permission to canvas all the staff about how to frame the question that we would discuss at the staff conference, and the question we agreed on was: "How can we work together at TEAR to make our experience truly life-giving to us and through us to all those we work for?" We agreed that John would officially sponsor the conversation, and I would facilitate it and submit suggestions for action to John, who would ensure that they got a fair hearing with the management and board.

Generally, it is inadvisable to facilitate an open space conversation within an organization where you work, since the findings of the conversation might put you in direct, serious conflict with the administration. However, I was prepared to take the risk because I cared about the future of TEAR.

We had a host of meaningful, enthusiastic conversations that intersected one another and mixed and morphed into one another. The key themes were about the need to maintain a culture of high trust and high transparency in TEAR throughout the restructuring process by prioritizing relationships and continuing to care for, nurture and empower people.

Since that staff conference, I have been asked to facilitate two more open space conversations in TEAR on how to maximize our creativity, wisdom and sustainability and how to remain open and keep taking risks in our work amidst a world of increasing caution and compliance. At the end of these conversations, we made the following suggestions:

> We need to practice common sense.
> We need to cultivate a culture of love, not fear.
> We need to create the space for robust debates.
> We need to see compliance as a means, not an end.
> We need to be prepared to push back when needed.
> We need to use an appreciative approach with people.
> We need to encourage people to "give things a go."
> We need to ensure there's freedom to make mistakes.
> We need to be able to learn to think outside the box.
> We need to take the risks to work outside of the box.[12]

Engaging TEAR through an open space conversation helped me examine my own concerns about the organization, but my role was that of a "carer," rather than a high-profile, in-your-face "confronter." My purpose was to be a fully present, but virtually invisible, facilitator, holding space open for others to reflect critically about their concerns with the organization themselves rather than putting forward that criticism myself.

A Transformed Way of Engaging Another Religion

By the time we started *Aashiana,* which was established by Indians for Indians, who come from many other religions (Hinduism, Buddhism, Jainism, Sikhism and Islam), I had come to realize that while I might have some knowledge of the "true truth," my knowledge of the "absolute true truth" was relative, limited, partial and incomplete. Since then, I have found that dialogue with people of other religions is not only meaningful, but also mutually enlightening.

12. "TEAR Staff Open Space Summaries And Suggestions," 1999, 11

After 9/11, I have focused on developing dialogue between Christians and Muslims in Australia. In my experience of meaningful interfaith dialogue, I have proceeded on the basis of three beliefs. First, there is only One God. Second, God is bigger than our own religion. Third, God can speak "truth through our religion and also through another's religion. As a confronter, the challenge for me has been to move from a position of "hostility" to a posture of "hospitality" towards that "truth."

Henri Nouwen says that "The German word for 'hospitality' is *gastfreundschaft*, which means friendship for the guest. The Dutch word for 'hospitality', *gastvrijheid*, means the freedom of the guest. Hospitality, therefore, means the creation of a free space where the stranger can enter and become a friend instead of an enemy."[13] In this sense, showing "hospitality to the truth" means that Christians and Muslims seek to create a free space in ourselves for the "truth of a stranger" or a "strange truth," which we can welcome and befriend.

The "strange truth" in a "strange language" that I have come to welcome as a friend through a more hospitable approach to dialogue with Muslims is the *Bismillah,* which stands for the Arabic phrase, *Bismillahi r Rahman r Rahim,* which is the invocation at the beginning of each *surah* in the *Qur'an* (except one). This beautiful, poetic phrase encourages me to seek to work "In the name of God the most merciful, most gracious and most compassionate." I have welcomed the *Bismillah* into my home and my heart.

For me, empathy is the heart of compassion. Empathy is the capacity for us to feel how others feel. In the context of interfaith dialogue, Christians and Muslims can seek to empathize with one another as people and try to feel how each other might feel. As we empathize with one another, we can develop interpersonal relationships that bridge the gaps of division, suspicion and opposition that have set people of our religions over against each other for ages.

In seeking to improve relationships between Christians and Muslims, most people opt for what I call the "problematic approach," which focuses on problems and tries to fix them. At first glance, this approach may seem to make sense, because if we want to improve our relationship with one another, we will want to identify any problems and then try to solve them. However, when we give the "problematic approach" a second thought, we realize that it is endlessly "problematic," because when we look for problems, we find lots of them, and the more we look for problems, the more problems we'll find, and the more we look at all those problems, the bigger,

---

13. Nouwen, *Reaching Out,* 48–51.

scarier and harder to deal with they become—until we often find ourselves so overwhelmed by all the problems that we become unable to solve them.

In dialogue between Christians and Muslims, I have seen this happen time and time again. Christians try to fix Muslims, Muslims try to fix Christians, and both sides end up overwhelmed by all the problems and completely battered and bruised by our cack-handed attempts to solve them. Such engagements do not lead to meaningful dialogue, but to the avoidance of meaningful dialogue. When I first met my Muslim colleague, Nora, she said she didn't want to meet me at first because she knew I was a Christian, and she was sick of Christians like me seeing her as a problem and trying to fix her.

Nora and I have discovered an alternative way to improve relationships between Christians and Muslims, which is the "appreciative approach." The "appreciative approach" does not focus on the "bad things" in others, but the "good things" in others. At first glance, this may not seem like a way to improve anything, because if we celebrate the "good things" in others, they won't make any real effort to get any better. But I have found that when we give the "appreciative approach" a second thought, we realize that it is the only approach that will make any of us want to do better, because when we notice the "good things" in each other, we enhance the "good things" in one another, and we can encourage one another to do "good things" more often. As we observe authenticity, honesty and integrity in the other every time we encounter it, and as we celebrate sensitivity, sincerity and vulnerability in the other each time we encounter it, our appreciation can lead to meaningful interfaith dialogue that bridges divides instead of widening them.

As I have already said, one of the really "good things" in Nora's religion that I have come to appreciate is the *Bismillah*, which Nora says contains the true essence of the Qur'an—indeed, the true essence of all religions. The more I have thought about the *Bismillah*, the more I have realized that it represents the best perspective of God within any religion. Both *rahman* and *rahim* are derived from the Semitic root *rhm*, which signifies the *womb* and *nourishing tenderness* and *lovingkindness*. *Rahman* describes the quality of limitless grace with which God embraces the whole world and all who dwell in it, while *rahim* describes the general embracing grace of God as it interacts with us in the particular circumstances of our lives, always proactive, prevenient and responsive. In talking with Nora, I have gladly and regularly affirmed how much better both our religions would be if we interpreted our sacred texts in a way that reflects a spirituality of the *Bismillah*. We have both come to believe that we should use this invocation as a hermeneutic to interpret our sacred texts in the light of God's nourishing tenderness and lovingkindness.

However, how does a "born again" confronter/carer like me affirm the "good things" that need to be celebrated, but still confront the "bad things" that need to be confronted? In Christian-Muslim engagement, people either do not confront the "bad things" that need to be confronted, or they confront the "bad things" that need to be confronted by criticizing them. But when we attack the "bad things" about the other in the name of aggressive apologetics, we make things worse by escalating the conflict that already exists.

As I have said many times, the words Jesus spoke to his disciples about how we can proceed with care when criticizing others have been transformative for me: "Why do you see the speck in your neighbor's eye, but do not notice the plank in your own eye? Or how can you say to your neighbor, 'Let me take the speck out of your eye,' while the plank is in your own eye? You hypocrite, first take the plank out of your own eye, and then you will see clearly to take the speck out of your neighbor's eye" (Matt. 7:3–5).

Nora and I encourage people not to be *critically projective* by attacking one another's religions and escalating the conflict, but to be *critically reflective* by helping one another to confront the "bad things" in our own religions and working to make things better. Such a critically reflective approach can help us work together to resolve the existing conflict between our religions.

Nora and I have both been influenced by the Maulana Wahiduddin Khan. The Maulana is a revered Muslim leader and Islamic spiritual scholar based in Nizamuddin, New Delhi, India, who has adopted peace as the mission of his life and nonviolence as the only method to achieve peace. I have read many of his books, including *The Prophet Of Peace*, and if you have read any of my books, you will notice that he has significantly influenced my approach to engaging Muslims.

The Maulana says that there are two ways we can engage our religions. The first is to "take pride in our religion" and to be "critically projective" of another's religion, which makes us more partisan, protective of our traditions and reactive against others who may question our traditions. The second way is to "be true to the spirit of our religion" and to be "critically reflective" of our own religion, which makes us more sensitive to the issues that we need to deal with in our traditions and more willing to question our traditions ourselves.[14]

As I mention above, Nora and I have adopted the second approach. For example, rather than criticize the violence in one another's traditions, Nora and I help one another confront the violence in our own traditions and host conversations within our own families of faith to help those who

14. Khan, *The Prophet of Peace*, 10–13.

share our religion reflect critically, safely, honestly and vulnerably on traditional interpretations of sacred texts that have been used as pretexts for violence, such as the "genocide commands" in Deuteronomy or the "sword verses" in the *Qur'an*.[15]

After trying for many years, my friend Greg Manning and I got to have a personal audience with the Maulana Wahiduddin Khan at his private residence in Nizamuddin when we visited Delhi in 2017. This was a great honor, and the Maulana graciously answered our questions for over an hour. Towards the end of our conversation, when I asked the Maulana for a word that I could take with me as a mantra, he quoted from his own English translation of the *Qur'an*, saying, "Good and evil deeds are not equal. Repel evil with that which is better; then you will see that one who was once your enemy has become your friend" (*Surah* 41.34).

The meeting I had with the Maulana reminded me of a meeting that I'd had with an Imam two years previously. On November 13, 2015, the day after the infamous Islamist terrorist attacks in Paris that left more than a hundred innocent Parisians dead, I met with Imam Jamal Rahman, a Sufi Muslim, at a coffee shop in Seattle. We talked about interfaith engagement between people in a world of pain and violence. In the course of our conversation, I asked Jamal what he would want to say on that day, as a Muslim leader, to the non-Muslims he met. I will never forget what he said: "What do I need to do that would bring healing to the hurt we have caused one another?"

On August 7, 2020, I met with Timothy Weeks. Four years earlier, in August 2016, when this Aussie teacher was lecturing in English at the American University in Kabul, he was kidnapped, with a colleague, at gunpoint by the Taliban. Tim and Kevin were finally freed in a prisoner exchange in November 2019, but during their three intervening "long and tortuous" years in captivity, Tim says they were often kept locked in dark rooms and subjected to random beatings.

In spite of the beatings, Tim told me that he didn't see his captors as "terrorists." Tim saw his guards as "humans" who, like himself, were caught up in a larger conflict beyond their control, being moved about the geopolitical chessboard in Afghanistan like disposable pawns. Tim said not all of his guards were cruel; even those who were, weren't cruel all the time. In fact, Tim said, some of his guards were extraordinarily kind, treating him really well, considering the limitations of the conditions they found themselves in. Tim told me he learnt to speak *Pashtun*, talked to his guards

15. See Deuteronomy 20:16–17 and *Qur'an* 9.5a.

about *Pashtunwali*, the "*Pashtun* way of life," and developed really meaning-ful relationships with some of them. Tim is adamant: "I don't hate them at all; some of them I have great respect for and, and great love for, almost." [16]

Some may see this "great love" as a symptom of the "Stockholm syn-drome" – the feelings of affection that many victims of kidnapping develop towards their captors. But I sensed Tim was sure the "great love" he felt, was much more than a "syndrome." Contrary to the express, explicit and repeated wishes of his captors, Tim converted to Islam, and his commit-ment to forgiveness, mediation and reconciliation has become a religious vocation.

To encourage Tim I gave him the gift of a book that tells the amazing story of a friend, Dan Terry, who lived in Afghanistan for almost forty years, *Making Friends Among The Taliban*.[17] Tim's eyes lit up when he saw the title and he assured me he would read it.

Tim is asking a variation of the question that Jamal says we should all be asking: "What do I need to do that would bring healing to the hurt we have caused one another?"

---

16. https://www.theguardian.com/australia-news/2019/dec/01/freed-taliban-hostage-timothy-weeks-says-he-never-gave-up-hope

17.. Larson, *Making Friends Among the Taliban: A Peacemaker's Journey in Afghanistan.*

EPILOGUE

I HAVE RECENTLY ATTENDED the funerals of some of my very dear friends, and I have been reflecting on the fact that I'm closer to the end of my life than to the beginning. This has led me to wonder, if this epilogue is the last message I have to give, what do I want to say?

The longer I live, the less and less I believe, but the little I believe, I believe more and more. There's a whole lot I used to believe, which I used to talk about day and night, that I just don't talk about anymore. I couldn't care less about it, and it doesn't make any difference to me whether it's true, or not, but there is one thing—among the many things I used to believe—that I still believe, and I still want to talk about it as passionately as ever before, and that is the wonderful love of God revealed in the ever-enchanting person of Jesus of Nazareth.

I believe God is love and that we are made by love, with love, for love. I believe that Jesus embodies God and incarnates God's love in his life. Jesus calls us to love God and to love like God in whose likeness we are created. Jesus shows us how we can really, truly and sincerely love others as we love ourselves, including not only neighbors, but also strangers, not only our friends, but also our enemies. And in Jesus, we see, that in the end, love is not in vain, love triumphs over hate, love wins.

As a toddler I believed in Jesus as my relative. My parents were pious people. My father was a pastor, and my mother was "in the ministry," too. We were a close family, and my parents talked to us about Jesus as if he were a member of the family. I don't recall seeing Jesus at our home, but Dad and Mum told us all about him. Each night before we went to sleep, they'd read us a story about him and show us pictures of him from an old storybook. I can still remember those pictures of Jesus even now. There was one of him carrying a lamb he'd found on his shoulders and another of him sitting with some kids, which was my favorite, because the kid he held on his knee looked a lot like me!

As a child I believed in Jesus as my friend. My parents migrated from England to Australia when I was eight years old. I was uprooted from the only place that I knew and separated from all the relatives I loved—with the exception of Jesus. Coming over on the boat, someone played "Somewhere Over The Rainbow" when we crossed the equator, but the antipodes proved to be anything but the magical Land of Oz for me. It was uncool to wear shoes to school, and trying to run around the playground in the midday sun on blistering hot, rock-hard bitumen in my little pink, soft, bare feet was torture. What made matters worse was that at that time in Australia, it was a crime to have a posh English accent, and so I was beaten unmercifully for being a "smart-mouthed pome bastard." Often I felt that Jesus was the only friend that I had in the world.

As an adolescent I believed in Jesus as my hero. When I read the gospels, I saw Jesus in a whole new light. He struck me as a man's man. He said what he meant and meant what he said. He believed in love and justice and stood up bravely for his beliefs. So Jesus became my role model. And I took every chance I could to "be like Jesus" and "do a Jesus." There was a little kid in our neighborhood that everybody thought was a few sandwiches short of a picnic. All the kids used to pick on him, but there was one big kid in particular who used pick on him a lot. "What would Jesus do?" I asked myself. "He'd lay his body on the line to stop the poor blighter from being bullied," I told myself. So I vowed that the next time I saw him being attacked, I'd intervene. As it turned out, when I did step in, I got beaten to a pulp and had to be rushed off to hospital, but my bruises only served to strengthen my admiration for the man who bravely laid down his life for his friends.

As an adult I believed in Jesus as my guru. I went to university in the 1960s, when revolution was all the rage, and I agreed with much of Marx's analysis of society, but I thought Christ's solutions to problems were far more radical than Marx's. In the 1970s I went to India, along with the rest of my generation, where I studied Krishna, Moses, Buddha and Mohammed. Much of what they said was the truth, but to me, Christ was the truth of which they spoke. So I have spent most of my life setting up intentional, multicultural, inter-religious communities based on the uniquely radical, outrageously inclusive, nonviolent principles of the Rabbi from Nazareth. And at present, my family and I are part the Waiters Union, which is committed to developing a discipleship community with disadvantaged groups of people in our hometown

These days, as an older man (or "Old Man," as a young indigenous pastor I support respectfully calls me), I feel I need to believe in Jesus more in terms of our savior. I guess it's because I have worked as hard as I can for salvation and seen more than my fair share of miraculous transformation in people's lives, and yet in many ways, things do not seem to be getting better—but worse. In spite of illusions of progress, more than 120 million people were killed in wars during the twentieth century. We watched with horror at the "terror" attack on America, but turned a blind eye to the alliance-sanctioned "war against terror." Then there is the climate emergency we ignore because of our addiction to greed. We are unwilling—or unable—to save ourselves. Unless we are all transformed by the redeeming love of God revealed in Jesus, we will all be losers; there will be no winners.

Given the fact that the heart of the gospel of Jesus is love, I believe it has been a total, unmitigated disaster that the word "love" is not mentioned—not even once—in the creeds, which are the founding documents of Christianity. Framed by belief about Jesus, but without reference to the love of Jesus, Christianity has brought about a brutal litany of crusades and slaughter, inquisitions, torture and terrible sexual abuse.

Jesus said, "You shall love the Lord your God with all your heart, and with all your soul, and with all your mind" and "You shall love your neighbor as yourself" (Matt. 22:38–39). This is the law of the universe. Paul got the message, for he said, "Owe no one anything, except to love one another; for the one who loves another has fulfilled the law" and "Love does no wrong to a neighbor; therefore, love is the fulfilling of the law (Rom. 13:8, 10).

Jesus said, "You have heard that it was said, 'You shall love your neighbor and hate your enemy.' But I say to you love your enemies and pray for those who persecute you so that you may be children of your Father in heaven; for he makes his sun rise on the evil and on the good, and sends rain on the righteous and on the unrighteous" (Matt. 5:43–45).

Paul got this message, too, for he said, "Bless those who persecute you; bless and do not curse them. Rejoice with those who rejoice, weep with those who weep. . . . Do not repay anyone evil for evil, but take thought for what is noble in the sight of all. . . . if your enemies are hungry, feed them; if they are thirsty, give them something to drink. . . . Do not be overcome by evil, but overcome evil with good" (Rom. 12:14–21).

It was said of Jesus that "having loved his own who were in the world, he loved them to the end" (Jn. 13:1). And Jesus said, "This is my commandment, that you love one another as I have loved you" (Jn. 15:12). Paul extolled the qualities of this love when he said:

> Love is patient; love is kind; love is not envious or boastful or arrogant or rude. It does not insist on its own way; it is not

irritable or resentful; it does not rejoice in wrongdoing, but rejoices in the truth. It bears all things, believes all things, hopes
all things, endures all things. Love never ends. . . Faith, hope,
and love abide, these three; and the greatest of these is love (1
Cor. 13:1–13).

I can remember a time recently when I shared these verses with a
bunch of weary, wrinkled, disillusioned activists who had struggled in vain
for change in my state since the buoyant days of the anti-Vietnam War Moratorium in the late 60's. Most of them were hard-core atheists, very cynical
about the role that religion had played in supporting the status quo, but they
had invited Ange and I, as "Godists," to come to their group to share with
them about how "God" sustained us in our struggle for justice, in spite of
our disillusionment.

After an in-depth session in which we all shared about our disappoint-
ments, I asked them if they would permit me to quote a verse of scripture,
and they replied saying rather skeptically: "Sure, man. Preach it, brother." So
I quoted this verse: "Faith, hope, and love abide, these three; and the greatest
of these – greater than faith and greater than hope - is love." I said, the scripture seems to be saying, "if we are disillusioned, and no longer have any faith
in the possibility of major change, or any hope that the next revolution won't
be another betrayed revolution, but we still have love - and still practice a
wholehearted commitment to caring, compassion and a radical concern for
the welfare of others - like so many of you do – in the final analysis, that is
what matters most."

When I finished saying this, I heard a few people say "Amen" and as I
looked around the room, I saw there were some people with tears in their
eyes. And it seemed to me, they felt that this word, from a "God" whom they
didn't believe in, had profoundly affirmed them in being the very best they
could be as human beings. As indeed it does for me.

It is said that the only apostle who was not killed when he was young
was John. It is said that when John was an old man, they used to carry him
into the congregation on a stretcher and ask him to preach the gospel to
them. And it is said that the gospel he preached was simply a gospel of love.
He'd say:

God is love, and those who abide in love abide in God and God
abides in them (1 Jn. 4:18). Beloved, let us love one another, because love is from God; everyone who loves is born of God and
knows God. Whoever does not love does not know God, for
God is love. (1 Jn. 4:7–8). In this is love, not that we loved God,

but that he loved us (1 Jn. 4:10). We love because he first loved us (1 Jn. 4:19). Since God loved us so much, we also ought to love one another (1 Jn. 4:11). How does God's love abide in anyone who has the world's goods and sees a brother or sister in need and yet refuses help? Little children, let us love, not in word or speech, but in truth and action (1 Jn. 3:17–18). No one has ever seen God; [but] if we love one another, God lives in us, and his love is perfected in us (1 Jn. 4:12).

And all I can say is, Amen!

WAITERS UNION ACTIVITIES

EXAMPLES OF PAST ACTIVITIES involving people from the Waiters network include: setting up the Queensland edition of *The Big Issue,* a national newspaper sold by homeless people as an employment-generation project; coordinating the inner-city, inter-church "Room in the Inn" crash beds pilot program for homeless women at risk in Brisbane; developing the "Hail and Ride Bus Service," which is now run by the Brisbane City Council and provides affordable transport to shops, hospitals and social services in the area.

At the time of writing, some of the activities that have supported or have been supported by people in the Waiters Union include our involvement with Aboriginal people in association with Aunty Jean, a local Aboriginal leader; our involvement with refugees in association with the West End Migrant and Refugee Support Group, Refugee Airfare Loans Scheme (RALS), the Refugee Sewing Group and Ethical Property Management (EPM), a social enterprise that aims to generate employment with refugees; our involvement in interfaith dialogue through Misbah, a Christian interfaith dialogue initiative in association with Australian Muslims Advocating the Rights of All Humanity (AMARAH); our involvement with people in public housing, boarding houses and hostels; our involvement with global justice issues through Servants, TEAR, Make Poverty History, Make Indigenous Poverty History and the Micah Challenge; our involvement in alternative, local economic ventures, such as Justice Products and Blackstar Coffee Roastery; our involvement in alternative, local environmental ventures, such as Local Power, which installs PV solar panels to generate electricity sustainably.

The Waiters Union also have hosted regular community meals and organizes community picnics or similar outings for people who live in hostels or different forms of supported accommodation. We have helped arrange community transport, using a minibus people to provide transport for people who would otherwise have difficulty attending activities.

We have promoted community fellowship by holding an evening service at St. Andrews Anglican Church in South Brisbane to provide people with an opportunity to contribute to a church service through leading, presenting, praying, sharing and so on—particularly those who do not typically have the opportunity to participate.

We have supported community households, such as the Princhester Street household and its predecessor the Bristol Street household, which provided people with opportunities to learn about intentional community and community involvement with marginalized residents by forming friendships and offering assistance with living skills, conflict resolution, advocacy and so on. Other group households have sprung up organically from time to time that are connected with the network. We have participated in Project Hope, a support network for church-based community workers in southeast Queensland. We also have organized "soup and doco" evenings once a fortnight, when people have gone dumpster diving, made veggie soup and watched hot-topic contemporary documentaries.

BOOKS BY DAVE ANDREWS

http://www.daveandrews.com.au/publications

- *Can You Hear the Heartbeat? A Challenge to Care the Way Jesus Cared* with David Engwicht. London: Hodder & Stoughton, 1989. (reissued as *Not Religion But Love*)
- *Building a Better World: Developing Communities of Hope in Troubled Times.* Sutherland: Albatross Books, 1996. (20th Anniversary edition - Melbourne: Morning Star Publishing, 2017)
- *Christi-Anarchy: Discovering A Radical Spirituality Of Compassion.* Oxford: Lion Publishing, 1999. Eugene: Wipf & Stock, 2012.
- *Not Religion, But Love: Practising A Radical Spirituality Of Compassion.* Oxford: Lion Publishing, 2001. Eugene: Wipf & Stock, 2012.
- *Jars Of Clay.* Chennai: EMFI, 2003.. (only available in India)
- *Compassionate Community Work: An Introductory Course For Christians.* Carlisle: Piquant Editions, 2006. (10th Anniversary edition - Carlisle: Piquant Editions 2016)
- *Living Community: An Introductory Course In Community Work.* Armidale: Tafina, 2007. (Anniversary edition – West End:Tafina 2019)
- *Plan Be: Be the Change You Want To See In The World.* Milton Keynes: Authentic, 2008.
- *Hey, Be and See: We Can Be The Change We Want To See in the World.* Milton Keynes: Authentic, 2009.
- *See What I Mean? See The Change We Can Be In The World.* Milton Keynes: Authentic Media, 2009.
- *People of Compassion.* Melbourne: TEAR, 2008. Eugene: Wipf & Stock, 2012.

- *A Divine Society: The Trinity, Community And Society*. Brisbane: Frank, 2009. Eugene: Wipf & Stock, 2012.

- *Learnings: Lessons We Are Learning About Living Together*. Brisbane: Frank, 2010. Eugene: Wipf & Stock, 2012.

- *Bearings: Getting Our Bearings Again In The Light Of The Gospel*. Brisbane: Frank, 2010. Eugene: Wipf & Stock, 2012.

- *Down Under: In-Depth Community Work* Melbourne: Mosaic, 2012. Morning Star, 2012

- *Out And Out: Way-Out Community Work* Melbourne: Mosaic, 2012. Morning Star, 2012.

- *Crux: The Place of the Cross in the Process of Transformation* Melbourne: Mosaic, 2013

- *Bismillah - Christian-Muslim Ramadan Reflections* Melbourne: Mosaic, 2011.

- *Isa - Christian-Muslim Ramadan Reflections* Melbourne: Mosaic, 2013

- *Ramadan - Christian-Muslim Ramadan Reflections* Melbourne: Mosaic, 2016

- *The Jihad Of Jesus: The Sacred Nonviolent Struggle For Justice*. Eugene: Wipf & Stock, 2015.

Books are available for purchase from

Wipf and Stock
http://wipfandstock.com/catalogsearch/result/?q=Dave+Andrews

Morning Star Publishing
http://www.morningstarpublishing.net.au

SONGS BY DAVE ANDREWS

http://www.daveandrews.com.au/songs

SONGS OF JOY AND SORROW

1 On the mainline (mp3) (sheet music)

2 The rebel Jesus (mp3) (sheet music)

3 I've got a friend (mp3) (sheet music)

4 My prayer is you (mp3) (sheet music)

5 Only certainty (mp3) (sheet music)

6 For our friends (mp3) (sheet music)

7 Time was when (mp3) (sheet music)

8 Tell to me now (mp3) (sheet music)

9 Only way to go (mp3) (sheet music)

10 Living in eternity (mp3) (sheet music)

11 This is my song (mp3) (sheet music)

12 Love, only love (mp3) (sheet music)

13 What a shame (mp3) (sheet music)

14 Have no fear (mp3) (sheet music)

15 Most dearly (mp3) (sheet music)

16 So good (mp3) (sheet music)

SONGS OF HOPE AND PROTEST

1 We Can Be (mp3) (sheet music)

2 Let Justice Roll (mp3) (sheet music)

3 Need Your Mercy (mp3) (sheet music)

4 Comfort Of Love (mp3) (sheet music)

5 Hey-Hey You Say (mp3) (sheet music)

6 Live My Life For You (mp3) (sheet music)

7 God's Love Is Good (mp3) (sheet music)

8 Set My Heart On Fire (mp3) (sheet music)

9 Hope For Nothin' Less (mp3) (sheet music)

10 In Everything There's Grace (mp3) (sheet music)

11 May The Wonder Come (mp3) (sheet music)

12 Comfort Of Love (Reprise) (mp3) (sheet music)

SONGS OF GRACE AND STRUGGLE

1 Jesus' song (mp3) (sheet music)

2 Love reigns (mp3) (sheet music)

3 Don't be afraid (mp3) (sheet music)

4 What do you want? (mp3) (sheet music)

5 I still long for love (mp3) (sheet music)

6 All I have to offer (mp3) (sheet music)

7 I believe in you (mp3) (sheet music)

8 Christ that bleeds (mp3) (sheet music)

9 What love is this? (mp3) (sheet music)

10 The way of Christ (mp3) (sheet music)

11 Praise the saints (mp3) (sheet music)

12 Light the candle (mp3) (sheet music)

SONGS OF LOVE AND JUSTICE

1 Kindness (mp3) (sheet music)

2 All we ever talk about (mp3) (sheet music)

3 Sorry (mp3) (sheet music)

4 What are we gonna do? (mp3) (sheet music)

5 We believe (mp3) (sheet music)

6 Not for me (mp3) (sheet music)

7 Jesus for prime minister (mp3) (sheet music)

8 Wanna (mp3) (sheet music)

9 Keep on goin' (mp3) (sheet music)

10 One day (mp3) (sheet music)

11 Do it (mp3) (sheet music)

BIBLIOGRAPHY

Alinsky, Saul. *Rules for Radicals: A Pragmatic Primer for Realistic Radicals.* New York: Vintage, 1971.

Andrews, Dave. "Aashiana: A Study of an Intentional Religious Community Located in New Delhi, India." Unpublished dissertation. Brisbane: Faculty of Social Work, University of Queensland, 1985.

————. *Building A Better World: Developing Communities of Hope in Times of Despair.* 20th anniversary ed. Sydney: Morning Star, 2017.

————. *Christi-Anarchy: Discovering A Radical Spirituality of Compassion.* Eugene, OR: Wipf & Stock, 2012.

————. *Crux: the place of the cross in the process of transformation.* Melbourne: Mosaic, 2013.

————. *The Jihad Of Jesus: The Sacred Nonviolent Struggle For Justice.* Eugene, OR: Wipf & Stock, 2015.

————. "Leaving Room For Doubt," Interview by Bryan Bishop. *International YWAMer* (Oct. 2003–Jan. 2004): 4–7.

————. "Letting Our Humanity Get the Better of Us." *Westender* 14, 5 (December, 2104): 9.

————. "My Struggle for Good Against Evil." *Zadok Papers* S226 (Autumn 2018): 3–4.

————. *Not Religion but Love.* Eugene: Wipf & Stock, 2012.

————. *Plan Be: Be the Change You Want to See in The World.* Milton Keynes: Authentic, 2008.

Andrews, Dave & Helen Beazley, eds. *Learnings: Lessons We Are Learning About Living Together.* Eugene, OR: Wipf & Stock, 2012.

Attali, Jacques. *Millennium.* New York: Random House, 1991.

Austin, Greg, Todd Kranock & Thom Oommen. *God and War.* Department of Peace Studies. Bradford: University of Bradford Press, 2003.

Barclay, William. *The Gospel of Luke.* Edinburgh: The St Andrew Press, 1975.

Barenblatt, Rachel, "Prayer for the Children of Abraham/Ibrahim." *Velveteen Rabbi* (20 Nov 2012) http://velveteenrabbi.blogs.com/blog/2012/11/a-prayer-for-israel-and-palestine.html.

Benner, David. *Surrender to Love.* Downers Grove, IL: InterVarsity Press, 2003.

Beuchner, Frederick. *The Magnificent Defeat.* San Francisco: Harper Collins, 1966.

Brown, Anthony. "The History of Musgrave Park," *GreenLeft* (21 November 1995) http://www.greenleft.org.au/node/10288.

Brueggemann, Walter. *The Prophetic Imagination*. Minneapolis: Fortress Press, 2001.

Carlson, M. *Performance: A Critical Introduction*. 2nd ed. New York: Routledge, 2004.

Cassidy, Michael. *The Politics of Love*. London: Hodder & Stoughton, 1991.

Catchim, Tim. *The Prophetic Ministry*. http://5qcentral.com/prophetic-catchim.

Christos, Carlos. *Letters from a Prisoner of Conscience*. London: Lutterworth, 1978.

Cook, Terry. "Australian pilots aborted US-assigned bombing raids during Iraq war." World Socialist Website (23 March 2004). https://www.wsws.org/en/articles/2004/03/raaf-m23.html.

Davey, Melissa. "'The whole nation is on board': inside the sanctuary movement to protect asylum seekers." *The Guardian Australia* (13 March 2016).

Dear, John. *The Beatitudes of Peace: Meditations on the Beatitudes, Peacemaking and the Spiritual Life*. New London, CN: Twenty-Third Publications, 2016.

Dumont, Louis. *Homo Hierarchicus: The Caste System and Its Implications*. London: Paladdin, 1972.

Ellul, Jacques. *The Political Illusion*. New York: A. A. Knopf, 1967.

Engwicht, David. *Towards an Eco-city: Calming the Traffic*. Sussex Inlet, NSW: Envirobook, 1992.

Gandhi, M. *The Message of Jesus*. Bombay: Bharitya Vidya Bhavan, 1971.

Hage, Ghassan. *Against Paranoid Nationalism*. London: Pluto Press, 2003.

Harland, G. *The Thought of Reinhold Niebuhr*. Oxford: Oxford University Press, 1960.

Hebden, Keith. *Seeking Justice: The Radical Compassion of Jesus*. Alresford, Hampshire: Christian Alternative, 2013.

Heschel, Abraham. *The Prophets*. New York: Harper Perennial Modern Classics, 2001.

Hiebert, Paul G. *Anthropological Reflections on Missiological Issues*. (Grand Rapids, MI: Baker Academic, 1994.

———. "Conversion, Culture and Cognitive Categories," *Gospel in Context*, 1(4) (October 1978).

Hill, Richard & Donna Mulhearn. *The Sacking of Fallujah: A People's History*. Culture and Politics in the Cold War and Beyond. Amherst: University of Massachusetts Press, 2019.

Hirsh, Alan and Tim Catchim. *The Permanent Revolution: Apostolic Imagination and Practice for the 21st Century Church*. San Francisco: Jossey-Bass, 2012.

Jung, Carl. *Collected Works of Carl Jung*, Vol.12. Princeton, NJ: Princeton University Press, 1981.

Khalid M. K. *Ma'an 'ala-l-Tariq: Muhammad wa-i-Masih*. Cairo: 1958.

Kornfield, Jack. *The Art of Forgiveness, Lovingkindness and Peace*. London: Rider, 2002.

Küng, Hans. *Christianity: Its Essence and History*. London: SCM, 1995.

Larson, Jonathan P. *Making Friends Among the Taliban: A Peacemaker's Journey in Afghanistan* Harrisonburg: MennoMedia, 2012.

Lincoln, Bruce. *Holy Terrors*. Chicago: University of Chicago Press, 2002.

Maulana Wahiduddin Khan. *The Prophet of Peace*. New Delhi: Penguin, 2009.

McClung, Floyd. *Living on the Devil's Doorstep: From Kabul to Amsterdam*. Seattle: YWAM Publishing, 2013.

Mulhearn, Donna. *Ordinary Courage: My Journey to Baghdad as a Human Shield*. Sydney: Murdoch, 2010.

Muller, Wayne. *Legacy of the Heart*. New York: Simon & Schuster, 1992.

Nouwen, Henri. *Reaching Out*. New York: Doubleday, 1975.

Owen, Harrison. *The Power of The Spirit*. San Francisco: Berrett-Koehler, 2000.

————. *Wave Rider*. San Francisco: Berrett-Koehler, 2008.

Parambi, Nimmi. *Dilaram: a New Approach to Therapeutic Community*. New Delhi: Department of Psychology, Delhi University, 1976.

Peck, Scott. *The People of the Lie*. New York: Simon & Schuster, 1983.

Perkins, Royce. "Dollar Distribution Targets Our Greed," *The Queensland Baptist* 64, 7 (August 1987): 2.

"Prophetic Kingdom Action." *On Being*. (November 1987): 19.

Rohr, Richard. *Prophets Then, Prophets Now*. Albuquerque, NM: Center for Action and Contemplation, 2006.

————. *Way of the Prophet*. Albuquerque, NM: Center for Action and Contemplation, 1994.

Sabbah, Michel & Rifat Kassis. "Cry for Hope: A Call to Decisive Action." Kairos Palestine (1 July 2020) https://bit.ly/3eR6Gvw.

Samuel, C.B. *An Evaluation of the Concept of Communes and its Scope for Application in Youth Ministry in Urban India*. Yavatmal: Union Biblical Seminary, 1978.

Shawqi, Ahmed. *Al-Shawqiyyat*. Cairo: Matbaʿat al-Istiqamah, 1950.

Sherwood, Yvonne. "Prophetic Performance Art (editorial)." *The Bible and Critical Theory* 2.1 (2006): 1.2.

Soelle, Dorothee. *Suffering*. Philadelphia: Fortress Press, 1975.

Stassen, Glen and David Gushee. *Kingdom Ethics*. Downers Grove, IL: InterVarsity Press, 2003.

Studdert-Kennedy, G.A. *The Best Of G.A Studdert-Kennedy*. London: Hodder & Stoughton, 1963.

Summo-O'Connell, Renata. ed. *Imagined Australia*. Bern: Peter Lang, 2009.

Taylor, J. V. *The Go-Between God*. London: SCM, 1972.

Tolkien, J.R.R. *The Letters of J.R.R. Tolkien*. London: George Allen and Unwin, 1981

Tyson, Paul. *A Divine Society: The Trinity, Community and Society*. Eugene, OR: Wipf & Stock, 2012.

Vonnegut, Kurt. "Cold Turkey." *These Times*, 10 May 2004.

Walker, Peter & Matthew Taylor. "Far right on rise in Europe, says report," *The Guardian* (7 Nov 2011) http://www.theguardian.com/world/2011/nov/06/far-right-rise-europe-report

Web, Carolyn. "Give the Gift of Refuge." *The Age* (23 March 2014).

Webbe, Gale. *The Night and Nothing*. New York: Seabury Press, 1964.

Wiesel, Elie. *Messengers of God*. New York: Simon & Schuster, 1977.

General Index

Author Index

Scripture Index

Milton Keynes UK
Ingram Content Group UK Ltd.
UKHW020650060823
426385UK00009B/203